Sewing
FOR
DUMMIES®
2ND EDITION

by Jan Saunders Maresh

WILEY

Wiley Publishing, Inc.

Sewing For Dummies®, 2nd Edition

Published by
Wiley Publishing, Inc.
111 River St.
Hoboken, NJ 07030-5774
www.wiley.com

WILEY

About the Author

Jan Saunders Maresh is a nationally known sewing and serging journalist and home economist. After graduating from Adrian College in Michigan, she became the education director of one of the largest sewing machine companies in the country, and then the director of consumer education for the largest fabric chain in the country. Both professional experiences give her a solid foundation in the home sewing industry, which she continues to serve with her many writing, marketing, and industry consulting projects.

In addition to writing for several home sewing publications, she is a best-selling author for several publishers, with 14 books to her credit. Many of her titles have been chosen as main selections for the *Crafters' Choice Collection,* a division of the Book-of-the-Month Club.

To promote her projects, Jan has been a frequent guest on several PBS television shows. Jan also makes regular appearances on the Home Shopping Network and the Home & Garden Network. One of her segments has been the most popular with viewers since the series started in 1995. When she's not writing (or running kids to soccer practice), serving as founder and president of her own direct sales company keeps her busy teaching and motivating consumers by helping them to create beautiful homes using her do-it-yourself home decor products.

Jan currently resides in Camas, Washington (just outside Portland, Oregon), with her husband, son, dog, and a collection of books, sewing equipment, fabric, and crafting products stashed in every available corner of her home.

Dedication

This book is dedicated to the memory of Chris Hansen, the wonderful illustrator of this book. Chris's incredible talent and extraordinary hand added clarity to my words about sewing (and those of many other writers in this industry) for over 30 years. He illustrated with a terrific sense of humor and an incredible knowledge of sewing, which made all of us better at our craft. The sewing community is much richer because of Chris and we all miss him.

Author's Acknowledgments

At age 7, I learned to sew under the watchful eye of my grandmother. When I had finished hand-stitching the set-in sleeves of a doll jacket, I cried and cried because it didn't look right. Grandma gently grabbed the jacket from me and turned the sleeves "inside out." It was a miracle — the jacket looked just like the one in the store. From that moment on, I was hooked on sewing. It's been an intimate part of who I am ever since. Thank you, Grandma, for being my first teacher.

A big-time thank you also goes to my parents, Ray and Bernice Saunders. Although I grew up on a strict budget, there was always money for fabric and plenty of praise for my handmade creations.

Thanks also to my most understanding and tolerant husband, Ted Maresh, who hardly mentions the dozens of boxes, packed closets, and my home office overflowing with fabric and sewing paraphernalia. Yes, I will start cooking again, now that the book is done. And a big thank you to my wonderfully patient son, Todd Moser, who has given up a lot of time with me so I could work on this book.

I have the most wonderful network of friends who have influenced what I've done in my life and career. You provide inspiration, knowledge, encouragement, and expertise, and I thank each of you from the bottom of my heart. Without you, this book would have been written by someone else. Thank you, Robbie Fanning, for teaching me so much about writing, sewing, and keeping life in perspective. Thank you, Jackie Dodson, for your incredible sense of humor, for your sewing help on a tight deadline, your creative genius, and friendship. Thank you, Gail Brown, for your constant encouragement and market savvy. Thank you, Karyl Garbow, for being a kindred spirit for almost 30 years. Thank you, Sue Hausmann, for your dedication to sewing education in our industry and for always sharing your wisdom with me no matter the time of day. Thank you, Judy Raymond and Maureen Dudley at Simplicity Pattern Company, for your help and support of this project and for publishing and promoting the *Sewing For Dummies* sewing patterns. Many more people have the courage to try sewing for the first time because of your efforts.

Thank you, Kate Singh, for the beautiful photographs and the kind treatment of the projects in this book. Thank you, Ally Geller, for the lovely home accessories that dressed up our room settings for those photographs. Thank you, Lisa Reed, for your tremendously talented hand and critical eye in illustrating the additional art included in this second edition. And thank you Natasha Graf, Traci Cumbay, Laurie Baker, and the team of incredible editors at Wiley Publishing that helped my words sound brilliant and encouraged my sense of humor about this craft I love so much. You are all truly amazing at what you do and how you do it.

Publisher's Acknowledgments

We're proud of this book; please send us your comments through our Dummies online registration form located at www.dummies.com/register/.

Some of the people who helped bring this book to market include the following:

Acquisitions, Editorial, and Media Development

Project Editor: Traci Cumbay

Acquisitions Editor: Natasha Graf

Copy Editors: Josh Dials, Laura K. Miller, Chad Sievers

Technical Editor: Laurie Baker

Senior Permissions Editor: Carmen Krikorian

Editorial Manager: Jennifer Ehrlich

Media Development Manager: Laura VanWinkle

Editorial Assistants: Courtney Allen, Melissa Bennett

Cover Photo: © F. Schussler/PhotoLink/ Photodisc/ PictureQuest

Cartoons: Rich Tennant, www.the5thwave.com

Composition

Project Coordinator: Adrienne Martinez

Layout and Graphics: Denny Hager, Joyce Haughey, Heather Ryan, Brent Savage

Illustrations: Chris Hansen, Lisa Reed

Proofreaders: Andy Hollandbeck, Charles Spencer, Aptara

Indexer: Aptara

Publishing and Editorial for Consumer Dummies

Diane Graves Steele, Vice President and Publisher, Consumer Dummies

Joyce Pepple, Acquisitions Director, Consumer Dummies

Kristin A. Cocks, Product Development Director, Consumer Dummies

Michael Spring, Vice President and Publisher, Travel

Brice Gosnell, Associate Publisher, Travel

Kelly Regan, Editorial Director, Travel

Publishing for Technology Dummies

Andy Cummings, Vice President and Publisher, Dummies Technology/General User

Composition Services

Gerry Fahey, Vice President of Production Services

Debbie Stailey, Director of Composition Services

Contents at a Glance

Table of Contents

Introduction

· ·

I love to sew. Period. First, there's the immediate gratification of completing a project using beautiful fabrics and great timesaving tools. Then there's the personal recognition — I get to admire my work and hear praise from my family and friends. On top of that, I save money sewing. Wow, what a hobby!

I'm betting that, after you have a couple of projects under your belt, you'll love to sew as much as I do.

About This Book

Sewing For Dummies, 2nd Edition, is a book for both absolute beginners and experienced sewers. If you're a stone-cold beginner, you may appreciate that I explain everything necessary to sew beginning-level projects and that I don't assume that you've ever even picked up a needle and thread before. If you've had some experience with sewing, *Sewing For Dummies,* 2nd Edition, still has something to offer — I give you tips and tricks that it took me years to pick up. All sewers can enjoy the projects in this book, no matter what their level of experience.

If you're new to sewing, I suggest that you start by reading the chapters in Parts I and II. You can find some fundamental information on sewing in those parts. After that, you can skip around from chapter to chapter in the book, reading about the types of sewing and the projects that interest you.

What's New in This Edition

With the home decorating craze in full swing, anyone who wants to beautify his or her home touches a piece of fabric. But then what? Never fear, *Sewing For Dummies,* 2nd Edition, is here. This time around, I tell you the best ways to put those creative juices into your home decor projects with tips, tricks, secrets, and fun projects I've used successfully in my own home, as well as in the homes of my family, friends, and neighbors. In this edition, you also find new illustrations that ensure your sewing success, an updated list of the most popular fabrics and how to use them, and even more innovative sewing short-cuts and techniques.

Conventions Used in This Book

As you sew, you're going to rely heavily on the tools in your Sewing Survival Kit, which I describe in Chapter 1. Keep it handy and well-stocked. You need it for just about every project listed in this book, and I wrote this book assuming that you have and use these tools.

You also see instructions throughout the book that can be completed by using a sewing machine or a serger. A serger is a specialized machine that saves a lot of sewing time; it sews the seam, overcasts the edge, and then cuts off the excess fabric from a seam allowance — all at the same time. I think of a serger like the microwave oven of sewing — you wouldn't want make an entire project on a serger, but it sure speeds up the process.

Foolish Assumptions

As I wrote this book, I made some assumptions about you and your needs:

- ✔ You don't yet know how to sew or are looking for a refresher course.
- ✔ You want to master the fundamentals of sewing.
- ✔ You're looking for tips and tricks to make your sewing and home decorating projects easier and more fun.
- ✔ You want to start sewing as soon as possible.

If this sounds like you, you've come to the right book!

How This Book Is Organized

I organized this book into six parts so that it's easy for you to find exactly the information you need.

Part 1: Hardware and "Softwear" for Sewing

In this part, I tell you about the hard and the soft tools you need for sewing and how to work with them, including your sewing machine, fabric, thread, and patterns.

Part II: Sewers! Start Your Engines!

Read the chapters in this part to find out how to do some things fundamental to sewing, including threading a needle, tying a knot, sewing on a button, sewing a seam, and hemming.

Part III: Fashion Fundamentals

When you sew clothing, you usually start out with a pattern and a set of instructions for putting the project together. For a beginner, these pattern instructions can sometimes be a little intimidating. The instructions may tell you to do something (like sew a dart or apply a zipper) that you don't know how to do. The chapters in this part help you decipher these sorts of techniques, which are essential to successful fashion sewing.

Part IV: Sewing for the Home

This part of the book lets you turn a little sewing knowledge into untold savings for your home. I show you how to sew pillows, duvet covers, dust ruffles, draperies and slipcovers, napkins, table runners, tablecloths, and more. Using the chapters in this part, you can create coordinated looks for almost every room in your home, quickly and inexpensively.

Part V: Alterations and Quick Fixes

Are you suffering from the "terrible too's" — clothes that are too tight, too loose, too long, or too short? Then read the chapters in this part when you want creative solutions to fixing what ails your clothing. I also show you how to do some basic repairs on holes, rips, and other mishaps.

Part VI: The Part of Tens

In this part, I share with you tips for mixing fabrics without creating home decor havoc, ways to avoid common mistakes when you start sewing, and important guidelines for sewing smarter and faster. I also include an appendix of resources to help you find the materials you need.

Icons Used in This Book

Throughout this book, I guide you toward important points by using the following icons:

Some sewing tools are essential to sewing, and others aren't essential but are still nice to have as you sew. Try out the tools mentioned next to this icon — you may find one that helps you quite a bit with the sort of projects you like to do.

Next to this icon, you find information that you should keep in the back of your mind as you sew. These points are key to creative and efficient sewing.

The information next to this icon tells you how to do something in the quickest and best way possible.

Make sure to read the text next to this icon. It can save you a lot of blood, sweat, and tears.

Where to Go from Here

I wrote this book to be your sewing companion. Instead of putting it on the bookshelf for future reference after you finish reading it and making the projects, use it actively each time you sew — whether at home or in one of the many sewing classes available at your local sewing machine dealer or fabric store. Keep it handy so that when pattern guide sheet instructions direct you to do something, you can check out this book to find the fastest, most efficient way to accomplish the task.

I've spent my professional lifetime amassing these sewing methods (and more), and they fuel my love affair with the craft every time I sit in front of the machine. My fervent hope is that after spending a little time with this book, a beautiful piece of fabric, and your beloved sewing machine, your own love affair with sewing will blossom. Enjoy!

Part I

Hardware and "Softwear" for Sewing

The 5th Wave   By Rich Tennant

"Ooo– crime scene tape. I'd love to get some of that for my sewing kit."

In this part . . .

To end up with a successful sewing project, you need to start out with good materials. These materials include your sewing machine, needles, thread, fabric, and pattern, among other things. I tell you about the very best tools for your sewing projects in this part. In addition, I tell you how to work with those tools after you have them, including how to navigate a sewing machine and how to lay out a pattern.

And just in case you're thinking that I don't give you anything fun to do in this part, you can think again. I include some low-sew projects guaranteed to impress your friends and family with how much you can do with your sewing machine.

Chapter 1

Assembling Your Sewing Kit

In This Chapter

▶ Putting together the tools you need for sewing

▶ Pressing tools and why they matter

▶ Figuring out which sewing machine parts do what

*L*ike most hobbies, successful sewing projects begin with a few good tools and a little know-how. Sure, you can collect some of these tools from your household: Those old scissors from the garage, the ruler from your desk drawer, and pins scavenged from freshly opened dress shirts, but you'll have a better sewing experience by using the tools intended for the job.

In this chapter, I list and explain the necessities — the tools I use just about every time I sew and that are essential for creating the projects in this book. I also give you some tips about additional tools that come in handy as your skills improve. So you can consider these tools your Sewing Survival Kit.

Keep your Sewing Survival Kit in a small fishing tackle box (other than your sewing machine and pressing tools, of course) or use one of the many sewing or craft organizers available through your local fabric store, craft store, or sewing machine dealer. Choose an organizer that has a handle and a secure latch so that you can easily carry it without dumping stuff all over the place.

Use the following as a checklist when you round up the tools for your Sewing Survival Kit; afterward, read the rest of this chapter to understand how each one works:

- ✔ Tape measure
- ✔ Dressmaker's shears
- ✔ Trimming scissors
- ✔ Fabric markers for light and dark fabrics

- ✔ Glass-head pins and pincushion (wrist or magnetic)
- ✔ Hand needles
- ✔ Sewing machine needles
- ✔ Seam ripper
- ✔ Invisible or removable transparent tape

Making Sure Your Sewing Measures Up

You use a *tape measure* for taking your own measurements, checking measurements on a pattern, and other measuring tasks. (See Chapter 4 for more information on patterns.)

All kinds of tape measures are available. I recommend that you use a plastic-coated fabric tape measure. This tape doesn't stretch, so you always get accurate measurements. Most tapes are ⅝-inch wide, the width of a standard seam allowance (see Chapter 6 for more on seams), and 60 inches long, like the tape measure in Figure 1-1. Many tapes come with both metric and imperial measurements and are two-toned, so you can readily see when the tape is twisted.

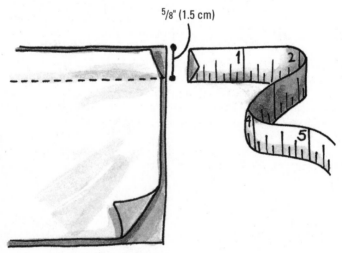

⁵/₈" (1.5 cm)

Figure 1-1:
Tape measures are ⅝-inch wide and 60 inches long.

Keep your tape measure handy by draping it around your neck, but remember to take if off when you leave the house — no one ever believes in this fashion statement.

NICE TO HAVE

Taking on small tasks with a seam gauge

A tape measure suffices for most measuring jobs, but for measuring small and narrow things, such as hems and buttonholes, use a *seam gauge*. This 6-inch ruler has an adjustable slide that moves up and down the length of the ruler. When you measure a hem, you use the slide to see how deep the hem is as you move the seam gauge all the way around the hemline. When measuring buttonholes, simply set the slide to the correct length and mark away.

NICE TO HAVE

One of my favorite rulers is a clear O'Lipfa ruler. It's 24 inches long and 5 inches wide, and is marked into quarter-inch increments across the width of the ruler — handy for cutting even strips in many home decor projects. (Read the following section to find out about rotary cutters.) The ruler and the mat together work like a T-square — helpful when marking and cutting perfect 90-degree squares or rectangles and for cutting strips. You can find a lot of clear rulers on the market — many longer than my ruler, but I find that I use my O'Lipfa almost every time I sew.

Cutting Up (Without Cracking Up)

If I could have only two cutting tools, I'd use the following:

✔ **8-inch bent dressmaker's shears:** Shears are the best tool for cutting fabric. They have one straight and one bent-angle blade, a round thumb-hole, and an oblong finger hole for comfortable, accurate cutting. The bent-angle blade gives your index finger a place to rest when you have a long cutting job. The bend in the blade also prevents you from lifting the fabric off the table, ensuring a more accurate cut.

✔ **5-inch trimming scissors:** These scissors have straight blades and two round holes for your finger and thumb. They come in handy for trimming smaller areas on a project and for clipping threads.

TIP

When shopping for shears or scissors, make sure that you test them on a variety of fabrics. They should cut all the way to the tips of the blades.

Some brands of scissors and shears are made of lightweight aluminum alloy. The lightweight models generally fit more comfortably in your hand, are usually a little cheaper than other models, and can be resharpened several times. However, with some brands, the lighter-weight blades may not cut as easily through heavy fabrics or multiple-fabric layers.

Steel scissors and shears are heavier, which means they easily cut through heavier fabrics and more fabric layers. Because each blade is made of one solid piece of steel, you can resharpen heavy scissors and shears more times than the lightweight variety, and they often stay sharper longer, too. But the heavier models are generally more expensive than their lightweight counterparts.

Regardless of the weight, scissors and shears with a screw joining the blades generally cut heavier fabrics and more layers than those that are riveted.

After you've plunked down money for a good pair of scissors and shears, don't let the family get hold of them and cut plastic, cardboard, wire, or anything you don't normally cut when sewing. The blades become rough and dull and not only will they chew or snag your fabric, but they also wear out your hand when you try to use them.

I also often use a pair of 3-inch *embroidery scissors.* The pointed blades are perfect for cutting out unwanted stitches and trimming laces, appliques, and hard-to-reach places.

After you decide you like to sew, treat yourself to a *rotary cutter,* which looks a lot like a pizza cutter, and a *cutting mat,* which protects the table and helps keep the rotary blade sharp. You use these tools without lifting the fabric off the cutting mat, so you can cut lines very accurately. Rotary cutters come in several sizes — I like the largest model because you can cut more, faster. But don't discard your shears; you need them for cutting intricate pattern pieces.

Cut edges can mean frayed edges, but you can put a stop to that with seam sealant. *Seam sealant* is a liquid that dries soft and clear so that you don't see any residue on the fabric and it won't snag or scratch. It comes in a small plastic bottle with a tip for easy aim. Dot it on a knot to prevent threads from coming out and dribble a bead at the cut edges of ribbon to prevent fraying.

Keeping your shears and scissors sharp

Dull scissors can make cutting a real drag: You have to work twice as hard to use them, and the results aren't nearly as good. Keep your shears and scissors sharp so they're a pleasure to use. After all, cutting is a big part of sewing, and if it's a chore, you won't like to sew.

Most sewing machine dealers sharpen scissors and shears. In addition, many fabric stores have a scissors-sharpener who visits the store periodically. After the pro finishes sharpening your shears or scissors, check that they cut to the point.

Making Your Mark

Sewing is an exact science, in many ways. When you sew, you must match up the pieces of your project precisely — otherwise you get the left sleeve in the right armhole and end up feeling like you're walking backwards all the time (find out more about sewing in sleeves in Chapter 10).

To help you match up your fabric pattern pieces exactly the right way, the pattern for a project includes *match points,* called notches and dots, which are printed right on the pattern tissue. To use these match points, lay the pattern tissue down on the fabric, pin the tissue to the fabric, cut out the pattern piece, and clip the notches and mark the dots from the pattern tissue to the fabric. (See Chapter 4 for more information on cutting out and marking patterns.)

Fabric markers made especially for sewing make transferring match points from the pattern to the fabric a quick and easy task. Use one of the following markers, depending on the kind of fabric you want to mark:

- **Disappearing dressmaker's chalk:** Excellent for marking dark fabrics, dressmaker's chalk disappears in about five days or when you wash or iron the fabric.

- **Wash-out pencil:** This pencil shows up well when marking dark fabrics and erases with a drop of cold water. It looks like a regular pencil with white, pink, or light blue lead.

- **Vanishing marker:** Best for marking light-colored fabrics, this felt-tipped marker usually has pink or purple ink that disappears in 12 to 24 hours, unless you live in a humid climate where marks can disappear in minutes.

- **Water-erasable marker:** This felt-tipped marker for light to medium-colored fabrics has blue ink that disappears with clear water or by washing the fabric. This marker works better than the vanishing marker if you sew in a humid environment.

The ink in vanishing and water-erasable markers uses a chemical that may react to the dyes and chemicals in synthetic fabrics. Always test markers on a scrap of fabric to make sure that you can remove the mark and that it doesn't come back when you press the fabric.

- **Invisible or removable transparent tape:** These are useful but not essential marking tools. Invisible tape has a cloudy appearance that you can easily see on most fabrics. Removable tape has the same adhesive as sticky notes and doesn't pull off the *nap* (fuzz) from velvet, corduroy, or velour. I use ½-inch-width invisible or removable tape as a stitching template for sewing in a zipper (see Chapter 9), as a guide for straight stitching (I talk about stitches in Chapter 5), and for a lot of other little jobs. Hide it from your family, though, or it may disappear when you really, really need it.

Pinning Down Your Projects

You need pins to sew. Period. You use them to pin the pattern to the fabric, pin the pieces of fabric together before sewing them, and for several other pinning jobs. Because pins are such a constant companion when you sew, buy some that keep your fingers happy.

I recommend using long, fine, glass-head pins. The glass head fits comfortably in your fingers when you pin through multiple layers of fabric, and the extra length makes pinning more secure. Plus, if you accidentally press or iron over the glass heads, they don't melt like the plastic ones may.

You also need a place to keep your pins. Some pins, like glass-head pins, come packaged in convenient plastic boxes that make great pin holders. But to save time, I wear a wrist pincushion so that my pins stay with me wherever I go.

A magnetic pincushion, available in a wrist or tabletop model, is handy in your cutting area and at the ironing board. Besides pins, small scissors and a seam ripper also stick to the magnetized surface. The magnetic cushion is also wonderful for picking up pins and stray metal objects that fall on the carpet.

Even though computerized sewing machines have improved, avoid getting the tabletop magnetic pincushion near yours because you may wipe out the machine's memory.

Pressing Issues

Why are you delighted when someone asks if your pie is homemade but insulted when someone points to your dress and asks, "Did you make that?" In sewing, if someone can immediately tell that your project is homemade, it's probably because something just looks . . . wrong. Usually this happens because the project wasn't pressed properly during construction. Using the right tools for pressing is just as important to sewing as using a sharp needle and thread that matches your fabric. Good pressing tools mean the difference between a project that looks good and a project that looks great.

Consider these points when choosing your tools:

- **Iron:** You need a *good* iron. I didn't say an *expensive* one — just a good one. Choose an iron that has a variety of heat settings and can make steam. Also, choose an iron that has a smooth *soleplate* (the part that heats up) and is easy to clean.

If you use *fusible products,* such as iron-on patches that melt when heated, you can easily gum up the iron. A non-stick soleplate makes it easy to clean and provides a smooth, slick surface for trouble-free pressing and ironing. Also, several newer brands of irons automatically turn off every few minutes, which is a real pain when you're ready to use the iron for sewing, so avoid buying an iron with this feature.

✓ **Ironing board:** Make sure you buy a padded ironing board. Without the padding, seams and edges press against a hard, flat surface that scars the fabric. This scarring shadows through to the right side of the fabric, so when a seam is pressed open it can look like ski tracks on either side of the seamline. The finished project has a shiny, overpressed look that's tough — if not impossible — to remove.

Choose a muslin or nonreflective ironing board cover: The silver, reflector-type covers are too slippery and sometimes get too hot, causing unnecessary scorching on some synthetic fabrics.

✓ **Press cloth:** A *press cloth* is essential for pressing a variety of fabrics, from fine silks to heavier woolens and wool blends. You place the press cloth between the iron and the fabric to prevent shine and overpressing. Use a clean, white or off-white 100-percent cotton or linen tea towel or napkin, or purchase a press cloth.

If you're considering a print or color-dyed fabric for a press cloth — don't do it. Dyes can bleed through and ruin your project. Terry cloth isn't a good choice, either. The napped surface of a terry cloth towel can leave the familiar terry texture on the fabric.

A professional dressmaker friend of mine loves using a cloth diaper for a press cloth. The diaper is white and absorbent, can be doubled or tripled depending on the use, and is a good size for many projects.

After you decide to make sewing a regular hobby and you feel comfortable investing a little extra money into your projects, consider purchasing the following tools:

✓ **Seam roll:** This fabric cylinder measures about 12 inches long by 3 inches in diameter. You use the roll to press seams open without leaving tire tracks on either side of the seam. Because of the shape of the seam roll, the seam allowance falls away under the iron and doesn't press through to the right side of the fabric.

✓ **Tailor's ham:** This stuffed, triangular-shaped cushion has several curves on it that simulate the curves on your body. You use the ham to press and shape darts, side seams, sleeves, and other curved areas on a garment.

Both the seam roll and the ham have a 100-percent cotton cloth side made out of heavy muslin-type fabric for pressing high-temperature fabrics such as cotton and linen and a wool side for pressing lower-temperature fabrics such as silks and synthetics.

Figure 1-2 shows you pressing tools in action.

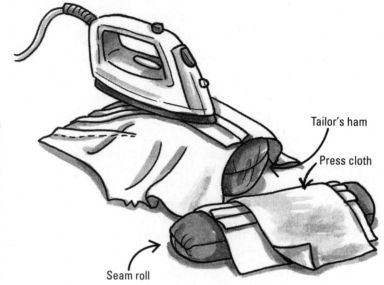

Tailor's ham

Press cloth

Figure 1-2:
Pressing tools that turn home-made into hand-tailored sewing projects.

Seam roll

Needing the Right Needles

Needles come in hand and machine varieties, and you can find many shapes, sizes, and types within each variety. The needle you select depends on the fabric you use and the project you want to sew.

Generally, the finer the fabric you work with, the finer the needle — the heavier the fabric, the heavier the needle.

Selecting needles for hand sewing

When selecting hand needles, choose a variety pack, and you have what you need for most basic hand-sewing projects. Variety packs vary from brand to brand but generally have from five to ten needles of various lengths and thicknesses. Some even have different-sized eyes.

In a pinch, you can use any hand needle as long as the point can easily penetrate the fabric and the eye doesn't shred the thread.

Fortify your fingertips with thimbles

Fingers are fabulous tools, but they leave a little to be desired when it comes to pushing a needle through heavy thicknesses of fabric. Protect the soft pads of your fingers from potential pain with a thimble, which is kind of like a little hard hat for your finger.

Thimbles come in a variety of sizes; choose a thimble that comfortably fits the middle finger on your dominant hand. Try on a variety of thimbles until you find one that's just right — and then use it! You can save your fingers a lot of wear and tear.

Selecting needles for sewing machines

For machine needles, size #11 (in American sizing) or #12/80 (in European sizing) works well for general sewing on about 80 percent of today's fabrics.

To make sure that you have the right size needle for the fabric, read your Operating Manual or ask your local sewing machine dealer. Some needles offer different point types designed to handle different stitching techniques and fabric types. For most projects, though, a multipurpose or Universal point works beautifully. Buy a package or two of #11 American multipurpose or #12/80 Universal European sewing machine needles and you should be all set.

When shopping for sewing machine needles, remember to take the make and model number of your machine with you. Some models can use only their brand of needle without causing harm to the machine. When in doubt, ask your local sewing machine dealer what to buy.

During the course of a project, a sewing machine needle gets used and abused, and when the needle becomes bent or burred (like the end of a blade of grass or a fish hook), the needle skips stitches and can snag the fabric. Unlike hand needles, your machine needle will need to be replaced frequently. The best machine needle for any project is a new one, so start each project with a new needle.

As ye sew, so shall ye rip

If you sew, you must stitch rip. Okay, so it may not be a biblical proverb, but it's a fact of sewing. When you make mistakes, you correct them by ripping out the stitches, or unsewing. For specifics on unsewing, see Chapter 5.

Make ripping stitches as pleasant as possible. Buy a sharp *seam ripper,* a little tool with a point that lifts the stitch off the fabric as the blade cuts the thread.

I've put too many unwanted holes in a project with a dull ripper simply because I had to push too hard to cut a stitch and ended up tearing right past the stitches into the fabric. When your seam ripper gets dull, throw it away and buy another one. You can't resharpen them.

Working with a Sewing Machine

Many folks drag out Aunt Millie's 75-year-old sewing clunker from the garage or basement, thinking it's good enough for a beginner. Turns out the instruction book for Millie's machine has long since disappeared, and just before completing a project, the machine becomes possessed by demons that sabotage every seam.

Just like your car, you want your sewing machine to be dependable. The machine doesn't have to be a race car, and it doesn't need every modern convenience known to man. It just needs to work well — every time.

Your local sewing machine dealer can show you a wide range of models and prices. Many dealers offer machines on a rental basis, and some dealers let you come into their classrooms and use a machine during open sewing time. You can also take Aunt Millie's machine into a dealer, have an honest assessment made about its general working condition and life span, and see if you can realistically count on using it.

Finding your way around a sewing machine

Acquainting yourself with the parts of the sewing machine and knowing how it works keeps you and your sewing machine out of trouble. Consider this section of the book your road map to navigating a sewing machine. I tell you all about the parts on a typical machine (shown in Figure 1-3) and what you use them for.

Of course, your sewing machine may look a little different from what you see in Figure 1-3. You may have a newer model, or you may be working on a serger (in which case, you should check out the section "Using a serger" later in this chapter). If things on your machine don't correspond exactly to what I show you, consult the operating manual that comes with your machine to see how the parts compare.

Needle

The most important part of the sewing machine is the needle. It's so important that I devote a section to the needle, "Selecting needles for sewing machines," earlier in this chapter.

Always start a new project with a new sewing machine needle. A new needle won't skip stitches or snag the fabric, and changing your needle regularly may save you from an unnecessary trip to the dealer just to find out that all you need is a new needle. (Ask me how I know this.)

Presser foot

Sometimes incorrectly referred to as a pressure foot, the *presser foot* holds the fabric firmly against the feed dogs (check out the section "Feed dogs," later in this chapter to . . . well, find out about feed dogs) so that the fabric doesn't flap up and down with each stitch.

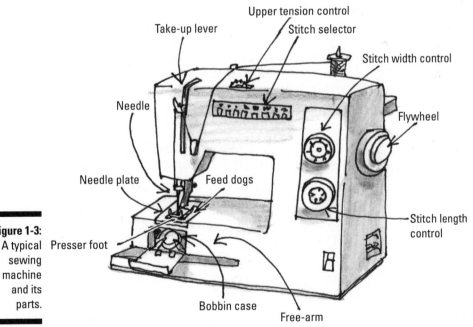

Figure 1-3:
A typical sewing machine and its parts.

Take-up lever

Upper tension control

Stitch selector

Stitch width control

Needle

Flywheel

Needle plate

Feed dogs

Stitch length control

Presser foot

Bobbin case

Free-arm

For most machines, you can buy different presser feet for specialty jobs. Most machines come with four or five of the most useful variations, including the following (shown in Figure 1-4):

- **All-purpose foot:** This foot, which is usually metal, works well on a lot of fabrics. The foot is often available with a Teflon coating for an even smoother sewing experience.

- **Embroidery foot:** Sometimes referred to as the *appliqué foot,* the embroidery foot is often made of a transparent material. The high, wide groove carved out on the underside allows the foot to glide over satin decorative stitches without smashing them into the fabric.

- **Blind hem foot:** This foot helps stitch a truly invisible hem (you can read more about hems in Chapter 7). The blind hem foot usually has a wide toe on the right and a guide (which may or may not be adjustable) and narrow toe on the left.

- **Button sewing foot:** This foot usually has very short toes and a nylon or rubber gripper designed to hold a button firmly in place (see Chapter 5 for clever ways to sew on buttons by machine and hand).

- **Quilting or edge guide:** This foot slides or screws on behind the ankle of the presser foot. The guide rides over the previous row of stitching for parallel rows of quilting or next to an edge for perfectly positioned topstitching. (See Chapter 5 for more about topstitching.)

- **Zipper foot:** Not surprisingly, you use this foot to sew in a zipper (see Chapter 9 for the details on zippers). The foot has one toe, and you can adjust it either by sliding the foot over or by snapping it on the other side of the ankle.

Figure 1-4: Typical sewing machine presser feet.

All-purpose

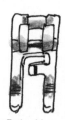
Embroidery

Blind hem

Zipper

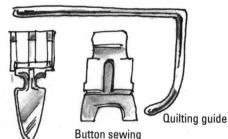
Button sewing

Quilting guide

Presser foot lever

Lift the *presser foot lever* to raise the presser foot. Doing so releases the upper tension so that you can remove the fabric.

The timesaving knee-lift feature, common on commercial sewing machines, is available on some brands of household sewing machines. The knee lift allows you to have both hands free when removing the fabric from under the presser foot or when pivoting the fabric around a corner.

Feed dogs

Feed dogs, sometimes referred to as *feed teeth,* are saw-shaped teeth or pads that move the fabric through the machine. You sandwich the fabric between the presser foot and the feed dogs, and as the needle stitches up and down, the feed dogs grab the fabric and move it under the foot.

Most machines allow you to sew with the feed dogs up or down. You do most sewing with the feed dogs in the up position; you use the down position mostly for mending or for free-machine embroidery, in which you move the fabric freely under the needle as it stitches.

Needle plate

Sometimes referred to as a *throat plate,* the *needle plate* rests on the bed of the machine and fits over the feed dogs. It has either a small round hole or an oblong hole that the needle passes through.

The needle plate often includes a series of lines that run in ¼-inch increments from the needle. These lines guide you as you sew a seam allowance, which you can read more about in Chapter 6.

For most sewing, you use the needle plate with the oblong hole. This way the needle has the clearance it needs and doesn't break when you use a stitch that zigzags from side to side.

Bobbin and company

A *bobbin* is a small spool that holds about 40 to 70 yards of thread. The machine uses the needle thread and the bobbin thread to make a stitch.

Machines usually come with three to five bobbins that are specially made for the machine's make and model. Bobbins are wound on a *bobbin winder.* Check your operating manual for proper bobbin winding and threading instructions. After you wind the thread around a bobbin, the bobbin fits into a *bobbin case,* and the thread can be pulled up through the needle plate, ready for stitching.

If you're winding a bobbin that has a hole in it, double and twist the thread end, poking the folded end of the thread through the hole from the inside of the bobbin out. Place the bobbin on the winder, holding the thread end tightly. Start winding until the thread breaks off. This way, when you get to the end of a bobbin, the wrong end of the thread doesn't accidentally get caught in the stitch.

Bobbin winding does differ according to brand, so check your operating manual for bobbin winding instructions. No matter what brand you use, though, don't overfill the bobbin if you want smooth sewing and the best stitch quality.

Free-arm

A *free-arm,* sometimes called an *open arm,* is a squared-off cylinder on the bed of the machine that lets you stitch around tubular areas, such as pant legs, sleeves, cuffs, and armholes, without ripping out a seam.

Flywheel

The right end of the machine has a *flywheel,* or *hand wheel,* that turns when you sew. The flywheel drives the needle up and down and coordinates the needle movement with the feed dogs when creating a stitch. On certain machines the flywheel allows you to manually control the needle, which helps you pivot fabric under the needle when sewing corners.

To pivot your fabric under the needle, simply turn the flywheel so that the needle is down in the fabric, lift the presser foot, pivot the fabric, lower the presser foot, and then continue sewing.

Depending on the machine model, some flywheels have a *clutch* or button that you must release when winding a bobbin. Consult your operating manual for specific instructions on bobbin winding.

Stitch-length control

The *stitch-length control* determines the distance the feed dogs move the fabric under the needle. When the feed dogs move with shorter strokes, the machine sews shorter stitches. When the feed dogs move with longer strokes, the stitches are longer.

Your stitch-length control gives stitch lengths in one of the following two ways, depending on the make and model of the machine:

- ✔ Millimeters (mm)
- ✔ Stitches per inch (spi)

Throughout *Sewing For Dummies,* 2nd Edition, I give you stitch length settings in millimeters (mm) and stitches per inch (spi).

The average stitch length for mid-weight fabrics is 2.5 to 3 mm/10 to 12 spi. For fine fabrics, use 1.5 to 2 mm/13 to 20 spi. (Anything shorter is almost impossible to rip out when you make a mistake.) For heavier fabrics, basting, or topstitching, use 3.5 to 6 mm/4 to 5 spi. (You can read more about basting and topstitching in Chapter 5.)

Stitch-width control

The *stitch-width control* sets the distance the needle moves from side to side. You always measure this distance in millimeters (mm).

Some sewing machines have a maximum stitch width of 4 to 5 mm. Others create stitches as wide as 9 mm. A 5-mm width does the trick for most utility sewing. (Throughout *Sewing For Dummies,* I give stitch-width settings in a range that works for most sewing machines.)

Needle position

Needle position refers to the position of the needle in relationship to the hole in the needle plate. In center needle position, you center the needle over the oblong hole in the needle plate. In left needle position, you set the needle to the left of center. In right needle position, you put the needle to the right of center.

A few older, less expensive models have either a permanent left needle position or a permanent center needle position. Most new models (made in the last 25 years or so) have an adjustable needle position. Adjustable needle position comes in handy when you topstitch, sew on buttons, and sew in zippers. Instead of manually positioning the fabric under the needle, you simply move the needle into the right spot by adjusting the needle position. The needle position control is usually around, near, or a part of the stitch-width control. If you can't locate it, read your operating manual.

Stitch selector

If your sewing machine does more than straight stitch and zigzag, it has a way for you to select a stitch. (See Chapter 5 for more information on basic sewing machine stitches.) The *stitch selectors* on older machines are dials, levers, buttons, or drop-in cams. Newer, computerized models have keys or touch pads that not only select the stitch but also automatically set the stitch length and width.

Upper tension control

In order to make uniform stitches, your machine requires a certain amount of tension on the thread as it sews. You adjust the tension using the *upper tension control,* which is usually located on the top or front of the machine.

The upper tension is usually marked in numbers — the higher the number, the tighter the tension, and the lower the number, the looser the tension. Some makes have the upper tension marked with a plus sign (+), meaning more tension, and a minus sign (-), meaning less tension.

The old adage "If it ain't broke, don't fix it" definitely applies to the upper tension control. Unless you have major problems with the fabric puckering or the thread looping, leave the tension alone. If you experience these problems, consult your operating manual or a qualified sewing machine dealer for advice on adjusting the tension.

Pressure adjustment

The *pressure adjustment,* which you can usually find above the bar that holds the presser foot, controls how much pressure the foot exerts against the fabric.

For most sewing projects you want to leave the pressure on the *full* setting. This way, the fabric doesn't slip and slide around under the foot, creating crooked seams while you sew. For some jobs, like sewing through very heavy fabrics or through multiple thicknesses or stitching complicated embroidery designs, lighter pressure works better. Consult your operating manual for specifics on your machine's pressure control.

Take-up lever

The *take-up lever* is very important in the threading and normal operation of the sewing machine. This lever pulls just enough thread off the spool for the next stitch.

Newer machines have a needle-up, needle-down function that automatically stops the needle in the up or down position without your having to manually turn the flywheel. Set this function for the up function, and the needle stops out of the fabric — you don't unthread the needle with the next stitch. Set it for the down function, and the needle stops in the fabric for easy pivoting around corners.

Speed control

Many newer machines have a *speed control.* It works like the cruise control in your car or the feature in your computer that controls the speed of your mouse. You adjust the speed control so that you can't sew faster than what feels comfortable.

Reverse button

At the beginning and end of seams, you often want to lock the stitches in some way so that they don't come out. You can tie off each seam by hand (ugh) or use your reverse button. Simply sew three or four stitches, touch the *reverse button,* and the feed dogs back up the fabric a couple of stitches. Release the button, and the machine resumes stitching forward. The stitches are then locked off and secure.

Maintaining your sewing machine

A little-known pest infestation runs rampant in the world's sewing machines — dust bunnies. These little guys can cause all sorts of problems for you, including the following:

- ✔ Skipped stitches
- ✔ Needle or bobbin thread looping when it shouldn't
- ✔ Noise and a lot of vibration
- ✔ General sluggish performance

You must keep lint dusted out from under the feed dogs and the area where the bobbin case sits in the sewing machine. When lint gets packed under the feed dogs your machine has a hard time making stitches.

Read your operating manual before you clean out the lint. You need a good lint brush with a lot of bristles. Some — but not all — machines come with a good one; if yours is skimpy, buy a new one.

Follow these general instructions to get rid of lint:

1. **Fluff out your brush until it looks like you've stuck it into a light socket.**

   This way, each bristle reaches into the lint-infested area and finds as much lint as possible.

2. **Unplug the machine.**

3. **Remove the needle, presser foot, needle plate, bobbin, and bobbin case.**

4. **If you can, remove the race area, snap off the race cover, remove the hook (Figure 1-5), and then memorize how the hook and race cover go back together.**

   Your operating manual most likely shows you how to fit the pieces together but find out *before* you start.

5. **Brush away the lint collected in and around the race area, especially under the feed dogs.**

6. **Put the race back together.**

7. **Plug in the machine and run it without the needle, needle plate, presser foot, bobbin, and bobbin case.**

8. **Now put everything back on your machine.**

   When replacing the needle, make sure the flat side goes to the back of the machine for a top- or front-loading bobbin. For machines with a side-loading bobbin, the flat side goes to the right.

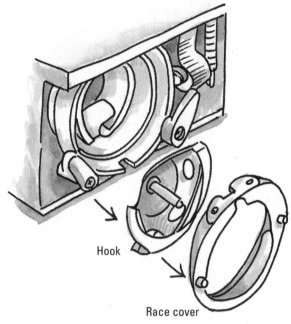

Hook

Race cover

Removing dust bunnies from your sewing machine sometimes involves taking the machine apart (and then putting it back together). Your best bet is to figure out how to clean the machine by taking the after-purchase lessons offered by most sewing machine dealers. For really heavy, once-a-year cleaning and tune-up, see your local sewing machine dealer.

Using a serger

A *serger* is to sewing as a microwave oven is to cooking. I love my serger because it really speeds up the sewing process by sewing a seam, finishing the edge (like the seams you see in ready-made clothing), and then cutting off the excess fabric in one step. You can use a serger to stitch a wide variety of fabrics, but it can't make buttonholes. A serger works much faster than a standard sewing machine, but it's not as versatile.

Most beginners start off on standard sewing machines. However, in case you want to sew on a serger, I give you special instructions where you need them throughout *Sewing For Dummies,* 2nd Edition.

Chapter 2

Selecting Fabric, Findings, and Interfacing

Remember how fun it was shopping for all the back-to-school stuff you needed? That's how I feel every time I start a new sewing or decorating project. I envision the finished project, get excited about the fun I'll have walking though a fabric store selecting just the right items for my new project, and then imagine the compliments I'll get from my friends and family when it's completed. And because everything you sew is custom-made, you never have to return something because it doesn't fit or isn't exactly what you wanted.

This chapter covers all the important information involved with sewing, including understanding fiber content (not the type that aids digestion, but the type that makes fabric), buying good fabric, what to do with decorative trims and findings, and the important purpose of a mysterious item called *interfacing*.

Choosing the Right Fabric for Your Project

Have you ever bought a good-looking, great-fitting pair of pants on sale, thinking that you are getting a smokin' deal — only to find that after the first washing, the pants fall apart, shrink more than a full size, or suffer from terminal wrinkling? Chances are that those bargain pants are plagued with poor fiber content.

You may wonder what makes a good piece of fabric and how to know whether you're getting the most for your fabric-buying dollar. With that in mind, the following section lists the advantages and disadvantages of common fibers.

You can often find a list of recommended fabrics on the back of pattern envelopes. This information about fibers and fabric comes in handy when selecting fabric and also when buying clothes off the rack.

Don't stray from the advice about the choice of fabric on the back of a pattern envelope — or I promise that the final product won't look as good or fit as well as you intended, even if you achieve the color you want.

Figuring out fiber

Fibers are the raw ingredients used to make up fabric. Fibers are important because they determine a fabric's characteristics, including

- ✔ **Feel:** Is it comfortable to wear?
- ✔ **Weight:** Is it too heavy? Too light?
- ✔ **Care:** Is it wash and wear, or does it need to be dry-cleaned?
- ✔ **Durability:** How does it hold color after washing or dry-cleaning?

Fibers break down into the following four categories:

- ✔ **Natural:** These fibers include cotton, silk, and wool. These natural fibers breathe, take dyes well, and drape beautifully. They also have a tendency to shrink, fade when washed, wrinkle, and stretch out of shape with moderate wear.

- ✔ **Man-made:** Acrylic, acetate, and rayon are high-profile members of this fiber group, which uses materials from plants that make cellulose. Acrylic is soft, warm, and resistant to oil and chemical stains, but sometimes acrylic fibers stretch out of shape and *pill* (form little fuzz balls) with wear. Acetate doesn't shrink, is moth resistant, and has wonderful drapeability; however, acetate can lose its color and shred with wear, perspiration, and dry-cleaning. Rayon (which has been referred to as the poor man's silk) breathes, drapes, and dyes well. Rayon also wrinkles and shrinks, so it must be dry-cleaned or hand-washed and pressed rigorously.

- ✔ **Synthetic:** Nylon, polyester, spandex (*Lycra* is a widely recognizable brand of spandex), and microfibers are among the hundreds of synthetic fibers, which are produced from refined petroleum or natural gas. Nylon is exceptionally strong, elastic when wet, abrasion resistant, lustrous, and easy to wash with low moisture absorbency. Polyester doesn't shrink, wrinkle, stretch, or fade. It's stain- and chemical-resistant, dyes easily, and is easy to wash. But, if you wear an all-polyester garment, you find that some polyesters don't breathe and are best when blended with natural fibers. Spandex is lightweight, smooth, and soft, and when you compare it with rubber, you'll find that it's stronger, more durable, and just as elastic. Microfibers take dyes well, are washable and durable, and have incredible strength and drapeability.

✔ **Blends:** Fibers are blended so the finished fabric has the advantages of the blended fibers. For example, a cotton/polyester blend washes, wears, and breathes because of the cotton fiber, and it doesn't wrinkle as much as 100-percent cotton because of the polyester fiber. Popular fabrics for sportswear are cotton/spandex blends, which allow for a close, comfortable-fitting garment that moves and bends without strangling your legs or waist.

You want fibers to fit your needs and lifestyle. For example, my mom doesn't like ironing or taking things to the dry-cleaners. So synthetic, easy-care fibers that are machine washable and dryable and that don't wrinkle are her fabrics of choice. My husband likes the breathable characteristics of cotton, linen, and wool. He doesn't mind going to the dry-cleaners and paying the price to have his shirts laundered and his suits cleaned and pressed. So, you guessed it, he's a natural-fiber guy.

Running down common fabric types

Woven fabrics are made on a loom similar to the one you may have used as a child to make potholders. The lengthwise yarns are called the *warp* and are the strongest yarns in the fabric. Crosswise yarns are called the *woof, weft,* or *filler.* Woven fabrics are stable in the lengthwise and crosswise directions but give a little when pulled on the *bias* — the diagonal to the lengthwise and crosswise grains. (See Chapter 4 for more on lengthwise and crosswise grains and the bias.)

Knits are constructed with a series of lengthwise loops called *ribs* and crosswise stitches called *courses.* Because of this looped construction, you treat knits differently when sewing than you treat woven fabrics. Most knits have crosswise stretch and lengthwise stability, so they move and conform to the body.

Because the fabric gives, knit projects usually need fewer shaping details — darts, gathers, or seams — than projects made of woven fabrics.

Check out this list of some of the most common woven fabrics available by the yard:

- ✔ **Broadcloth:** A light- to mid-weight evenly woven cotton or silk fabric used in men's shirts. Broadcloth is also made in wool for fine wool suiting.

- ✔ **Brocade:** Originally made of heavy silk with an elaborate pattern of silver or gold threads, affordable brocade is now made from synthetic fibers and has a heavy, embossed appearance. Brocades are used both in apparel and in home decor projects.

- ✔ **Chambray:** A light- to mid-weight evenly woven cotton or cotton blend you find in work clothes, shirts, and pajamas. Chambray is usually made with a colored warp yarn and a white filler yarn. This fabric resembles denim but is lighter in weight.

- ✔ **Chenille:** Derived from the French word for *caterpillar,* chenille is a plush, fuzzy yarn used to create fabrics for upholstery and bedding.

- ✔ **Chintz:** A closely woven plain weave cotton or cotton/polyester blend often used in curtains and draperies. This fabric is printed with figures — most commonly with flowers — and has a smooth, shiny, or glazed finish.

- ✔ **Corduroy:** A mid- to heavy-weight cotton *weft pile* (fuzzy ribbed) fabric that is woven or shorn, creating the distinct ribs on the lengthwise grain. Corduroy comes in various rib widths, solid and printed, and is commonly used in children's clothing and sportswear.

- ✔ **Crepe:** A pebbly-surfaced woven or knitted fabric. Because of the pebbly surface, crepes snag more and don't wear as well as even weaves like poplin. Crepe is most often used in women's dress clothing, such as suits, dresses, and blouses.

- ✔ **Damask:** Named for the ancient city of Damascus, damask is flatter than brocade and is reversible with a different pattern color on the opposite side. The designs are usually elaborate and were originally woven in silk. Today's damasks are made of cotton or linen, and may be blended with synthetic or man-made fibers.

- ✔ **Denim:** A strong mid- to heavy-weight twill weave fabric in which the warp yarn is a color (usually blue) and the filler yarn is white. Denim is available in many weights, depending on the end use, and is great for jeans, jackets, skirts, and home decor projects.

- ✔ **Double knit:** A mid-weight knitted fabric in which both sides are knitted identically. Double knit keeps its shape and has good recovery. Use double knit to make dresses, tops, skirts, and jackets.

- ✔ **Doupioni:** A flat-finished silk with a very subtle linen-look of *slubbing* — little irregularities in the fiber that give the fabric a noticeable texture. Because silk dyes beautifully and has such a supple hand, doupioni is used in apparel and in home decor. It's a fairly fragile fabric, so when using it in home decor projects, keep it out of direct sunlight because sunlight breaks down the fabric.

- **Duck:** A heavy-weight, tightly-woven cotton or linen fabric available in plain or twill weaves. Duck and canvas are used interchangeably and make great aprons and slipcovers. (Don't try adding a raspberry glaze to this duck.)

- **Eyelet:** An embroidered cotton available by the yard for blouses and dresses or in narrower widths as trim. The distinct embroidery has holes that are overcast with zigzag stitches.

- **Flannel:** A light- to mid-weight plain or twill weave cotton or wool fabric. Cotton flannel that's brushed has a soft, fluffy surface and is used for work shirts and pajamas. Wool flannel isn't usually brushed and is used as a suiting.

- **Fleece:** A light- to heavy-weight *hydrophobic* (water-hating) double-sided polyester knit used in pullovers, jackets, mittens, booties, blankets, slippers, and scarves. A common trade name for this type of fleece is Polarfleece. You can also find sweatshirts in fleece made with cotton and cotton/polyester blends.

- **Gabardine:** A strong mid- to heavy-weight woven twill fabric made from several fibers or fiber blends. You see it in sportswear, suiting, raincoats, and pants.

- **Interlock:** A fine lightweight knit used in T-shirts and other sportswear. Interlock is generally made of cotton and cotton blends and is very stretchy.

- **Jacquard:** Damasks, tapestries, brocades, matelasse, and upholstery fabrics with elaborate figures are all jacquard fabrics woven on a loom named for its inventor, Joseph Jacquard.

- **Jersey:** A fine light- to mid-weight knit used in better sportswear, tops, and dresses. Jersey comes in solid colors, stripes, or prints.

- **Matelasse:** Matelasse is a French word meaning "to cushion or pad," and refers to fabric with a quilted surface produced on a jacquard loom. Matelasse blankets are popular in modern bedding.

- **Microfiber:** This fine-quality polyester fabric is called a microfiber because the fiber itself has a smaller diameter than silk. Microfiber fabrics come in varying weights from lightweight dressmaking fabrics to heavier twills and velvets. Because it's made of polyester, a microfiber doesn't breathe very well, so when choosing a pattern, choose one that fits loosely.

- **Poplin:** A mid- to heavy-weight, tightly woven fabric with a fine horizontal rib. Poplin is usually made of cotton or a cotton blend and is wonderful for sportswear, children's clothing, and outerwear.

- **Satin:** This term refers to a fabric's weave. Satin can be made of cotton, silk, synthetic fibers, and blends. Many types of satin fabrics are used on both clothing and home furnishings, but all have a distinct shiny appearance because of the way the fabric is woven.

✓ **Toile de Jouy:** Often just called *toile,* this typically cotton or linen fabric is printed in a single color on a solid background with scenes, landscapes, and people, depicting life in 18th-century France. It's currently a very popular fabric in French Country home decor.

✓ **Tricot:** A fine, sheer, single knit with vertical ribs on the right side of the fabric and crosswise ribs on the wrong (back) side of the fabric. Stretch the fabric across the grain and it curls to the right side of the fabric. Use tricot for making lingerie. Tricot is also made into fusible interfacing. (See "Investigating Interfacing" later in this chapter for the details.)

✓ **Tulle:** Open netting made of knotted, geometrically shaped holes. Made in several weights, Tulle ranges from very fine, used in bridal and dance wear, to heavy nylon netting, used in other crafting projects. Tulle is made of silk or nylon and ranges in width from 45 inches to 120 inches.

✓ **Velour:** A woven or knitted fabric with a thick, short *pile* (little hairs standing up from the fabric) and usually dyed into deep, dark colors. Use knitted velour for tops and robes and woven velour in home decor projects. Velour is a more casual fabric than velvet (see next bullet). Velour requires a *with nap* layout (see Chapter 4).

✓ **Velvet:** A woven silk or synthetic fabric with a short pile. Use velvet for eveningwear, tailored suits, and home decor projects. Velvet requires a *with nap* layout (see Chapter 4).

✓ **Velveteen:** A woven cotton fabric with a short pile, made similarly to corduroy but without the ribs. Use velveteen in children's clothing, home decor projects, and eveningwear.

✓ **Worsted:** A fine, closely woven wool fabric with a hard, smooth surface. Worsteds make great suiting because they're very closely woven and wear like iron.

Reading labels and bolt ends

In the fabric store, you see the fabric wrapped around *bolts* — cardboard flats or round tubes. Flat bolts of fabric stand at attention on tables, and tube-type bolts are stored upright in a rack or threaded with a wooden dowel and hung horizontally for easy viewing. At the end of flat bolts, you find a label that tells you many important things about the fabric, including the fiber content, care instructions, price per yard, and often the manufacturer. Tube bolts often have a hangtag that contains the same information as the bolt-end label.

The fabric's width determines how much fabric to purchase for a particular project. Reading the back of your project's pattern envelope helps determine how much fabric to buy based on the fabric width. (See Chapter 4 for more information on reading pattern envelopes.)

The most common fabric widths are as follows:

- ✔ **42 to 48 inches wide:** Most woven cotton, cotton blends, novelty prints, dressmaking, and quilting fabrics come in this width.
- ✔ **54 to 60 inches wide:** Many knits, woolens, and home decor fabrics come in this width.

Occasionally, you find a fabric that is 72 inches wide, and sheer fabrics, such as bridal tulle, come up to 120 inches wide.

Getting Notions about Findings

Tapes, trimmings, ribbons, piping, laces, elastics, and zippers are all lumped together under the category of *sewing notions* or *findings* — presumably because you need to find and gather them together before making a project.

The back of your pattern envelope tells you exactly which findings and notions you need for a particular project. (Chapter 4 tells you more about pattern envelopes.)

Some pattern envelopes list notions that aren't essential for the completion of the project. If you don't want use a notion that the envelope calls for, ask the sales associate at the fabric store if you really need the notion before crossing it off your shopping list.

Bias tape

Bias tape is a long, continuous strip of woven cotton/polyester blend fabric. Bias tape conforms to a straight edge, such as a seam allowance, and can be easily shaped to fit a curve or hem edge.

Bias tape comes in several configurations, including single fold, extra wide, double fold, hem facing, and hem tape. Your project's pattern envelope tells you which type of bias tape you need.

Braid

You use braid to cover an edge or to embellish a fabric's surface. *Fold-over braid* is used to trim the edges. *Middy* and *soutache braids* are flat, narrow braids often seen on sailor suits and band uniforms. Middy braid has several fine ridges that run the length of the braid, and soutache braid has one deep groove in the center that runs the length of the braid.

Elastic

Elastic comes in many different configurations and widths, depending on how you use it:

- **Drawstring elastic:** This knitted elastic has a drawstring running through the center of it — perfect for use in drawstring shorts and sweat pants.

- **Elastic braid:** Looks like middy braid but stretches. Use it in a casing at the wrist or waist (see Chapter 16 for more information on casings). Swimwear elastic is an elastic braid treated to resist wear in salt and chlorinated water.

- **Elastic cord:** This cord is heavier than elastic thread and can be zigzagged over for a soft, stretchy wrist treatment.

- **Elastic thread:** Use this for shirring fabric (see Chapter 16), for hemming swimwear (see Chapter 7), and for other decorative applications.

- **Knitted elastic:** This elastic is soft and extremely stretchy. When you stretch knitted elastic while sewing, the needle slips through the loops of the knit so that the elastic doesn't break down or grow larger than the cut length during the sewing process.

- **Non-roll waistband elastic:** This elastic works wonderfully through a waistline casing or at the waistline of pull-on shorts, pants, or skirts. The ribs of this elastic keep the elastic rigid so that it doesn't bend or curl in the casing.

Lace

Lace, which is sold by the yard, comes in the following flavors:

- **Hem lace:** This lace is flimsy and straight on both edges like lace insertion (see later in this bulleted list). Because it's used on the inside of a garment at the hem edge, hem lace doesn't have to be expensive or sensational to do the job.

- **Lace Beading:** This machine-made lace trim has straight edges and a row of openwork holes running down the center so that ribbon can be woven though it. It's often used as a channel for a ribbon drawstring.

- **Lace edging:** It can have either a straight edge or a scalloped edge. You use lace edging to trim a hem or cuff edge, most often in heirloom sewing. You also use lace edging to trim the edge of tucks.

✔ **Lace eyelet:** This lace is made of a woven cotton or linen and features little holes in the fabric or *eyelets,* which are finished with short, narrow zigzag stitches called *satin stitches.*

✔ **Lace insertion:** This narrow lace has straight edges so that you can easily insert it between two other pieces of lace or fabric. Insertion lace is most often used on heirloom garments, which are garments with old-fashioned styling.

Piping and cording

Piping and cording have lip edges and are sandwiched between two pieces of fabric at the seamline. A *lip edge* is a flat flap of fabric or braid that's attached to the edge of the cording for easy application. The most common types of piping and cording include the following:

✔ **Cord-edge trim:** You use this trim mostly in home decor projects. One edge of this trim has a twisted cable cord; the other edge is a lip edge. The lip edge is stitched to the cable cord, and you can remove it by pulling one end of the chain stitch thread. (See Chapter 15 for more information on using cord-edge trim in your home decor projects.)

✔ **Filler cord:** This cord fills the center of piping that's wrapped and stitched with fabric. Filler cord comes in a wide range of widths.

✔ **Piping:** Piping is purely decorative. You use it to trim the edges of slip-covers, pillows, and cushions. In clothing, use piping at the edge of pockets, cuffs, collars, and yokes in seamlines.

Ribbons

Ribbons come in hundreds, if not thousands, of configurations, fiber contents, widths, colors, finishes, textures, and edges. You can use ribbons for every-thing from trimming apparel to decorating floral arrangements. I list three common types of ribbon, but you have a whole world of ribbons to explore:

✔ **Grosgrain ribbon:** This ribbon — which is pronounced grow-grain, not gross-grain — has a ribbed texture and is very easy to sew. Use it on children's clothing because it doesn't snag easily or for trim on some-thing tailored.

✔ **Satin ribbon:** It has a smooth, shiny texture. Use it on more formal pro-jects and where you need a dressier look.

✔ **Silk ribbon:** Great for hand or machine embroidery, silk ribbon comes in various widths and is a popular ribbon for adorning handmade projects.

Rickrack and twill tape

Rickrack comes in many widths and colors. Use it on the surface of a garment to disguise a hem crease that you can't press out, or use it to peek out at the edge of a pocket in a seam allowance for extra interest.

Twill tape is made with a twill weave. It comes in narrow, medium, and wider widths and is very stable. Because of its stability, you can use twill tape to stabilize shoulder seams and other areas in a garment that may stretch or droop out of shape.

Shirring tape

When making a home decor dust ruffle, such as a shirred skirt that goes around a sink or dressing table, use one of the shirring tapes available by the yard (see Chapter 17 for more on making dust ruffles). Shirring tapes come with two, three, or more cords woven into a sheer, almost transparent, woven tape. Simply sew the shirring tape on the edge of the fabric and between the gathering cords, and then pull on the cords in the tape for fast, even gathers.

Zippers

Zippers come in a variety of types and configurations, including the following (see Chapter 9 for all things zipper):

- **Conventional nylon coil zipper:** The cool thing about this zipper is that it can heal itself — if the zipper splits, you simply zip the pull up and down, and the split *heals*. The zipper can handle only a few such splits, so use a coil zipper in garments for adults in nonstress areas.

- **Invisible zipper:** When sewn in properly, an invisible zipper ends up looking like a seam.

- **Molded-tooth zipper:** This zipper has individual zipper teeth made either of metal or nylon. The zipper is quite durable, which makes it great for kid's clothing, outerwear, backpacks, jackets, and sleeping bags.

Investigating Interfacing

Interfacing is an additional layer of fabric used to give high-wear areas of a garment more shape and durability. Use interfacing inside cuffs, waistbands, neck facings, and front plackets (the parts of shirts where the buttons and button holes sit) so those areas hold their shape.

If you think you can save some time and money by omitting the interfacing called for in the pattern, think again. Your project is sure to look, well, *awful.* It just doesn't hold up, the collar and cuffs wrinkle and pucker . . . you get the picture.

Interfacing comes in the following forms:

- ✔ **Knitted:** Made of nylon tricot, this interfacing is wonderful for use with knit fabrics because it has the same stretchy quality as the fabric. Lay out the pieces so the stretch goes in the same direction as the fabric pieces.

- ✔ **Nonwoven:** This interfacing is the easiest to use because you can lay it out any way you please.

- ✔ **Woven:** You lay out this interfacing along the same grainline as the fabric pieces. If your fabric pattern piece is cut on the lengthwise grain, the interfacing pattern piece should be cut on the lengthwise grain as well. (See Chapter 4 for the details on cutting out patterns.)

You can also choose between *fusible* interfacing, which you iron onto the fabric, and *sew-in* interfacing, which you apply the old-fashioned way — by sewing it onto the garment. (I love fusible interfacing. After properly fused, it stays where you want it, and because fusible interfacing is used frequently in ready-to-wear garments, you get a more professional finish on your handmade originals.)

What's the best type of interfacing to use? It depends on the fabric. When selecting interfacing, choose one that has a weight and fiber content similar to your fabric so that the end product is easy to care for. If in doubt, consult the sales associate at the fabric store for help on selecting an interfacing that's compatible with your fabric.

Preshrinking Your Fabric

Before laying and cutting out your project and before sewing a stitch, you must *preshrink* your fabric. Preshrinking allows you to see how your fabric behaves — it shows you how much your fabric shrinks, whether or not the colors run, how much it wrinkles, and other important characteristics.

As soon as you get back from the fabric store, preshrink your fabric. If you preshrink and put off the project, you don't have to wonder, "Did I preshrink my fabric already?"

For washable fabrics, preshrink your fabric as you would the finished project. For example, if you plan to wash your finished garment in the washing machine with regular-strength detergent and then dry it in the dryer, wash and dry your fabric in the same way to preshrink it.

After preshrinking, press your fabric smooth and flat. Now the fabric is ready for the layout and cutting process (see Chapter 4).

Also preshrink any trims, tapes, and piping you plan to use with your project. Wrap them around your hand and remove your hand from the trim, creating a *hank*. Put a rubber band around the hank and wash it along with the project's fabric.

For dry-clean-only fabrics and zippers, set your steam iron for high steam. Hold the iron above the surface of the fabric, letting the steam penetrate the fibers, but without soaking the fabric or zipper. Line dry the fabric and then press the fabric with a dry iron (not set on the steam setting).

Fusible interfacing can be tricky — unless you preshrink it

If fusible interfacing isn't fused according to the manufacturer's instructions, it can shrink after you wash the project, causing a rippled bubbly appearance. It can also detach from or become too crisp for the fabric, resulting in a stiff, boardy look that screams H-O-M-E-M-A-D-E.

Preshrinking woven or knitted fusible interfacing reduces the chances of such disasters. I preshrink these types of interfacings by soaking them in hot tap water until they're completely wet and then letting them air dry.

Fusible tricot, which is a wonderful lightweight knitted interfacing, curls terribly when you preshrink it. So I cut out my pattern pieces on the bias, and the tricot behaves beautifully in the finished project without preshrinking. Other fusible interfacings that work well without preshrinking are the nonwoven variety, provided that you follow the manufacturer's instructions for application printed on the plastic interleaving wrapped around the interfacing. These directions tell you everything you need to know about using the product, including important information such as how to cut out the pattern pieces, how hot to set your iron, and how long to leave the iron on the fabric.

Chapter 3

Closing In on Threads and Other Closers

*I*n this chapter, you deal with issues of closure. And no, I'm not talking about the latest self-help craze, but rather closures in sewing. Besides finding out about threads that close seams, you take a closer look at buttons, snaps, snap tape, hooks and eyes, and hook and loop fasteners.

Selecting the Thread for Your Project

All-purpose sewing thread is the type and weight of thread that works well for most fabrics. You can find several all-purpose brands at your local fabric store or sewing machine dealer.

Some all-purpose threads are a cotton-covered polyester; other all-purpose threads are 100-percent polyester or 100-percent cotton. Ask your sewing machine dealer what thread brand works best in your machine. After you select the appropriate thread, unwrap a little bit from the spool and look closely at it. Check that it has a smooth, even appearance. Take that unwrapped strand of thread and place it on your fabric. You want the thread color to be slightly darker than your fabric for a good match.

Surging ahead with serger thread

All-purpose polyester, all-cotton, or cotton-covered polyester serger threads are fine, 2-ply threads available in a few basic colors on cones that can hold up to 1,000 yards of thread. (A *ply* is a finer, slightly twisted strand used to make the thread.) When three, four, or five separate threads are used to serge a stitch, the finer serger thread creates a smoother seam finish than the 3-ply all-purpose sewing thread used on a conventional sewing machine. Because it's a finer thread, serger thread should be used only on the serger and not for all-purpose sewing with your sewing machine.

If you see five spools of thread for a dollar, run the other way. This "bargain" is promotional thread made with short fibers, which get lumpy and fuzzy very quickly. The lumps cause uneven thread tension, creating puckered seams that you can't press flat. The extra fuzz may also cause skipped stitches because it packs into and under the feed dogs (see Chapter 1 for more on feed dogs), impeding proper stitch formation. So use good thread and clean out fabric lint from the race area of your machine (see Chapter 1 for directions) frequently for smooth sewing.

Focusing on Fast and Fabulous Fasteners

Without the fasteners described in this section (and shown in Figure 3-1), you couldn't keep your pants up or your shirt closed! In this section, I give you a brief introduction to these closers. You find the specific use and application of many of the fasteners I list here in the projects throughout the book.

The following fasteners all come in a variety of sizes, shapes, and colors. The back of your pattern envelope tells you which (if any) of these fasteners you need and exactly which type and size of fastener to use.

Without further ado, I give you some fabulous fasteners:

- **Buttons:** Buttons (and their corresponding buttonholes) close a garment, and they may have a decorative function as well. (See Chapter 5 for tips on sewing on buttons.) When selecting them, decide whether you want a bold statement or a subtle one to guide your color choices. Also remember basic design principles by using contrasting buttons to draw the eye vertically or horizontally. Tone-on-tone buttons usually don't draw the eye anywhere, which may be exactly what you want for a particular project.

When selecting buttons, stick to the size guidelines suggested on the back of the pattern envelope. This way the buttonhole position and spacing correspond to the button size for an easy, proportional application. The easiest buttons to make buttonholes for are flat 2- or 4-hole buttons. (Refer to Chapter 9 for specific instructions on making buttonholes to fit your buttons.)

✔ **Snaps:** You use sew-on snaps to close necklines on dresses, blouses, and baby clothes, among other uses. You use the *gripper-type* sport snaps on active sportswear and outerwear. (See Chapter 9 for more on sport snap application.)

✔ **Snap tape:** Snap tape is a soft twill tape with a row of snaps running the length of it. Snap tape is as fast to undo as hook and loop fastener and much more flexible. You use snap tape on baby clothes and home decor projects.

✔ **Hooks and eyes:** You use hooks and eyes at the top of a zipper to keep the neckline closed and in shape. You can also use a specially designed hook and eye at the waistband of skirts and pants.

✔ **Hook and loop fastener:** Better known by the trade name Velcro, hook and loop fastener comes in many weights, colors, and widths. Some types of this fastener are fusible; others have a peel-and-stick backing.

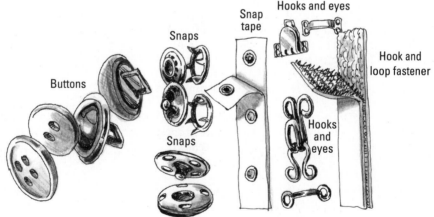

Figure 3-1: You find fasteners of all shapes and sizes at your local fabric store.

Making a Low-Sew Greeting Card

I think of buttons as the jewelry on a project. You can get some practice handling these little gems and ease into sewing by creating the easy-to-make project in this section.

Want to wow your friends and family? Sew a card. My long-time friend Jackie Dodson designed this one. Jackie crafts these one-of-a kind treasures by using ribbons, buttons, stamps, old postcards, plus other odds and ends collected from garage sales and flea markets. She even photocopies old photographs of friends and family members and adds them to her cards. So dig through that trunk, find that box of mementos in the attic, or clean out your closets and drawers. You can find a lot of material and inspiration from stuff you already have on hand.

To make this version, a Christmas card, you need the following supplies:

- One blank card and envelope
- Red, green, and gold tissue paper
- Threads that contrast with the papers (Optional)
- One 4-inch-x-8-inch piece of tracing paper
- A pencil
- A pair of sharp scissors
- A glue stick (available at your local craft store)
- One star-shaped gold button for the top of the tree (Optional)

You can find special papers and blank cards with matching envelopes at art supply stores and craft stores. Papers are available by the 8½-x-11-inch sheet, in a package (if you're doing all the same color scheme or more than one of the same card), and in different textures and colors. Some papers are different colors on each side. Also, don't overlook designer tissue papers!

To create the card, just follow these steps:

1. **To form a frame for the front of the card, cut the red tissue paper into a rectangle slightly smaller than the face of the card.**

2. **Glue-stick the rectangle to the front of the card, positioning the rectangle so that the margin at the bottom is a little wider than at the top.**

   Don't overglue. When you add stitching to the card, the glue can gum up the needle, causing it to skip stitches.

3. **Cut a rectangle that's slightly smaller than the red rectangle out of the green tissue paper.**

   The green rectangle fits inside the red rectangle, so be sure that you have the border you want.

4. **Make the tree pattern and trace it onto the green tissue paper.**

Using your tracing paper, trace the half-tree pattern shown in Figure 3-2. Cut out the pattern. Center the foldline of the pattern down the length of the green rectangle. Trace around only the branch side of the pattern. (In the next step, you cut the branches on one side of the tree, and then you fold the tree open to make the whole tree.)

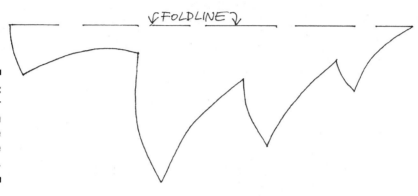

Figure 3-2:
Trace over this pattern to make a tree template.

If you want to make more than one card, transfer the pattern to card stock so it doesn't wear out.

5. **Using your sharp scissors, cut the half-tree pattern out of the green paper and fold it back at the foldline, as shown in Figure 3-3.**

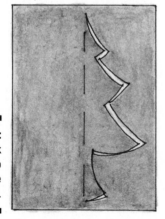

Figure 3-3:
Fold back the paper to complete the tree.

6. **Glue the green rectangle over the red rectangle so that the border is even all the way around.**

7. **(Optional) Sew decorative borders around the inside of the rectangles.**

   Thread your sewing machine with thread that contrasts with the paper (gold thread works well). Set your sewing machine for a 3 mm/9 spi straight stitch and sew ⅛ inch inside the edges of each rectangle without sewing through the tree. Figure 3-4 shows how your seam will look. Pull the threads to the back of the card and tie them off. (Chapter 5 tells you more about straight stitching, and Chapter 6 explains tying off threads.)

8. **(Optional) Glue or sew a star-shaped button on the top of the tree.**

   See Chapter 5 for hand or machine button-sewing instructions.

Figure 3-4:
Decorative borders sewn with contrasting thread give your card extra panache.

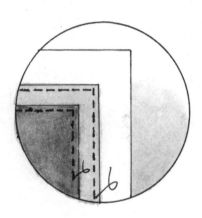

Sewing Fast with Place Mats

In about an hour, you can turn everyday place mats into a one-of-a-kind vest or jacket — and no one will ever guess your secret (until they sit down for dinner, anyway). The place mats' finished sides and edges add to the overall garment design, and the back and front of the mats completely line the projects, making them reversible. Whether you're tall, short, thin, chunky, old, or young, this fashion accessory is a welcome and novel addition to any wardrobe.

As you prepare to make these place mat fashions, keep the following pointers in mind:

✔ **Choose all-cotton place mats:** I used rectangular mats measuring about 12-x-18 inches to make the vest and jacket you see in the color pages of this book, but you can make this project with oval-shaped mats, too.

✔ **Choose soft and pliable place mats:** If the mats are too stiff, you may look like a scarecrow because you won't be able to put your arms down to your sides.

✔ **Pick mats with two attractive sides:** Both the front and the back of the place mat show in the finished project. Decide which side of the mat you want as the right side by holding it up to your chin and letting the *lapel* fold over at the center front.

✔ **Preshrink cotton mats before putting your creation together:** Simply wash, dry, and press the mats the same way you plan to take care of the finished project.

✔ **Use a zipper foot for fabric-bound edges:** Stitching next to fabric-bound edges of a place mat is easier when you use a zipper foot (see Chapter 9). The foot has a single, narrow toe and adjusts to either side of the needle for the most accurate stitching. For other types of mats, an all-purpose foot works just fine.

Piecing together a place mat vest

This vest is the definition of versatile — it looks great with jeans or over a turtleneck or a summer dress, and you can make it (using only four placemats!) for anyone from a petite 10 year old to a generously proportioned adult.

To make this project, you need the following materials in addition to your Sewing Survival Kit I describe in Chapter 1:

✔ Four cotton place mats

✔ Thread to match the mats

✔ Two buttons of a color, shape, and size that complement the place mats

✔ Pearl cotton (looks like a twisted embroidery floss and comes on a ball) or embroidery floss in a color that complements the colors in the mats

✔ One tapestry or large-eye hand needle

Follow these steps to make the place mat vest:

1. **On a table, turn two place mats vertically, overlapping and pinning them together ¼ inch at the top and 4 inches at the bottom (see Figure 3-5).**

   Remember, the sides of the mats you want to show are facing out. This part is the center back and may be adjusted out or in, as needed, before you start sewing.

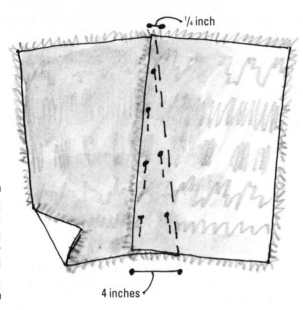

¼ inch

4 inches

Figure 3-5:
Overlap the
placemats
along their
vertical
edges.

2. **Create the shoulders of the vest by overlapping two more mats about ½ inch at the short ends. Pin the seams, stopping 5 to 6 inches from the center front (see Figure 3-6).**

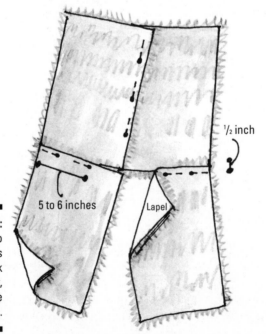

½ inch

5 to 6 inches   Lapel

Figure 3-6:
Pin two
more mats
to the back
of your vest,
creating the
shoulders.

Doing so allows the mats to fall open at the neckline, creating lapels.

This step creates the side seams. Make sure the spaces left open are large enough to comfortably fit your arms. Overlap the seams for mats with fabric-bound or hemmed edges. Place seams with wrong sides together for mats with fringed edges.

3. **Place the long sides of the mats together, pinning from the bottom up 6 to 7 inches (see Figure 3-7).**

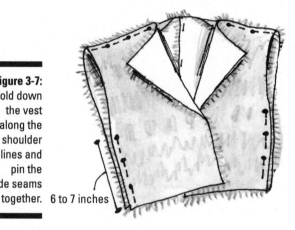

Figure 3-7:
Fold down the vest along the shoulder lines and pin the side seams together.

6 to 7 inches

4. **Try on the vest and adjust it to fit.**

If the vest is too big, overlap the mats at the center back a little more (as shown in Figure 3-8), and then pinch in and pin a pleat on both sides of the overlap until you like how the garment fits (see Chapter 8 for more information on pleats). If the vest is too small, narrow the overlap at the center back.

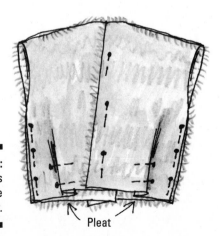

Figure 3-8:
Use pleats to customize the fit.

Pleat

5. **Set your machine like this:**
   - **Stitch:** Straight
   - **Length:** 3 mm/9 spi
   - **Width:** 0 mm
   - **Foot:** All-purpose

6. **Unpin the side seams so that the vest is flat and pinned together only at the shoulder seams and center back overlap.**

   Doing so makes the actual sewing easier.

7. **Stitch the center back overlap and the overlap at both shoulders.**

   Sew each overlap by guiding a presser-foot-width away from the edge of the place mats. Backstitch at the beginning and end of each line of stitching.

8. **Re-pin the side seams together (refer to Step 3) and then double-check the fit by trying on the vest.**

   If the vest is too boxy, make larger side seams. If it's too skimpy, make smaller side seams.

9. **Stitch the side seams, backstitching at the top and bottom of each seam.**

10. **Turn back and gently press the lapels and armholes.**

11. **Using the tapestry or large-eye hand needle and the pearl cotton or embroidery floss as the thread, secure the armhole cuffs in place at the shoulder seam by sewing on a button, which holds the cuff in place.**

    See Chapter 5 for more information about sewing on buttons.

Creating a place mat jacket

Simply add two more place mats to the place mat vest (see the preceding section) to create sleeves for this clever jacket.

To make this project, you need the following materials in addition to your Sewing Survival Kit, which I tell you about in Chapter 1:

- ✔ Six cotton place mats (I used ones that already had hand blanket stitching around the edges)
- ✔ Thread to match the mat
- ✔ Three buttons in a contrasting color (Optional)
- ✔ Pearl cotton (looks like a twisted embroidery floss and comes on a ball) or embroidery floss in a color that complements the place mats (Optional)
- ✔ One tapestry hand needle

Follow these steps to make the place mat jacket:

1. **Follow Steps 1 through 7 for the place mat vest.**

2. **Open the vest flat, center the long sides of two more mats over each shoulder seam, and pin the two new mats to the jacket, overlapping the long sides ½ inch.**

    These two mats (I call them *sleeve mats*) create the sleeves.

3. **Sew the sleeve mats to the body of the jacket along the long edges, as shown in Figure 3-9.**

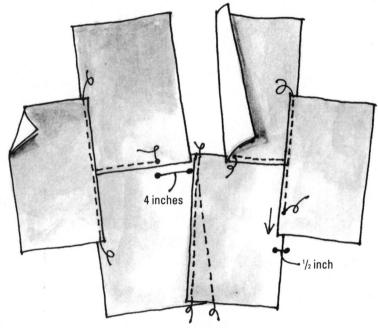

4 inches

½ inch

Figure 3-9: Overlap two mats along the sides of the vest mats to add sleeves.

4. **Place, pin, and sew the jacket side seams (right sides together and backstitching at both ends of the seam).**

5. **Place and pin the long, free edges of the sleeve mats, right sides together, to complete the sleeves.**

    Make sure to pin the underarm seams up to the edge of the mats that you're using for the sleeves.

6. **Sew the underarm seams the length of the sleeve mats, backstitching at both ends of each seam.**

7. **Place, pin, and sew the jacket side seams, right sides together, back-stitching at both ends of each seam.**

The jacket has an *air hole* where the sleeves and side seams come together under the arm.

8. **Turn back and gently press the lapels and the cuffs on the sleeves.**

To create the embellished look of the jacket you see in the color pages of this book, you need to do a little hand stitching. Using a single strand of No.8 pearl cotton or embroidery floss, decorate the lapels and the overlap at the center back with small, hand-running stitches (see Chapter 5 for more information on hand-running stitches). You can then attach three large contrasting buttons to the lapels for a unique look.

Chapter 4

Working with Patterns

In This Chapter

▶ Selecting the right pattern

▶ Reading the pattern and the pattern envelope

▶ Laying out and cutting the pattern

▶ Marking why-fors and how-tos

*B*esides starting with a good piece of fabric and a pattern that fits your figure type, the business of laying out, cutting, and marking the pattern pieces correctly, as you see in this chapter, are the foundations to your sewing success. After you understand these important steps, you'll zoom toward a finished project.

Shopping for Patterns

Patterns are marketed through pattern magazines, which you can find on the newsstands at your local bookstore or grocery store. You can also find patterns in pattern catalogs at fabric stores that carry fashion fabrics (fabrics that are made into clothing as opposed to fabrics that are made into home decor, craft, or quilting projects). Besides catalogs, these stores also display some brands that have specially priced or promotional patterns on spinner racks for easy access.

Stores that specialize in home decorating fabrics often don't carry clothing patterns. However, regional and national fabric chain stores often carry both types of fabric, plus quilting fabrics and supplies and everything else you need to complete clothing, home decor projects, crafting projects, quilting projects, and more.

What comes first, the pattern or the fabric?

For me, the pattern or the fabric can first pop into my head. Sometimes, I'm inspired by a design I see in a department store, boutique, or movie, and I look for a pattern to match that design.

Other times, the fabric speaks to me, and I look for a pattern that works well with the fabric. Even if you're just starting out with sewing, feel free to let your creative juices flow in either direction.

In addition to commercial patterns made by companies such as Burda, Kwik Sew, McCalls, Simplicity, Stretch & Sew, and Vogue/Butterick, independent pattern companies may or may not have a catalog. You can find their patterns in specialty sewing and fabric stores, craft and quilt stores, and sewing machine dealerships. If you can't find what you're looking for in your local fabric chain store, take a creative field trip and find these other retailers. They may have just the pattern you desire.

In most pattern catalogs, sections identify projects by categories, which range from dresses and children's clothing to crafts and home decor projects. Within those categories, you often find patterns categorized by degree of difficulty, usually placing emphasis on those projects that are easy to sew.

Even a pattern labeled *easy* or *quick* may be difficult and time-consuming for a rookie. Many pattern instruction writers assume that you have a certain amount of general sewing knowledge. If you're a real beginner, look for patterns with few seams and simple lines.

The *Sewing For Dummies* patterns, published by Simplicity Pattern Company, are a perfect choice. They have the latest projects and the easiest-to-follow sewing directions you can find. If you're in a quandary about a particular pattern, have a sales associate at the fabric store help you.

Sizing Things Up for Fashion Sewing

Determining your pattern size for a garment can be a humbling experience. Patterns for adults usually run smaller than ready-to-wear sizes — sad but true. Patterns for children have the opposite problem and run larger than ready-to-wear sizes.

That means, for example, that if you usually wear a size 10 dress, you may find yourself buying a size 12 pattern!

And I have more bad news. For measurement accuracy, someone else must take and record your measurements. You just can't get accurate measurements by yourself, so don't even try it. Find someone you trust, swear them to secrecy, and start measuring. (See Chapter 1 if you're in the market for a measuring tape to take your vital statistics.)

Dressed in your underwear or a leotard, tie a piece of narrow ribbon or elastic around your waist. Don't cinch the ribbon too tight. Wiggle around until the ribbon or elastic finds your natural waistline. If you can't find your waistline, put the elastic where you wear a belt. It's important to locate your waist to take your measurements and decide your figure type.

Have your helper take the following six measurements (Figure 4-1 shows you the exact placement of each measurement):

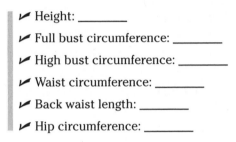

- ✔ Height: _____
- ✔ Full bust circumference: _____
- ✔ High bust circumference: _____
- ✔ Waist circumference: _____
- ✔ Back waist length: _____
- ✔ Hip circumference: _____

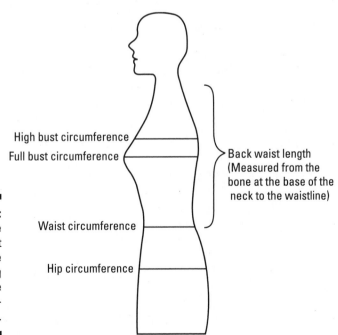

Figure 4-1:
Determine the correct pattern size by taking these measurements.

High bust circumference
Full bust circumference
Back waist length (Measured from the bone at the base of the neck to the waistline)
Waist circumference
Hip circumference

Take these measurements to the catalog counter. Somewhere in the front or back of the pattern catalog you can find measurement charts. Using your height and back waist length, determine your figure type (Junior, Misses/Miss petite, Unisex, and so on), and then compare your other measurements with the charts in the catalog to find the size that comes closest to your measurements. That's your pattern size. Write your size, the brand name of the pattern, and the pattern number (usually a four-digit number) on a piece of paper and head over to the pattern drawer.

Stores file patterns numerically by brand. So after you find the brand, the pattern number, and your size, pull the pattern from the drawer. Find your size on the chart on the back of the pattern envelope to see how much fabric you need to buy.

The Pattern and All Its Parts

Nothing can be more intimidating than trying to figure out all the hieroglyphics on the various parts of a pattern as shown in Figure 4-2. I tell you just what you need to know about pattern parts in this section.

Reading the front of the pattern envelope

On the front of the pattern envelope you often see several style variations of the same project. In the world of sewing, people call these style variations *views*. One view may have a collar, long sleeves, and cuffs. Another view may have a V-neck and short sleeves.

In home decor patterns, you may have several views in one pattern for a basic window treatment. Another pattern may have several pillow views. A third has several options for chair covers. Views simply give you style options on creating the same basic project.

Reading the back of the pattern envelope

The back of a pattern envelope contains the following information about your project:

  ✔ **The back of the project in detail:** The front of the pattern usually just shows the front of your project. The back of the pattern shows you the back of the project. You see details like kick pleats or a back zipper — information that you want to know about before buying the pattern.

✓ **A description of the project by view:** Always read the description of a project on the back of the pattern envelope. Drawings and photographs can deceive, but this written description tells you exactly what you're getting.

✓ **How much fabric to buy:** This information is based on the width of the fabric you choose, the view you make, your size, and whether your fabric has nap or not. (See Chapter 2 for more information on fabric widths.)

If your fabric has nap, the pattern requires you to buy a little more fabric. Your fabric has nap if it falls into any of these categories:

- **Contains a one-way design:** Dancing elephants printed in the same direction, for example. If you cut out some of the pattern pieces in one direction and other pattern pieces in the opposite direction, you find elephants dancing right side up on part of the project and upside down on another part of the same project. You need extra fabric so that you can get all your elephants going in the right direction.

- **Has a fuzzy texture:** Such as velvet, corduroy, Polarfleece, and some sweatshirt fleeces. When brushed in one direction, the fabric is smooth; when brushed in the other direction, it's rough. This texture difference translates into a color difference. You need more fabric to cut out the pattern pieces in the same direction.

- **Contains an uneven stripe:** For example, fabric with three colored stripes — red, blue, and yellow. To match the stripes at the seams, you need extra fabric because you have to lay out the pattern in the same direction. If you lay out the front and back pattern pieces in opposite directions, you cut the stripes on the front, going from red, to blue, to yellow. And you cut the stripes on the back so that they go from yellow, to blue, to red. When you sew the seam together, the stripes don't match at the side seams. See the section "Laying out plaids, stripes, and one-way designs," later in this chapter, for more information.

- **Contains an even or uneven plaid:** The color bars in a plaid must match both vertically and horizontally. If the plaid is even, the color bars have the same spacing and are in the same order in both directions along the selvage, which means you can lay out the pattern pieces in both directions. In an uneven plaid, the color bars aren't symmetrical in one or both directions, so you need to lay out all the pattern pieces in the same direction. You need more fabric to make either kind of plaid match. See the section "Laying out plaids, stripes, and one-way designs," later in this chapter, for more information.

✓ **List of notions needed for specific views:** These notions include items such as the number and size of buttons, the zipper length and type, elastic width and length, shoulder pad style and size, hooks and eyes, and so on.

Figure 4-2:
Front and
back of a
pattern
envelope.

It's what's inside that counts

Inside your pattern envelope, you find the following items necessary for your project:

✔ **Pattern pieces:** Some pattern pieces are printed on large pieces of tissue paper. Others are printed on sturdy pieces of white paper called *master patterns.*

To preserve the master pattern or a tissue paper pattern with multiple sizes for reuse, simply trace the size you need onto a piece of pattern tracing material. (You can get this material at most fabric stores or through sewing mail-order catalogs.) This way, you can trace off another view or cut out a project for someone else who is a different size without destroying the master pattern.

✔ **Key and glossary:** These references help you decipher the markings on the pattern pieces.

- **Pattern layout:** This guide shows you how to lay out the pattern pieces on the fabric yardage for each view.

- **Step-by-step instructions for putting the project together:** Depending on your knowledge of sewing, you may find this set of instructions (called a *pattern guide sheet*) clear as day — or as mud. Don't worry, though — this book tells you what you need to know to decipher the instructions.

The project instructions may run more than one page. If they do, staple the pages together in the upper-left corner and post them in front of you as you sew. You can easily check off each step as you finish it. If you don't have a place to post the sheet, set it next to your sewing machine, folded to the section you're working on, for a handy reference.

Some home decor projects, such as pillow patterns, include tissue or paper pattern pieces. Others, such as sofa slipcovers and some window treatments, don't include a paper pattern because they don't use a standard size or style of sofa or window. In these patterns, you find printed, step-by-step instructions that look like the pattern guide sheet that comes with a typical pattern.

Decoding the pattern pieces

Look at your pattern pieces. You have only one sleeve, half of a front top, half of a back top pattern, half of a facing, half of a collar, and so on. Did the company forget to print the whole pattern?

Because you fold the fabric in half the long way (usually with the right side of the fabric to the inside), you lay the pattern pieces out and cut them on a double fabric layer. So, most of the time, you need only half of the pattern to make a complete garment.

All pattern pieces have the following information printed on or near the center of each pattern piece:

- **Pattern number:** If you accidentally mix together pattern pieces of different projects, these numbers can help you figure out which pieces belong to which projects.

- **Name of the pattern piece:** These names are pretty straightforward — sleeve, front pant, and so on.

- **Letter or number of the pattern piece:** These identifiers help you find all the pattern pieces for the view you're making.

- **Size:** Many pattern pieces show several sizes; each size is marked clearly, so you shouldn't have too much trouble keeping them straight.

- **Number of pieces you need to cut:** Often, you need to cut more than one of each pattern piece.

These pattern markings appear around the periphery of the pattern pieces:

- **Cutting line:** This heavy, outer line on the pattern piece lets you know where to cut. Sometimes you see scissors symbols on this line.

- **Seamline or stitching line:** You usually find this broken line ¼ to ⅝ inch inside the cutting line. Multiple-sized patterns may not have a seamline printed on the pattern. Read the pattern guide sheet to determine the width of the seam allowance. (Chapter 6 tells you more about seams.)

- **Notches:** You use these diamond-shaped match points on the cutting line for accurately joining pattern pieces together. You may find single notches, double notches, and triple notches all on one pattern.

- **Circles, dots, triangles, or squares:** No, this isn't a geometry lesson — these shapes indicate additional match points that aid in the construction, fit, and ease in putting the project together. For example, large dots on the pattern may indicate where you gather a waistline.

- **Place on fold brackets or symbols:** Use these symbols to lay out the pattern piece exactly on the fold, which is also the lengthwise grain of the fabric. When you cut out the pattern piece and remove the paper pattern, the fabric opens into a full piece.

- **Lengthen or shorten directives:** Based on your measurements, your body may be longer or shorter than the paper pattern piece. These double lines show where you can cut the pattern apart to lengthen it or fold up the pattern piece to shorten it.

- **Darts:** Broken stitching lines meet at a point to create the dart. Some patterns also have a solid line that runs the length of the dart showing where you fold the fabric to create the dart. (See Chapter 8 for more information on darts.)

- **Center back and center front:** These directions are clearly labeled with a solid cutting line or *place on fold* symbol. If the pattern has a solid cutting line, it has a seam down the center front or center back. If, instead, you place the center front or center back on the fold and cut it out, you don't have a seam down the center front or the center back.

- **Zipper position:** This symbol shows the zipper placement. The top and bottom markings (usually dots) show you the length of the zipper. (See Chapter 9 on specifics for putting in a zipper.)

- **Grainline:** The most important pattern marking, the grainline symbol is a straight line that usually has arrowheads at each end. The grainline parallels the *selvages* (finished edges) of the fabric. See the section "Placing the pattern pieces on-grain," later in this chapter, to find out why this marking is critical for your sewing success.

- ✔ **Directional stitching symbols:** These symbols, which often look like small arrows or presser feet symbols, indicate the direction you sew when sewing the seam.

- ✔ **The hemline:** This direction on the pattern shows the recommended finished length of the project, which varies from person to person. But, even though the hemline may vary, the *hem allowance* (the recommended distance from the hemline to the cut edge) doesn't. See Chapter 7 for more information on hem depths.

Figure 4-3 shows the full gambit of markings you may find on a pattern piece.

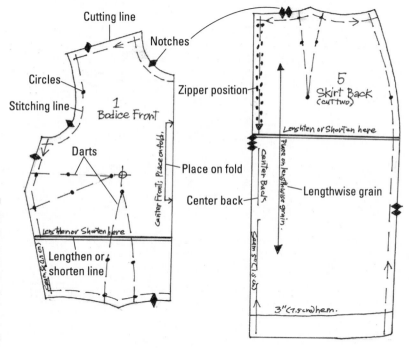

Figure 4-3: Markings on tissue pattern pieces are the road-map to your project.

Laying Out the Pattern

Before laying out the pattern on the fabric, you need to understand some basic fabric terminology. Why? Let me put it to you this way: Understanding the parts of the fabric and cutting your pattern pieces on-grain means that seams stay pressed and straight, pant legs and sleeves don't twist when you wear them, and the creases in your pants stay perpendicular to the ground.

Getting to know your fabric

If you hear the word *grain* and think of oatmeal, you're not quite ready to lay out your pattern. Knowing your way around a piece of fabric is crucial to your sewing success. Take a look at Figure 4-4 to acquaint yourself with fabric's four key facets:

- ✔ **Selvages:** The finished edges where the fabric comes off the looms, the selvages are parallel to the lengthwise grain.

- ✔ **Lengthwise grain or grainline:** The grainline runs the length of the fabric, parallel to the selvages. On knit fabrics, the lengthwise grain is usually more stable and less stretchy than the crosswise grain.

- ✔ **Crosswise grain:** This grain runs across the width of the fabric, from selvage to selvage and perpendicular to the lengthwise grain. On knit fabrics, most of the stretch is usually across the grain.

- ✔ **Bias:** 45 degrees between the lengthwise and crosswise grains.

Preparing the fabric

Using fabric straight off the bolt is a little like eating an unbaked apple pie: You can do it, but the results are not going to be good. You skip an important step if you do not preshrink and press your fabric before you begin. (See Chapter 2 for more information on preshrinking; you're on your own for the apple pie.)

Even after preshrinking and pressing your fabric, you may notice a crease running down the center of the goods — that's where the fabric was folded on the bolt. You can press this pesky crease out of most fabrics by sprinkling equal parts of white vinegar and water on a press cloth and then laying the press cloth on the crease between the iron and the fabric, pressing until the fabric dries.

After you press the fabric, refold it to the original bolt fold so that the selvages are even.

Take a look at the fabric: When you fold it in half so the selvages are together, are the raw edges perpendicular to the selvages and the selvages parallel to one another? If not, the fabric may have been cut off the bolt unevenly, or the fabric needs to be pulled back on grain. To do so, unfold the fabric again, pull it on the bias (as shown in Figure 4-4), and straighten it. If you have a large piece of fabric, get a helper to pull the yardage from one corner while you pull on the yardage from the opposite corner.

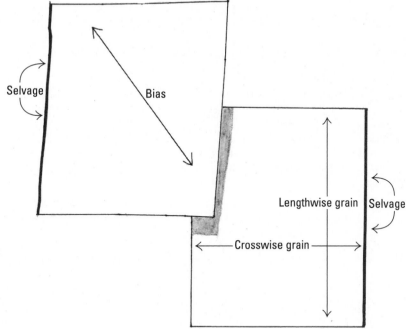

Figure 4-4:
The parts
of a piece
of fabric.

Knowing right from wrong

The *right side* of the fabric is the pretty side that everyone sees. Many fabrics are on the bolt with the right side folded to the inside to keep it clean. The *wrong side* of the fabric is the inside that nobody sees when you wear the project. When you lay out the pattern for cutting, be sure that you lay out all the pattern pieces as shown in your pattern guide sheet instructions.

The pattern guide sheet shows the right side of the fabric shaded in a darker color than the wrong side of the fabric so you can see what's going on in the step-by-step illustrations.

Placing the pattern pieces on-grain

Each pattern piece shows a *grainline* or *place on fold* symbol (which is also the lengthwise grain. See the section "Decoding the pattern pieces," earlier in this chapter, for more information on the chicken scratches you find on pattern pieces). The grainline allows you to cut the piece *on-grain*, meaning that the pattern piece lines up with the lengthwise grain of the fabric.

Pattern piece storage made easy

Trying to put the pattern pieces back into the envelope after using them is like putting toothpaste back into the tube. Instead, tape a gallon-sized plastic freezer bag to your sewing machine. Put the pattern envelope, extra pattern pieces, and guide sheet into this bag — I find it much easier than using the pattern envelope, and everything fits.

When you finish with each pattern piece, fold it so that the pattern number, name, and company name show. This way, if you forget to mark something, you can see it through the freezer bag and locate it easily without unfolding and shuffling through multiple paper pattern pieces.

Lay out and cut your fabric on a large table or counter. If you don't have a large table to cut on, buy a foldable cutting board available through your local fabric store. Buy a large, flat sheet of corrugated cardboard with a fold in the middle, which usually comes with an inch and a metric grid printed on it. Lay it on a small table and you have an instant workable cutting space. When you finish using the board, simply fold it up and slide it under your bed or behind your dresser. Even though you can lay out and cut on the floor, your back will thank you for using a cutting board, table, or counter.

Follow these steps to lay the pattern pieces on the fabric:

1. **Find and cut apart the paper pattern pieces you need to make your project view; set them aside.**

   When you cut the paper pattern pieces apart, don't cut them out right on the cutting line; leave a little of the paper past the cutting line. Leaving the extra paper makes cutting out the paper pieces faster and easier.

2. **Locate the lengthwise grain or place on fold symbols on the paper pattern pieces.**

   On a flat tabletop and before laying the pattern on the fabric, mark over these symbols, using a highlighter, for easy reference.

3. **Fold and then lay the fabric on a table or cutting board, as shown in the pattern guide sheet instructions.**

   If the fabric is longer than your table or cutting board, prevent the excess fabric weight from stretching and pulling on your fabric by folding it and laying it on the end of the table.

4. **Following the layout the pattern guide sheet suggests, lay out the pattern on-grain, making sure that the grainline is parallel to the selvages as shown in Figure 4-5.**

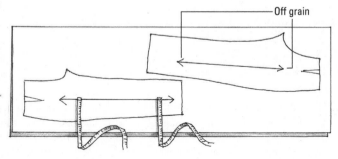

Figure 4-5:
The grainline of your pattern should be parallel to the selvages when you lay out a pattern.

Check that each pattern piece is placed precisely on-grain by poking a pin straight down into one end of the grainline, measuring the distance from the top of the grainline to the selvage, and then measuring the distance from the bottom of the grainline to the selvage. Be sure to pivot the paper pattern so that each end of the pattern piece is equidistant from the selvage. However, use this technique only if a cutting board or table pad protects your tabletop.

Now you're ready for pinning and cutting. See the section "Pinning and Cutting Out the Pieces," later in this chapter, for more information.

Laying out plaids, stripes, and one-way designs

You don't often see perfectly matched plaids and stripes in ready-to-wear garments — unless you want to spend a lot of money. Garment manufacturers find it tough to match designs because they stack many layers of fabric as high as 12 inches and then cut out each pattern piece with a jigsaw. That system lets them cut 100 left sleeves at once, but it leaves little room for precision.

As a home sewer, though, you cut one garment at a time, so you can more easily get a perfect match with a one-way design, stripe, or plaid.

Save yourself a major headache: If you plan to use fabric with a plaid, stripe, or one-way design, avoid patterns that say "not suitable for plaids, stripes, or one-way designs." Princess lines (seams that run from the shoulder seam, over the bust, and down to the hemline) and patterns with long vertical darts are also hard to match if you use this kind of fabric.

Because you need more fabric when working with these patterns, remember to use the *with nap* yardage requirements found on the back of the pattern envelope.

One-way designs

Your fabric contains a one-way design if the pattern makes sense only when you view it from one direction. For example, fabric printed with dancing elephants makes sense only if all the elephants dance right side up. To make all the elephants dance right side up all over the project, you have to lay out all the pattern pieces in the same direction.

When working with a one-way design, consider the following factors:

✔ **Size of each design in the print:** If the fabric has a small-scale, all-over print, you don't need to worry so much about matching the design. If the scale of the print is large, you want the design to match across the front, over to the sleeves, and to the back of the garment.

Placement is important when working with a large-scale print. For example, you don't want a print with big red balloons to end up with a balloon at both bust points. You also don't want sailing ships positioned over your derriere because it may seem like some major waves toss them around when you walk — so think before you cut.

✔ **Size of the repeat of the pattern:** This size means the distance between each repeating design on the fabric. If the repeat is ½ inch, a small example, you may not have to match it. If the repeat is 4 inches, though, the repeat is large and should be matched.

Even and uneven stripes

Stripes have bars of color printed, knitted, or woven either horizontally or vertically in the fabric. Stripes come in two varieties:

✔ **Even stripe:** This pattern has an even number of color bars, and all the color bars are the same width. Think of a T-shirt knit with a 1-inch white stripe and a 1-inch blue stripe. When working with an even stripe, you can lay out pattern pieces in either direction (with the top edge of the pattern at the top of the fabric or the top edge of the pattern at the bottom of the fabric), and the stripes match.

✔ **Uneven stripe:** This pattern has the same- or different-width stripes and an odd number of color bars. For example, a T-shirt knit with horizontal stripes with a 1-inch red stripe, a ½-inch white stripe, and a 1-inch blue stripe has an uneven stripe pattern. If you cut the pattern pieces in opposite directions, the stripes don't match: The color bars line up as red, white, and then blue on one piece and as blue, white, and then red on the other piece.

As a beginning sewer, you need to steer clear of uneven stripes. If you're unsure whether the fabric you chose is an even or uneven stripe, ask the fabric store sales associate to identify it for you. If you don't, you're asking for A.S.F.S. — Acute Sewing Frustration Syndrome.

Even and uneven plaids

Plaid fabrics have color bars printed or woven into the fabric both horizontally and vertically. Plaids come in two different flavors:

✔ **Even plaid:** The color bars in an even plaid match in the lengthwise and crosswise directions. To check for an even plaid, fold the fabric in half the long way (like when you lay out the pattern for cutting) and then turn back a corner, folding it on the bias (see the section "Getting to know your fabric," earlier in this chapter, for information on the bias). If the top layer of plaid forms a mirror image of the bottom layer, you have an even plaid. You can match even plaids more easily than uneven plaids.

✔ **Uneven plaid:** This plaid may or may not match in one or both directions and as a result is more difficult to work with. Use the test in the "Even plaid" bullet above to determine whether you have an even or uneven plaid on your hands. If, when you fold down a corner, the plaid isn't a mirror image, you may want to choose another plaid. Until you have considerable experience in laying out and cutting fabric, avoid uneven plaids.

Uneven plaids present problems for the beginning sewer because of the matching difficulty they present. If you're unsure whether or not the fabric you may choose is an uneven plaid, ask the fabric store sales associate to identify it for you. As your skills improve, start with a small, even plaid and gain some confidence before tackling the uneven plaids.

After pinning the pattern piece to the fabric, use an air-soluble marker to draw the design onto the pattern tissue, following the dominant color bars as shown in Figure 4-6. Remove the pattern piece that you draw over and place it on the fabric so that the color bars on the plaid or stripe you see marked on the pattern paper match those on the fabric.

Figure 4-6:
Match a
plaid by
drawing
over the
design on
the pattern
tissue.

Lay out twice and cut once

The following tips help in laying out a pattern for large, one-way designs, stripes, and even plaids:

- ✔ **Centering:** Decide what you want in the center of the project and fold the fabric there, matching the stripes, plaid, or one-way designs across the width and length of the fabric. Doing so may mean that the selvages aren't even. You may also have to pin the fabric together every few inches or so to keep the fabric from shifting when you lay it out and cut it according to the pattern.

- ✔ **Placement:** Generally, you place the dominant stripe or color bar in a project directly on, or as close as possible to, the hemline edge. This arrangement means placing the hemline marked on the pattern tissue along the dominant color bar of the fabric. Avoid the dominant stripe, color bar, or big red balloons across the bust or at the fullest part of the hips.

- ✔ **Crosswise matching:** Use the notches on the pattern pieces to match the fabric design from piece to piece. For example, to match the design at the shoulder seams, notice where the notches on the pattern pieces fall on a particular color bar and within the plaid itself.

Crosswise matching is easiest when you center the first pattern piece on the fabric where you want it. After you center the pattern, take the pattern piece you want to match the fabric to and place it over the first, matching the notches.

Pinning and Cutting Out the Pieces

Pin the pattern piece to the doubled layer of fabric so that the pins go through both fabric layers and are perpendicular to and inside of the cutting line. This prevents the fabric from shifting during the cutting process. (See the section "Laying Out the Pattern," earlier in this chapter, for more information on folding your fabric to create a double layer.)

My grandmother taught me to pin parallel to the cutting line. While researching the *right* way to pin for this book, I realized I've been doing it *wrong* all these years but still had beautiful results. So here's the message: Whenever you find a way of doing anything in sewing that you like and that works, use it.

You don't need to pin every inch. Just pin at the notches and everywhere the pattern changes direction. On long, straight edges, such as pant legs and sleeve seams, place pins every 4 inches or so.

Cut out your pattern pieces using a pair of sharp dressmaker's shears. (See Chapter 1 for more information on choosing the right scissors for cutting.) For accuracy, cut in the middle of the solid cutting line marked on the pattern tissue, trying not to lift the fabric off the table too much when cutting.

Rather than cutting around each individual notch, save time by cutting straight across the notches on the cutting line. After you completely cut out the pattern piece, go back and, with the tips of your sharp scissors, snip into the notch about ¼ inch. A single notch gets one snip in the center of the notch; a double notch gets two snips, one in the center of each notch; a triple notch gets three snips. When you go to match up the pattern pieces at the notches, just match up the snips — a fast and accurate task.

On Your Mark!

After you cut out the pattern pieces and fuse on any necessary interfacing (see Chapter 2), you're ready for marking. Marking is important because you don't want to get halfway through a project, notice that the pattern guide sheet tells you to sew from this mark to that mark, and realize that you forgot to mark something (or thought it wasn't important). You have to stop what you're doing and rifle through your paper pattern pieces to locate the appropriate one. Next, you have to look for that pesky little mark and transfer the mark to your fabric before going any further.

Save yourself time and frustration — mark the dots, circles, squares, or triangles, even if you think that you won't need them later. Trust me, you will.

Making the marks that matter

You need to mark the following things from your pattern pieces onto your fabric:

- ✔ Darts (see Chapter 8)
- ✔ Pleats (see Chapter 8)
- ✔ Tucks (see Chapter 8)
- ✔ Dots, circles, triangles, and squares (see the section "Decoding the pattern pieces" earlier in this chapter)

When you begin constructing a project, you transfer the pattern marks indicating darts, tucks, pleats, and the other symbols to your fabric pattern pieces for a very good reason: To see and understand what the drawings and text in the pattern guide sheet instructions mean for you to do. For example, when marking a pleat, tuck, or dart, instead of marking the entire stitching line, simply mark the dots on the stitching lines. When you put the right sides together for sewing, pin the project together by matching the dots; sew from dot to dot (pin to pin). For specific instructions on marking and sewing darts, tucks, and pleats, see your pattern guide sheet instructions.

Using the right tool at the right time

You find many marking tools on the market, but using pins, disappearing dressmaking chalk, and an air- or water-soluble marking pen is the easiest way to go. Chapter 1 gives you more information on these tools.

Use the following marking techniques, depending on the type of fabric you use in a project:

- ✔ **Mark light-colored fabrics by using your air- or water-soluble marker.** Place the point of the marker on the tissue pattern at the dot or circle, as shown in Figure 4-7.

  The ink bleeds through the pattern tissue, the first layer of fabric, and then to the second layer of fabric for an accurate mark. You can easily remove the marks from either marker with clear water.

✔ **Mark dark fabrics by using your disappearing dressmaker's chalk.**
Push pins through the pattern paper and both fabric layers at the dots,
as I show in Figure 4-8. Open the fabric between the layers and mark
both layers where the pins enter the fabric.

When marking with chalk, I prefer marking the wrong side of the fabric.
The mark is easier to see and doesn't show on the right side of the
fabric. But be careful: When you iron or press over the disappearing
chalk, steam sometimes removes the mark, which is okay when you
want it to disappear and maddening when it happens accidentally.

✔ **Mark hard-to-mark fabrics by pin-marking.** Push the pins straight
through the fabric on both fabric layers. Carefully remove the pattern
paper by tearing it over the pin heads. Pull apart the fabric layers. The
pins pull right up to the heads and accurately mark the fabric, as you
can see in Figure 4-9.

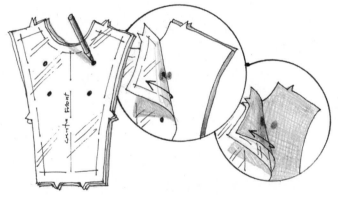

Figure 4-7:
Mark light-
colored
fabrics
with an air-
or water-
soluble
marker.

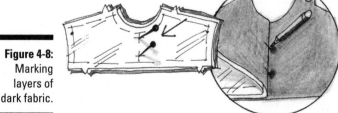

Figure 4-8:
Marking
layers of
dark fabric.

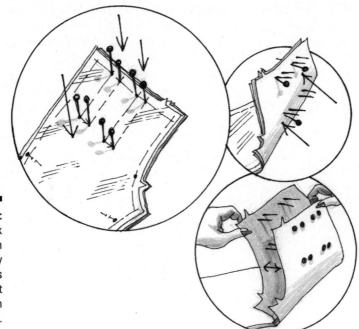

Figure 4-9:
Mark
pattern
pieces by
pushing pins
straight
through both
fabric layers.

Part II
Sewers! Start Your Engines!

The 5th Wave   By Rich Tennant

"Roger! Check the sewing machine's connection to the PC. I'm getting e-mails stitched across my curtains again."

In this part . . .

The chapters in this part focus on the fundamentals of sewing. If you're a stone-cold beginner to sewing, you should definitely appreciate the step-by-step information in this part about threading a needle, sewing many common types of hand stitches, using an iron effectively, finishing fabric edges, sewing seams, and hemming, among other fun sewing fundamentals. If you have sewn before, you may be tempted to skip over the chapters in this part — don't! Each of the chapters includes several tips and hints that help even a more experienced sewer. Plus, this part contains some really great sewing projects — don't miss them!

Chapter 5

Sewing 101

*W*hether you quilt, embroider, mend, or construct a project, you need a needle, thread, fabric, and some sewing know-how. This chapter covers the important sewing fundamentals.

Threading the Needle

When a motorist *threads the needle* on the freeway, she weaves in and out of traffic, almost hitting other cars in the process. Although threading the needle in sewing is much less dangerous, it does require some skill.

Hand needles

To begin threading a hand needle, reel off a strand of thread about 18 to 24 inches long. Longer threads tend to tangle and wear out before you use them up.

Starting with the end of the thread that comes off the spool first, cut the thread cleanly and at an angle with a sharp pair of scissors. Cutting at an angle puts a little point on the thread so that it slips easily through the eye.

The cheapest sewing notion on the market is your own saliva. Moisten the thread end to help it glide right through the needle's eye.

Some needles have very small eyes; some people have very poor eyesight. A *needle threader,* which you can find at your local sewing supply store, can help with tight threading situations. To use a needle threader, poke the fine wire through the eye of the needle, push the thread end through the wire loop, and then pull. The wire grabs the thread and pulls it through the needle's eye, as shown in Figure 5-1.

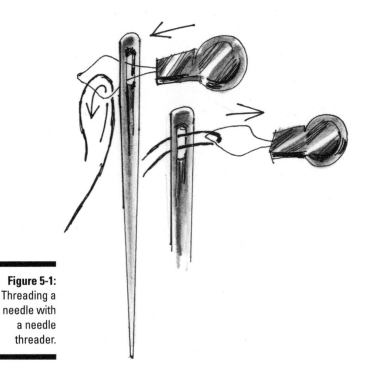

Figure 5-1:
Threading a
needle with
a needle
threader.

Self-threading hand needles make threading even easier. To use a self-threading needle, hold the needle and a length of thread in one hand. Pull the thread end across the self-threading eye so that the thread lies in the notch. Snap the thread into the notch until it clips into place, as shown in Figure 5-2. If the thread keeps coming unthreaded after many uses, you've worn out the self-threading eye, so throw away the needle and use a new one.

No amount of spit helps thread a tapestry needle because the embroidery floss or yarn commonly used with these needles tends to get frizzy at the end. Just fold over the end of the floss or yarn and poke it through the eye, as shown in Figure 5-3.

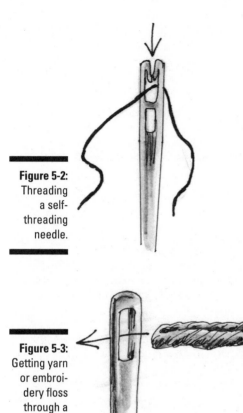

Figure 5-2:
Threading
a self-
threading
needle.

Figure 5-3:
Getting yarn
or embroi-
dery floss
through a
tapestry
needle.

Machine needles

A *machine needle*, meaning a needle for a standard sewing machine or serger, has a round and a flat side, as shown in Figure 5-4. (See Chapter 1 for more information on sewing machines and sergers.)

For sewing machines with a *side-loading bobbin* (meaning that the bobbin goes in the left side of the machine), the flat side of the needle base faces to the right. For most sergers and sewing machines with *top- and front-loading bobbins* (meaning that the bobbin goes in the front or drops into the top of the machine's bed where the fabric rests on the machine when sewing), the flat side of the needle base faces to the back.

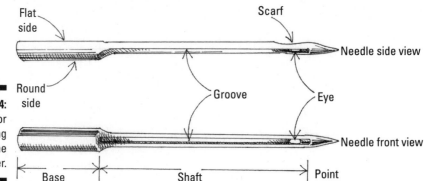

Figure 5-4:
A needle for
a sewing
machine
or serger.

Make sure that you position the needle properly for your kind of machine. The long groove running the length of the shaft protects the thread as it stitches up and down through the fabric. The scarf, the little indentation behind the eye, creates a loop that enables the bobbin thread to lock with the top thread, making a stitch. If you put the needle in the machine backwards, nothing works right.

The anatomy of a machine needle makes threading it easier than threading a hand needle. Instead of spitting on the thread, just follow these steps:

1. **Lick your finger and then rub it behind the eye of the needle.**

2. **Cut the end of the thread cleanly and at an angle.**

3. **Starting just above the eye, run the end of the thread down the shaft in the front groove until the thread pokes through the eye.**

   When the thread hits the eye, the moisture pulls the thread through it, and you're ready to sew.

Tying the Knot

You may think that having a knot in your thread is a bad thing. It may be if you didn't put it there and the thread tangles when you don't want it to. Not to worry, however, if the knot stops the thread from pulling completely through the fabric when you sew on a button and at other times where you want to anchor the end of the thread.

When preparing to write this book, I took an unofficial poll of my sewing buddies to discover whether right-handed sewers tie a sewing knot with their right hand. (I'm right-handed, and I do.) I found out that how you tie a knot doesn't seem to have a thing to do with the dominant hand; what feels natural when it comes to knot tying depends on the way you were taught.

I don't want to leave anyone out! The following steps tell both lefties and righties how to tie a sewing knot:

1. **Hold the thread between your thumb and index fingers and wrap a loop of thread around the tip of your opposite index finger, as shown in Figure 5-5.**

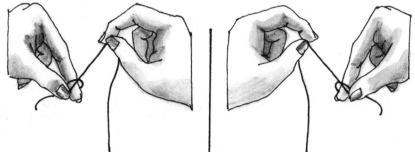

Figure 5-5:
Make a
loop.

2. **Roll the loop between your finger and against your thumb so that the loop twists, as shown in Figure 5-6.**

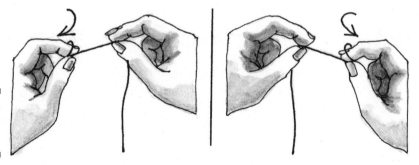

Figure 5-6:
Twist the
loop.

3. **Slide your index finger back while rolling the thread until the loop is almost off your finger, as shown in Figure 5-7.**

4. **Bring your middle finger to the twisted end of the loop, remove your index finger, and firmly place the middle finger in front of the twisted thread against the thumb, as shown in Figure 5-8.**

5. **Pull on the thread with the opposite hand to close the loop and form the knot.**

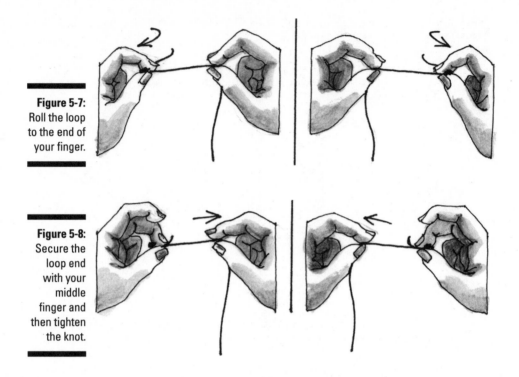

Figure 5-7:
Roll the loop to the end of your finger.

Figure 5-8:
Secure the loop end with your middle finger and then tighten the knot.

Straight Talk on Hand Stitches

Any given sewing job may entail several types of stitches, and you definitely need the right stitch for the job. For example, you shouldn't use a hand-basting stitch to permanently sew together a pair of overalls; the stitches are too far apart, and your overalls fall apart the first time you attempt to lift that bale or tote that barge. In this section, I familiarize you with the basic hand stitches and their uses.

The securing stitch

In hand sewing, you secure the end of a stitch by sewing a knot — regardless of the stitch. To sew a knot, take a small backstitch and form a loop over the point of the needle. When you pull the thread through the loop, it cinches the thread and secures a knot at the base of the fabric (see Figure 5-9). When securing a high-stress area, sew two knots.

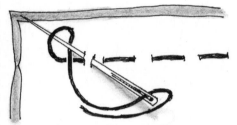

Figure 5-9: Use this technique to securely fasten a hand-sewn stitch.

The hand-basting stitch

You use hand-basting stitches to temporarily hold two or more layers of fabric together. (See the section "Basting: The Key to a Better Fit," later in this chapter, for more information.)

Each basting stitch should be about ¼ inch long with less than ¼ inch in between each stitch. When you use stitches with thread that contrasts with the fabric, the stitches are easier to pull out after you sew in the permanent stitches.

Working from right to left (for right-handers) or from left to right (for left-handers), weave the point of the needle in and out of the fabric, working it through the fabric (see Figure 5-10).

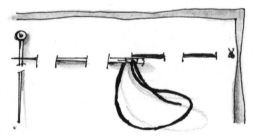

Figure 5-10: You baste by simply weaving the needle in and out of the fabric.

The running stitch

You use this very short, even stitch for fine seaming, mending, and gathering. The stitch is short and tight and, as a result, is usually permanent. I use it to quickly or temporarily repair a seam that comes apart.

To make a running stitch, weave the point of the needle in and out of the fabric making very short (1/16-inch), even stitches before pulling the needle through the fabric (see Figure 5-11).

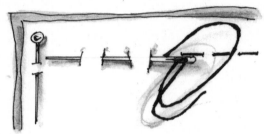

Figure 5-11:
Use short, even stitches when fashioning running stitches.

The even backstitch

The even backstitch is the strongest hand stitch. Because of its durability, you use this stitch more often when repairing a seam on dense, heavier fabrics than you would repair with the running stitch.

To create the even backstitch, pull the needle up through the fabric and poke the needle back into the fabric half a stitch behind where the thread first emerged. Bring the needle up half a stitch in front of where the thread first emerged (see Figure 5-12). Repeat for the length of the seam.

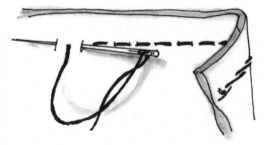

Figure 5-12:
The even backstitch is extremely strong.

The blind hemming stitch

You take these stitches inside the hem allowance between the hem and the garment (see Chapter 7 for more information on the fine points of hemming). With a little practice, a fine needle, and fine thread, good blind hemming stitches don't show on the right side — hence the name *blind*.

You need to turn up the hem allowance and press it into place before you use the blind hemming stitch. You should also finish the edge of the hem by pinking the edge or overcasting (see Chapter 6 for more on edge finishes).

Fold the hem allowance back ⅜ inch and take the first short stitch ¼ inch from the hem edge. Take the next short stitch by catching only a thread of the fabric. Continue with stitches spaced about ½ inch apart, catching the hem allowance in a stitch and taking as fine a stitch as possible into the garment. Stitch back and forth between the hem allowance and the garment around the hemline until you complete the blind hemming (see Figure 5-13).

Figure 5-13: Blind hems require fine stitches about ½ inch apart.

The slant hemming stitch

This stitch is the fastest — but least durable — of the hemming stitches because so much thread is on the surface of the hem edge. (If you've ever caught your heel in your hem and pulled it out, you may be the victim of a slant hemming stitch.) So use the slant hemming stitch only if you're in a hurry and you're hemming the bottom of a blouse that you tuck in. Take a stitch around the hem edge and then up through the garment, catching only a thread of the garment fabric (see Figure 5-14).

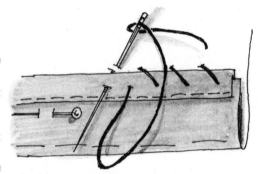

Figure 5-14: The slant stitch is quick and easy but not too durable.

The hemming slipstitch

You use the hemming slipstitch when working with (guess what?) a folded hem edge. This stitch is very durable and almost invisible. (See Chapter 7 for more information about hemming.)

Fasten the thread to the hem allowance by poking the needle through the fold of the hem edge and bringing it up through the fabric. With the point of the needle, pick up one thread from the garment and work the needle back into the fold of the hem edge (see Figure 5-15). Then repeat the process.

Figure 5-15: The hemming slipstitch is very durable and nearly invisible.

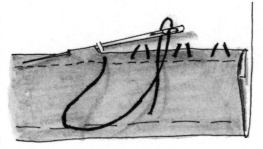

The even slipstitch

You can join two folded edges by using the even slipstitch. Most often, this stitch comes into play when you want to repair a seam from the right side because the seam is difficult to reach from the wrong side of the project.

Fasten the thread and bring it out at the edge of the fold. Taking fine stitches, work the needle, slipping it through the fold on one edge and drawing the thread taut. Take another stitch, slipping the needle through the opposite, folded edge (see Figure 5-16).

Figure 5-16: Use the slipstitch to join two folded edges or seamlines together.

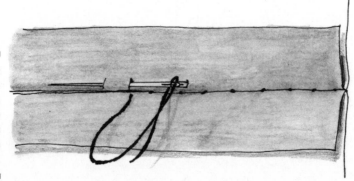

Making Machine Stitches Work for You

My parents gave me a sewing machine for my high-school graduation. After threading the machine, the first thing I did was to try all the stitches. I had no idea what they did and thought I wouldn't use most of them. Later, during my professional training as a home economist with White Sewing Machine Company, I discovered that the various stitches save time and produce more professional results.

Instead of sewing on buttons by hand, I found out I could use the zigzag stitch and buttons almost never fall off. Instead of using the time-consuming hand seam-finishing techniques from my college tailoring classes, I discovered I could finish the raw fabric edges with my sewing machine, using one of the many overcasting stitches discussed in this section and in Chapter 6. I produced beautifully machine-stitched hems in a fraction of the time it took to hem by hand. I cut my sewing time in half, and my projects looked better than ever. Finding out how to use these stitches was an epiphany, and I'm happy to share this practical knowledge with you.

The basic machine stitches

Figure 5-17 shows the basic machine stitches. Of course, your machine may offer more, or fewer, of these stitches. Compare them with what's available on your sewing machine. I bet you find a good selection.

- **Straight:** You use the straight stitch for basting, seaming, and topstitching.

- **Zigzag:** Increase the stitch width to make zigzag stitches. The fabric moves under the presser foot at the same time the needle moves from side to side. You use the zigzag stitch for stitching around appliqués, making buttonholes, sewing on buttons, and embroidering. The zigzag stitch is as practical as it is fun.

- **Three-step zigzag:** When used on the widest width, the ordinary zigzag stitch pulls the fabric into a tunnel, and the fabric rolls under the stitch — not very desirable. The three-step zigzag stitch eliminates this problem. The needle takes three stitches to one side and then three stitches to the other side, keeping the fabric flat and tunnel-free. Use the three-step zigzag for finishing raw edges, sewing on elastic, mending tears, and making decorative effects.

- **Blind hem and stretch blind hem:** The blind hem stitch is designed to hem woven fabrics so that the stitches are almost invisible when you look at the right side of the garment. The stretch blind hem stitch has an extra zigzag or two that stretches to invisibly hem knit fabrics. Both stitches have decorative applications, too.

✔ **Overlock:** Many of the overlock-type stitches on today's sewing machines are designed to stitch and finish seams in one step, simulating the overlock stitches that you see on ready-to-wear garments. Some of these stitches work well on woven fabrics; some work better on knits.

✔ **Decorative:** Decorative stitches fall into two basic categories: closed, satin-type stitches (such as the ball and diamond) and open, tracery-type stitches (such as the daisy and honeycomb). The stitch sampler belt you see in the color pages of this book is decorated with both types of stitches (see Chapter 19 for instructions on how to make this belt). You can program many newer machines to combine these stitches with other stitches, elongate the designs for a bolder decorative effect, and even stitch someone's name.

The newest high-end sewing machines can also create intricate embroidery designs (like the ones you see on ready-to-wear garments) by using *embroidery cards*. Embroidery cards can store several large, intricate motifs, like memory cards for a digital camera. Some machines also offer scanners, which allow you to add additional patterns to the machine's stitch library. Contact machine manufacturers to find out about all the options (see the appendix).

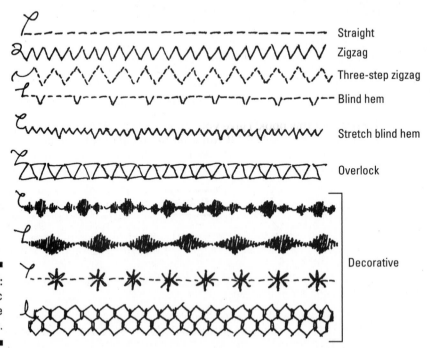

Straight

Zigzag

Three-step zigzag

Blind hem

Stretch blind hem

Overlock

Decorative

Figure 5-17:
Basic
machine
stitches.

Selecting a stitch type

If your sewing machine does more than straight stitch and zigzag, the machine must give you some way to select the stitch you want to use.

Older machines have dials, levers, buttons, or drop-in cams as *stitch selectors*. Newer, computerized models have keys or touch pads that not only select the stitch but also can automatically set the stitch length and width. Consult the operating manual that comes with your sewing machine to get the specifics on how to select a stitch type.

Selecting the length of the stitch

The length of the stitch determines the stitch's durability. Short stitches (1 to 3 mm, 13 to 60 spi) are very strong and are meant to be permanent. Longer stitches are usually temporary or used as a decorative topstitch (see the section "Topstitching" later in this chapter).

The distance the feed dogs move the fabric under the needle determines the *stitch length*. When the feed dogs move with shorter strokes, stitches are short. When they move with longer strokes, stitches are longer. (See Chapter 1 for more information on feed dogs.)

You measure stitch length two different ways — in millimeters (mm) and in stitches per inch (spi). The setting used depends on the brand and model of your machine.

Throughout this book, I give you the necessary stitch length settings both ways. Check out Table 5-1 if you want to compare stitch length in millimeters to stitch length in stitches per inch.

Table 5-1	Converting Stitch Lengths
Stitch Length in Millimeters	*Stitch Length in Stitches per Inch*
0.5	60 (fine setting)
1	24
2	13
3	9
4	6
5	5
6	4

Use the following as a general rule for stitch lengths:

- ✔ The average stitch length for mid-weight fabrics is 2.5 to 3 mm/10 to 12 spi.
- ✔ The average stitch length for fine fabrics is 2 mm/13 to 20 spi.
- ✔ For heavier fabrics, basting, or topstitching, use 4 to 5 mm/5 to 6 spi.

Setting the stitch width

The *stitch-width* control sets the distance the needle moves from side to side while creating a stitch. You don't need to worry about the stitch width when sewing straight stitches — just set it to 0 (zero).

All machines measure the stitch width in millimeters (mm). Some makes and models have a maximum stitch width of 4 to 6 mm. Others create stitches as wide as 9 mm.

Is wider better? When it comes to decorative stitches, it usually is. For the more practical stitches used in seam finishing, blind hemming, or making buttonholes, a narrower (2- to 6-mm) width works better.

Throughout this book, I give machine stitch-width settings in a range that works for most makes and models.

Stitching-in-the-ditch

You use this simple technique to tack down facings and to tack up a quick cuff or hem. Just follow these steps:

1. **Place the crack of the seam right side up and perpendicular to the presser foot so that the needle is poised over the seamline.**

2. **Using a straight stitch, sew so that the stitches bury themselves in the crack of the seam, as shown in Figure 5-18.**

Instead of backstitching, pull threads to the wrong side of the project and tie them off (see Chapter 6 for more on tying off threads).

Topstitching

Topstitching is an extra line of stitching sewn on the right side of the fabric that parallels a seamline or sews a hem. You see topstitching on the right side of a project, so it needs to look good. Your pattern instructions tell you exactly where on the project to topstitch.

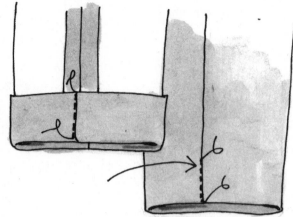

Figure 5-18:
Secure
cuffs and
facings by
stitching-in-
the-ditch

To execute the topstitch, place the project under the needle, right side up, and stitch at the right spot. Because topstitching is usually an important part of the overall garment design, you use a longer stitch length than for seaming, and you tie off the threads (see Chapter 6) instead of backstitching at the end of each topstitched seam.

Starting and Stopping

Make sure that you properly start and stop your sewing machine and serger to prevent hurting your equipment or ruining your fabric. For smooth and easy sewing, follow these techniques for starting and stopping stitches.

... with your sewing machine

Lower the presser foot onto the fabric before sewing a stitch. If you don't, the fabric flops all over the place as the needle goes up and down, and you don't get anywhere. You may even jam up the machine . . . bummer. After a few seams, lowering the foot becomes second nature.

Also, pull the top and bobbin threads to the right or to the left of the needle before lowering the foot. This way, the foot pressure holds the threads firmly, and they don't tangle or jam at the beginning of a row of stitching.

Stop sewing at the end of the fabric, stopping with the take-up lever at the highest position (see Chapter 1). If you don't, you may unthread the needle with the next stitch. Next, lift the presser foot, pulling out several inches of thread. To remove the fabric from the machine, cut the threads, leaving a

6- to 7-inch thread tail on the fabric and 2 to 3 inches of thread behind the foot. Most machines have a thread cutter near the needle, or you can cut threads with a pair of scissors.

. . . *with your serger*

Starting and stopping with sergers is easier than with sewing machines because sergers are designed for speed and durability. Leaving the presser foot down and with a short thread chain coming off the back of the foot, you simply butt the fabric edges under the toe of the foot and step on the foot pedal. When the serger starts, it grabs the fabric — and you're off and running.

To stop, gently pull the fabric as it comes out of the serger behind the foot, keeping constant, gentle tautness. Serge off the edge, creating a thread chain behind the foot. Stop serging and cut the thread chain, leaving enough on the fabric to tie off threads or to weave back under the stitches.

Basting: The Key to a Better Fit

Basting in sewing is nothing like basting a turkey in the kitchen. In sewing, *basting* means to temporarily hold pieces of a project together. You can hold them together with your hands (called *finger-basting*), with long-hand or machine stitches (called *hand-basting* or *machine-basting*), or with pins (called *pin-basting*). You can easily remove the long stitches and pins to check and adjust the fit before permanently sewing the seam together.

My seventh-grade home economics teacher made me hand-baste an entire project together before machine stitching. It took forever, and I thought that it was a real waste of time. Now that I don't have to answer to my home-ec teacher, I don't baste whole projects together, but I do pin- or machine-baste in the following circumstances and suggest that you do, too:

- ✔ When you're not sure how one pattern piece fits into another
- ✔ When you need to check and adjust the fit of the project

Use a contrasting thread color to find and pull out your basting more easily. If you're machine-basting, use contrasting thread in the bobbin case. (See Chapter 1 for more information on the bobbin case.)

To baste two pattern pieces together, start by placing and pinning the right sides together and then use either of the following methods:

✔ **Pin-basting:** Pin parallel to and ⅝ inch from the cut edge. For small areas, such as a shoulder seam, pin every 1 to 2 inches. For larger areas, such as the side seam on a pair of pants, pin every 3 to 4 inches.

✔ **Hand-basting:** Thread your hand needle and run a row of hand-basting stitches along the seamline.

✔ **Machine-basting:** Set the stitch length to a long 4-mm/6-spi straight stitch and slightly loosen the upper thread tension. Stitch along the seamlines. Remember to put the tension back to normal when you finish basting.

Some sewing machines have an automatic machine-basting function that makes stitches from about ¼ to 1 inch long. If your machine has this function, remember to use it. It can save you time and effort.

To prevent needle breakage when machine-basting or sewing, remove the pins before the foot reaches them, as shown in Figure 5-19.

If you're working on a fairly close-fitting project, add all elements that affect the fit of the project before basting. If you don't, your basting doesn't give you an accurate picture of what the project will look like. For example, you may work on a dress bodice that includes darts and shoulder pads. You should first sew and gently press the darts as shown in the pattern guide sheet. Next, pin in the shoulder pads and then baste the side seams together. You can then try on the bodice and get a fairly good idea of what the final product will look like.

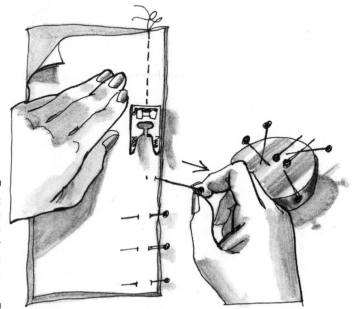

Figure 5-19: Remove pins before running over them with your sewing machine.

Sewing on Buttons

For many people, sewing on a button is an introduction into the world of sewing. Sewing on buttons is a great way to get started because it shows you the importance of technique when doing anything with a needle and thread — even something small.

Yes, you can avoid a mishap by correctly sewing on a button, which you can do either by hand or on the sewing machine. If I replace or move one button, I sew it on by hand. If I make something that requires sewing on several buttons at once (the front of a shirt, for example), I use my machine.

By hand

Follow these steps to sew on a button of any size by hand:

1. **Mark the spot on the fabric where you want the button to go, using a fabric marker or dressmaker's chalk from your Sewing Survival Kit.**

2. **Pull off a strand of thread 18 to 24 inches long.**

   A thread that's longer than 24 inches tangles and may break before you sew on the button.

3. **Thread the needle (as described in the section "Hand needles" earlier in this chapter), pulling one end of the thread to meet the other so that you have a double thread.**

4. **Knot the ends of the thread as described in the section "Tying the Knot" earlier in this chapter.**

5. **From the top right side of the project, stab the needle all the way through the fabric so that the knot ends up on the mark.**

6. **Bring the needle back up and all the way through the fabric, a short stitch (not more than ⅛ inch) away from the knot.**

7. **Thread the button on the needle through the left hole, pushing it firmly against the surface of the fabric, and then pull the thread up as shown in Figure 5-20.**

8. **Create a *spacer* by placing a toothpick, matchstick, or hand-tapestry needle on top of the button between the holes.**

   This technique gives you enough thread to raise the button off the fabric's surface so that you have room to button the buttonhole. The extra room the spacer creates is called a *thread shank*.

Figure 5-20:
Thread the
button on
the needle.

If you are sewing on a button with a shank (a little loop on the underside of a blazer button, for example), the shank of the button acts as an automatic spacer, raising the button off the surface of the garment for easy buttoning, so you don't need the toothpick.

9. **Push the needle down through the hole on the right (the one directly opposite the hole you started with — see Figure 5-21). Pull the thread tight.**

   Repeat this process, stitching up through the left hole and down through the right hole one more time for each set of holes so that you secure the button with two passes of the needle.

Figure 5-21:
Use a
spacer
to make
a thread
shank
for easy
buttoning.

10. **After you stitch the button on, remove the toothpick.**

11. **Poke the needle through a hole in the button (it doesn't matter which one) so that the needle comes out between the button and the fabric.**

   Take a look at what's going on between the button and the fabric: Those connecting threads running out the back of the button into the fabric make the base of the thread shank.

12. **Wrap the thread around these connecting threads three times to secure the thread shank, as shown in Figure 5-22.**

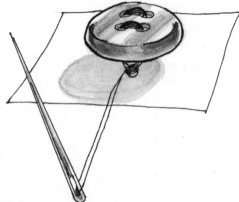

Figure 5-22:
Create a
thread
shank.

13. **Tie a knot by pushing the needle through a thread loop as it goes around the shank and pulling the thread tight.**

14. **Repeat Step 13 and clip the thread close to the shank.**

By machine

If you have several buttons to sew on at one time, consider using your machine to help you with the job. To use this technique, you need a glue stick, a button-sewing foot for your machine, or a presser foot shank with a removable presser foot sole (check your operating manual to see if your model has this feature).

Just follow these steps:

1. **Mark the spot on the fabric where you want the button to go, using a fabric marker or dressmaker's chalk from your Sewing Survival Kit.**

2. **Dab the back of the button with a glue stick and place the button over your mark.**

3. **Prepare your machine with the following settings:**

   - **Stitch:** Zigzag
   - **Length:** 0 mm (0 spi)
   - **Width:** 4 mm
   - **Foot:** Button-sewing, all-purpose, or foot shank without the sole
   - **Feed dogs:** Down
   - **Needle position:** Left (see Chapter 1)

4. **With the presser foot up, turn the flywheel by hand, stabbing the needle through the left hole in the button; lower the presser foot or the foot shank.**

   For a four-hole button, start with the holes farthest away from you.

5. **Slide a toothpick, matchstick, or tapestry needle over the button, between the holes and perpendicular to the foot or the foot shank.**

   Adding this spacer raises the button off the fabric's surface so that the buttonhole doesn't gap and lies smoothly under the button.

   Sometimes, the foot has a helpful little groove that holds the spacer in place.

6. **Check that the needle clears each of the holes in the button by taking a couple of zigzag stitches, moving the flywheel by hand, as shown in Figure 5-23.**

   Adjust the stitch width, if necessary.

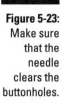

Figure 5-23:
Make sure
that the
needle
clears the
buttonholes.

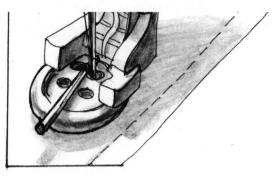

7. **Slowly step on the foot control and stitch, counting five stitches — zig left, zag right, zig left, zag right, zig left.**

   For a four-hole button, lift the foot and move the project so that the needle is over the front two holes, and then sew five more zigzags to secure the front of the button.

8. **Move the stitch width to 0 (zero), place the needle over one of the holes, and step on the foot control again, taking 4 to 5 stitches in the same hole.**

   This step helps to secure and knot the stitches.

9. **Lift the foot and remove the project, reeling off a 7-inch tail of thread.**

10. **Remove the spacer so that you can use it to sew on the other buttons, if necessary.**

11. **Proceed to the rest of the buttons, repeating Steps 4 through 10 until you've sewn on all the buttons.**

12. **Pull the needle and bobbin threads between the button and the fabric so that you're ready to create a thread shank, as follows:**

    - Thread a large-eye tapestry needle with the 7-inch thread tail from the needle and, between the button and the fabric, pull the tail through any hole in the button.

    - Thread a large-eye tapestry needle with the 7-inch thread tail from the bobbin and pull the tail through the fabric between the button and the fabric.

    - Thread both tails through the needle's eye and wrap the thread tails around the connecting threads three times, creating a thread shank to secure the button.

13. **Push the needle through a thread loop as it goes around the shank, pulling the thread tight. This action ties a knot.**

14. **Repeat Step 13 and then clip the thread close to the connecting threads.**

Creating a button collage greeting card

Practice your hand and machine button-sewing technique by making the decorative greeting card shown in Figure 5-24. You not only get more bang for your gift-card buck, but you also impress the heck out of the lucky recipient.

To make this great greeting card, you need the following tools (in addition to the tools in your Sewing Survival Kit, which I tell you about in Chapter 1):

- Four to five inches of 2- to 2½-inch-wide ribbon, trim, or belting (I use Guatemalan belting, which you can usually find at craft and fabric stores)

- Handmade paper (available at craft, art supply, or scrapbook stores) that complements the colors in the belting

- One 3-inch length of rickrack

- One 5-inch length of rickrack

- Three 4-hole buttons that complement the colors in the belting

✔ One color of all-purpose thread that contrasts to the colors of the papers

✔ One blank card and envelope (available at your local craft store)

✔ A ruler

✔ A glue stick

✔ Seam sealant, such as FrayCheck (see the appendix)

✔ A pencil

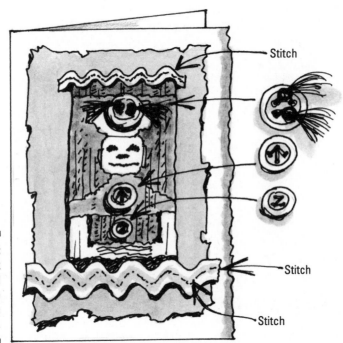

Stitch

Stitch

Stitch

Figure 5-24:
Rickrack
trim and
buttons give
the card a
3-D effect.

After assembling your tools, follow these steps to create a card that makes a lasting impression:

1. **On the handmade paper, lightly pencil-mark a rectangle slightly smaller than the front of the blank card.**

2. **Rip a rectangle out of the handmade paper, as shown in Figure 5-25.**

   Lay the paper and ruler on the table. Lay the edge of the ruler along one of the pencil lines of the paper. Holding the ruler down with one hand, pull up on the paper with the other hand, ripping the paper against the edge of the ruler. Repeat this process for the other three sides of the paper. Because you're using handmade paper, the edges should look rough.

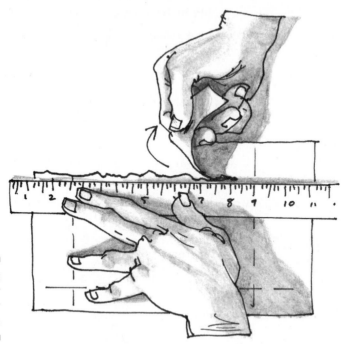

Figure 5-25:
Use a ruler
to rip your
paper.

3. Center and glue the ripped paper rectangle on the front of the card using the glue stick.

4. Cut the ends of the rickrack and belting and spread a fine bead of seam sealant on them to prevent fraying. Let the ends dry.

5. Center the belting strip on the rectangle and glue the strip in place over the handmade paper rectangle.

6. Glue the rickrack to the edges at the top and the bottom, covering the raw edges of the belting.

7. Set up your machine like this:

- **Stitch:** Straight

- **Length:** 3 mm/9 spi

- **Width:** 0 mm

- **Foot:** All-purpose

8. Stitch the rickrack trim on the card by following the shape of the zigzags on the rickrack (refer to Figure 5-24).

9. **Sew on three buttons either by hand or with your machine.**

   If you use Guatemalan belting, stitch one button at the top of the head and center the other two down the belting. Making this card is a creative process, so if you want sew the buttons on somewhere else, go ahead and have fun.

Pressing Matters

What's the difference between ironing and pressing?

- ✔ You *iron* by pushing and pulling a hot iron across the fabric in a side-to-side motion to smooth out wrinkles.

- ✔ You *press* by using an up-and-down motion as you firmly push down on an area of the fabric with an iron. Pressing is most commonly used to shape an area when sewing or when pressing out wrinkles in a knit.

When smoothing out wrinkles on knits such as t-shirts, use the up-and-down pressing motion. Ironing knits distorts and stretches the fabric out of shape, sometimes permanently.

In the instructions for the projects in *Sewing For Dummies,* 2nd Edition, I ask you to either press or iron. Now you know the difference (read more about pressing tools in Chapter 1).

Why press and iron as you sew?

Sewing changes the texture of the fabric wherever stitching occurs. Seams pucker a bit due to the thread, the fabric, the stitch used, or the shape of the pattern pieces, so for the seam to look good after sewing you must smooth it out by pressing.

Pressing up and down with the iron sets the stitches so that they become part of the fabric. Ironing back and forth smooths the seam and puts the fabric back as close to its prestitched state as possible. If you don't press and iron while constructing a project, the seams stay as they come out of the sewing machine or serger and the project has a rough, puckered, unfinished look.

A Seam Stick is made of a very smooth, hard wood and curved like a seam roll (see Chapter 1 for more on pressing tools). The stick is much longer and narrower than a seam roll so you can easily slip it into a sleeve or pant leg and press these longer seams without repositioning the tool 4 to 6 times. The Seam Stick is a wonderful addition to your pressing tools.

When and where to press

Press every seam right after you sew it and every time the pattern guide sheet tells you to.

Use a hotter steam setting for natural fibers, such as silk, cotton, wool, and linen. Use lower synthetic-temperature settings for man-made and synthetic fiber fabrics. Depending on your iron, you may or may not be able to use steam at these cooler settings. If you're in doubt about what works best on your fabric, do a test-press on a fabric scrap using the iron with and without steam.

Be careful to set your iron for the appropriate temperature for the fiber content of your fabric (see Chapter 2 to read about fiber content). An iron that's too hot melts the fiber and creates unwanted shine that never presses out.

Follow these steps to properly press a seam:

1. **Press the seam flat and together, setting the stitches in the fabric.**

2. **Press the iron over the seamline from the wrong side of the fabric to set, or *blend*, the stitches in the fabric.**

3. **Position the iron so that you press the seam allowance together from the seamline out toward the edge (see Figure 5-26).**

4. **Press a ⅝-inch seam open over a seam roll and a ¼-inch seam to one side.**

Figure 5-26:
Press along the seamline to set the stitches. Press seams open over a seam roll or to one side.

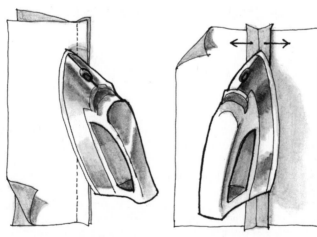

Your pattern guide sheet may instruct you to press other items throughout the course of a project. Don't try to cut corners by skipping these instructions.

 Make pressing easy on yourself by setting up your pressing area close to your sewing area. If your chair is on wheels, lower the ironing board to a comfortable height so that you can use your iron and ironing board from a seated position.

Pressing napped fabrics

Napped fabrics like velvet, velour, corduroy, and Polarfleece all have a fuzzy texture that can crush under iron pressure. Follow these tips when pressing napped fabrics:

- **Polarfleece:** Don't press Polarfleece.

- **Velour:** Lightly press velour by using a good deal of steam and pressing from the wrong side using a press cloth.

- **Corduroy:** Press and iron corduroy from the wrong side of the fabric.

- **Upholstery velvet:** Upholstery velvet is designed for sitting, so the nap doesn't crush as easily as it does with dressmaking velvet and cotton velveteen. Nonetheless, you should also press upholstery velvet from the wrong side using a press cloth.

- **Velvet:** Velvet practically crushes when you look at it. Lay a large scrap of velvet or a terry cloth towel on the ironing board, nap side up. Lay the napped side of the velvet you're pressing against the napped side of the towel and carefully press it from the wrong side.

Chapter 6

Sewing Sensational Seams

- -

In This Chapter

▶ Finishing the seams before you begin

▶ Making sure your seams stay put

▶ Uncovering secrets to sewing straight seams

▶ Unsewing when things go wrong

▶ Seam-shaping shortcuts

- -

Simply put, you form a seam every time you sew two pieces of fabric together. You need straight seams, curved seams, and corner seams to build a project. After you sew a seam, you beat a seam into submission with the iron, scissors, and the sewing machine to keep its shape.

Before you sew two pieces of fabric together, though, you must do a little preparation work. Strangely enough, you finish a seam before you begin it!

Finish the Edges First!

Seam finishing is what you do to the fabric edges to prevent them from raveling. Finishing the seams also gives the project a neat, polished look.

The following seam finishes are for woven fabrics. If you're working on a knit, skip ahead to the section "Sewing straight seams," where you stitch and finish the seams of knit fabrics at the same time.

Pinking your edges

Pinking the raw fabric edges is a quick way to finish a seam. You do pinking by trimming the raw edge of a single layer of fabric with a pair of *pinking shears,* which are shears with a zigzag pattern on the blades. Pinking shears work best on woven fabrics because the blades cut clean little zigzags into the fabric, thereby preventing the raw edges from raveling.

Don't use pinking shears on a knit fabric. The blades chew up and snag the fabric beyond recognition. Skip ahead to the section "Sewing straight seams" for information on sewing seams on knits.

Don't cut out a project with pinking shears and think that you're saving a step — a pinked cutting line isn't accurate. Instead, cut out your pattern pieces using your dressmaker's shears. Remove the paper pattern and pink the raw edges of each pattern piece, one layer of fabric at a time.

Using your sewing machine or serger

You finish (or *overcast*) the raw edges on a fabric so that the seam allowance (the fabric from the seam to the cut edge) doesn't ravel up to the *seamline* — the line of stitches that joins the fabric pieces together to make a seam. Woven fabrics ravel, so you need to finish the edges by using stitches on your sewing machine or your serger. Knits don't ravel, but the edges on a knit sometimes curl and are hard to press flat, so you handle the seams a bit differently (see "Seaming Fabrics," later in this chapter).

Just follow these steps to finish woven fabric edges as shown in Figure 6-1:

1. **Set your sewing machine like this:**

   - **Stitch:** Three-step zigzag
   - **Length:** 1 to 1.5 mm/20 spi or fine
   - **Width:** 5 to 6 mm
   - **Foot:** All-purpose

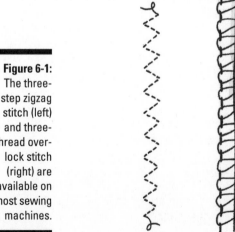

Figure 6-1:
The three-step zigzag stitch (left) and three-thread over-lock stitch (right) are available on most sewing machines.

If you're using a serger, set your serger like this:

- **Stitch:** Three-thread overlock
- **Length:** 3 mm
- **Width:** 5 mm
- **Foot:** Standard

2. **With either the right or the wrong side up, start sewing or serging the raw edge, guiding the fabric so that the stitches catch the fabric on the left and sewing just off the edge at the right.**

   Because you use these stitches to finish the edge of the fabric rather than to construct a seam, you don't need to backstitch (see the "Securing Your Seams" section to find out more about backstitching).

Securing Your Seams

When sewing a seam with a straight stitch, you want to secure the stitches at the beginning and end so that the stitches don't pull out during construction. You can prevent stitches from coming unstitched in two ways:

- ✓ By backstitching at the beginning and end of the seam
- ✓ By tying off the threads

Backstitching or not

Most machines have a backstitch or reverse button, lever, or function (see Chapter 1). To secure a seam with backstitching, simply sew the first two or three stitches and then touch the reverse button. The machine automatically sews backward until you release the reverse button. Backstitch at the beginning and at the end of a seamline (see Figure 6-2), and you have all the stitch security you need!

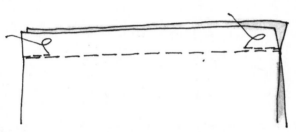

Figure 6-2: Keep your seams in place with back-stitching.

Only backstitch when using a straight stitch. Backstitching with a zigzag or more complex stitch globs up the thread, creates knots that you can never rip out if you make a mistake, and may damage your sewing machine.

Sometimes you don't know how something fits until you sew it together and try it on. When you aren't sure that you want a seam to be permanent, just sew the seam without backstitching and leave the thread tails free at both ends of the seam. Removing stitches that haven't been backstitched is easier.

Tying off threads

You may want to tie off threads rather than backstitching at the point of a dart or at the beginning and end of a line of topstitching — like topstitching around a sleeve hem, for example. Tying off the threads is less bulky — important at the point of a dart — and it just plain looks better than backstitching.

When tying off threads, lift the presser foot and remove the fabric, pulling off and cutting a length of thread at least 8 inches long. Then, from the wrong side of the stitching line, pull up on the bobbin thread. The pulled thread brings a loop to the wrong side. Now grab the loop and pull it through until both threads are on the same side of the fabric. Tie off the threads as follows:

1. **Starting with thread tails at least 8 inches long, hold the threads together and form a loop as shown in Figure 6-3a.**

2. **Bring both threads around and through the loop, working the loop to the base of the stitch as shown in Figure 6-3b.**

3. **Holding the threads with your thumb, pull them taut so that the loop forms a knot at the base of the fabric at the stitching line as shown in Figure 6-3c.**

Figure 6-3:
Tie off threads so they don't ravel.

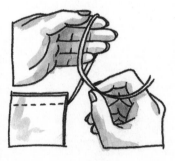

a.   b.   c.

The standard in seam allowances

A pattern piece indicates the seam allowance by a line that shows you where to stitch the pattern pieces together. As a rule, you can count on the following seam allowances as industry standards:

✔ ⅝ inch for woven garments

✔ ½ inch for home decorating projects

✔ ¼ inch for knit fabrics

Look on your project's pattern guide sheet if you're unsure about the seam allowances for your project.

Seaming Fabrics

Sewing a seam is kind of like driving a car. In fact, I passed my driver's test on the sewing machine before I could sew a stitch (or drive a car). I had to prove that I could control the sewing machine — that I could start, stop, maneuver both inside and outside curves, and turn corners safely. Thank goodness I didn't have to parallel park!

Consider this next section your driving test and put the pedal to the metal and sew some seams.

Sewing straight seams

For straight seams every time, follow these steps:

1. **Set your machine like this for woven fabrics:**

   • **Stitch:** Straight

   • **Length:** 2.5 to 3 mm/10 to 12 spi

   • **Width:** 0 mm

   • **Foot:** All-purpose

   Set your machine like this for knit fabrics:

   • **Stitch:** Zigzag

   • **Length:** 1 to 2 mm/13 to 24 spi

   • **Width:** 1.5 to 2 mm

   • **Foot:** All-purpose

This traditional seaming technique is used mostly on woven fabrics when applying a ⅝-inch seam allowance. Knit fabrics use ¼-inch seams, and you stitch and overcast them together, as I show you in the upcoming section "Sewing ¼-inch seams."

2. **Place and pin your pattern pieces so that the right sides of the fabric are together.**

   From now on, when you see the words *place the right sides together*, you'll know what they mean. Use as many pins as it takes to hold the edges together so that they don't slide around. The more you sew, the closer you can estimate how many pins you need for a particular job.

   For easy pin removal, pin perpendicular to the seamline so that the pin heads are toward your dominant hand and the pins either enter or exit the fabric about ¼ inch from the edge of the fabric. (See Chapter 5 for more about using pins when sewing.)

3. **Place the seam under the presser foot and line up the edge of the fabric with the appropriate seamline marked on the needle plate.**

   On the needle plate, look for a set of lines to the right of the needle. Depending on your machine, the lines may be marked as ⅝, ½, and so on; sometimes you find just plain old lines. Placing the bulk of the fabric to the left, line up the raw edges of your fabric along the ⅝-inch line. If you have everything lined up properly, the needle should be poised to hit the fabric right on the ⅝-inch seamline.

   If your needle plate has plain old lines, place your sewing tape measure under the needle so that the long length of the tape is to the left. Poke the needle into the tape at the ⅝-inch mark and lower the foot. Make sure the short end of the tape lines up with the ⅝-inch line in the needle plate. Remember which line is needed for the ⅝-inch seamline or place a strip of tape, aligning the edge of the tape with the ⅝-inch line.

4. **Lower the presser foot onto the fabric and stitch, backstitching at the top and bottom of the seam. (See "Backstitching or not," earlier in this chapter, for more information.)**

   If the needle hits a pin, both can break, sending shards all over the place. Unless you plan on wearing safety goggles when you sew, pull out the pins before sewing over them.

   Slow down when you seam a curve. Using the line in your needle plate, guide the edges along the appropriate line for an even sewing distance along the length of the curve.

5. **Press the seam flat and together. From the wrong side, press the seam open. (See Chapter 5 for more information on pressing.)**

To match a plaid perfectly, put one pin on every other color bar so one pin goes in from *east to west* and the next goes in from *west to east,* like in Figure 6-4. (Check out Chapter 4 for more about matching plaids.) As with any other seam, remember to pull out the pins before sewing over them.

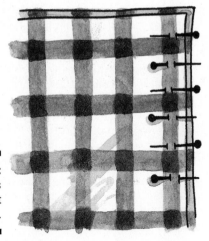

Figure 6-4:
Pin plaids
for a perfect
match.

Turning corners

When turning a corner in the car, you slow down and stop, look both ways, and then turn. You do the same when turning a corner in sewing. Follow these steps, and you make good-looking corners every time:

1. **Using a fabric marker, mark the corner on the wrong side of the fabric with a dot so that you know exactly where to stop and pivot.**

   After you stitch several corners, you have a good idea of where to stop sewing to turn a corner without marking the corner first.

2. **As you approach the corner, slow down and stop, with the needle all the way into the fabric.**

3. **Leaving the needle in the fabric, lift the presser foot and pivot the fabric around the needle so that the other edge of the fabric lines up with the appropriate line in the needle plate.**

4. **Lower the presser foot and start sewing again. Easy, isn't it?**

Sewing ¼-inch seams

When seaming a T-shirt, sweatshirt, and other active knit sportswear fabrics, you usually stitch and press a ¼-inch seam to one side.

Some patterns call for ¼-inch seam allowances; others call for ⅝-inch seam allowances. If the pattern you're working with calls for the wider seam allowance, instead of trimming it to ¼ inch, leave it wider to allow for fitting and then trim it off later. Exceptions are those areas where you apply ribbing at the neck edge and cuffs — trim those to ¼ inch before sewing. You can make ¼-inch seams in one or two steps, depending on your sewing machine's capabilities.

This technique for seaming knits is called the two-step method because you sew the seam with two separate passes through the sewing machine. It also works better on most fabrics when using ⅝-inch seam allowances and then trimming them to ¼-inch after sewing.

Follow these steps to sew ¼-inch seams:

1. **Set your sewing machine like this:**
   - **Stitch:** Zigzag
   - **Length:** 2.5 to 3 mm/10 to 12 spi
   - **Width:** 1.5 to 2 mm
   - **Foot:** All-purpose

2. **Place and pin your pattern pieces so that the right sides of the fabric are together.**

3. **Place the seam under the presser foot so that the needle stitches ⅝ inch from the raw edge and sew.**

4. **Set your sewing machine like this:**
   - **Stitch:** Three-step zigzag
   - **Length:** 1 to 1.5 mm/13 to 24 spi
   - **Width:** 4 to 5 mm
   - **Foot:** All-purpose

5. **Guiding to the immediate right of the tiny zigzag stitches, sew the second row of stitching with the three-step zigzag stitch, as shown in Figure 6-5.**

Figure 6-5:
Two-step ¼-
inch seam.

If you used a ⅝-inch seam allowance, trim the excess fabric up to, but not through, the stitches.

6. **Press the seam to one side.**

See Chapter 5 for details about pressing a seam.

Serging ¼-inch seams

You can serge ¼-inch seams in one step on your serger by using a four-thread overlock stitch. The straight stitch within the seam allowance is an insurance policy. If you pop a seam, the extra row of stitching prevents the seam from coming completely unraveled.

1. **Set your serger like this:**

   - **Stitch:** 4-thread overlock

   - **Length:** 2.5 to 3mm (10 to 12 spi)

   - **Width:** 4 to 5 mm

   - **Foot:** Standard

2. **Place and pin the seam, right sides together, so the pins are parallel to the seamline and about 1 inch from the cut edge.**

   This way you don't accidentally serge over pins and ruin your serger.

3. **Serge the seam, guiding the raw edge by either the ¼-inch or ⅝-inch line on the needle plate of your serger.**

   The serger automatically trims off the excess seam allowance, giving a nice, ¼-inch finished seam (see Figure 6-6).

Figure 6-6:
¼-inch
seam sewn
with a
serger.

Differential feed, abbreviated D.F., is a feature on many sergers that prevents the unnecessary stretching out of stretchy fabrics. Without D.F., serged knit seams can distort, ending up longer than they should. These distorted seams throw off the look and fit of a garment. If you're in the market for a new serger, buy a model that has this feature. Check out your operating manual to find out how it works.

Seaming knit ribbing

The knitted bands found on T-shirt and sweatshirt necklines and cuffs are called *ribbing*. My favorite type of ribbing has spandex blended with cotton or nylon (see more about fibers and fabrics in Chapter 2) and doesn't bag out of shape with a lot of washing and rough wear.

The following steps show you how to create the flattest and most invisible seam for ribbing:

1. **Cut the ribbing as described in your pattern.**

2. **Set your machine like this:**
   - **Stitch:** Overlock
   - **Length:** Longest
   - **Width:** 5 to 6 mm
   - **Foot:** Embroidery

3. **Using a ¼-inch seam allowance, sew the ribbing into a circle, seaming the short ends together as shown in Figure 6-7.**

4. **Finger press the seam to one side, and then turn the ribbing so it makes a circle with the seam on the inside of the band.**

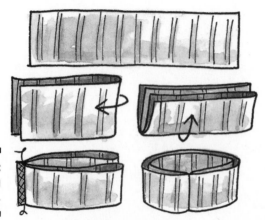

Figure 6-7:
Seaming
knit ribbing.

Sewing or serging ribbing into an opening

When you see how fast and easy applying ribbing into an opening is, you'll want to put ribbing on everything in sight.

Follow these steps to attach your ribbing like a pro:

1. **Fold the ribbing band in half the long way, so the seam is on the inside of the band.**

   If the ribbing curls and you find it difficult to handle, baste the raw edges together (see Chapter 5) using a 4 mm-length (6 spi), 4 mm-width zigzag stitch.

2. **Use pins to mark off the opening into quarters.**

   In a round neckline, for example, the pins mark the center front, left shoulder seam, the center back, and the right shoulder seam. This process is called *quarter marking*.

   Until you get more practice, you may find marking the ribbing and opening into eight equal parts, rather than four, is easier.

3. **Quarter mark the ribbing, making sure the seam will be placed at the center back of the opening.**

4. **With the right sides together, line up the ribbing and the opening so the pin marks match up, and pin the ribbing into the opening as shown in Figure 6-8.**

5. **Set your machine like this:**

   - **Stitch:** Overlock
   - **Length:** Longest
   - **Width:** 5 to 6mm
   - **Foot:** Embroidery

   Set your serger like this:

   - **Stitch:** 4-thread overlock
   - **Length** 2.5 to 3 mm
   - **Width:** 4mm
   - **Foot:** Standard

6. **Sew a ¼-inch seam with your sewing machine or serger (see the section "Seaming Fabrics" earlier in this chapter.)**

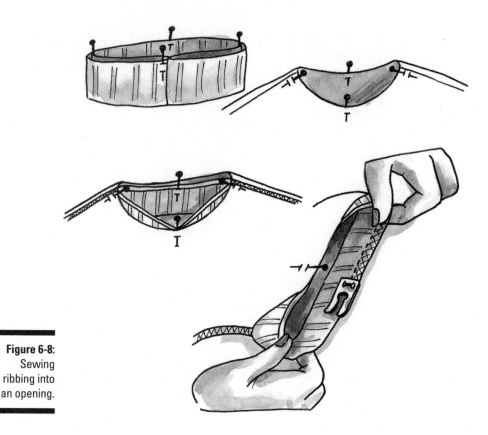

Figure 6-8:
Sewing
ribbing into
an opening.

Let 'Er Rip

You may think that if you're a careful sewer you won't make mistakes that you need to rip out . . . WRONG. Ripping is part of sewing, no matter how experienced you are. But I do have a rule: Don't rip it out if you can live with it. The mistake may actually look worse after you fix it than it did before you ripped it out. So sleep on it, look at your project with new eyes in the morning, and then decide if doing it over is worth the extra effort.

Now that you know when to rip, look at the easy ways to do it. My two favorite methods are using a seam ripper (see Chapter 1 to read more about a seam ripper) and pulling the needle and bobbin threads.

A *seam ripper* has a very sharp point that lifts a stitch away from the fabric and a knife-edge that cuts the thread in one smooth motion.

Work the point of the ripper under the stitch and cut through the thread. After you cut the stitch, gently tug open the seam until another stitch holds the seam closed. Cut this stitch with the ripper and pull the seam open as before until you have *unsewn* the distance you want to open (see Figure 6-9).

Do   Don't

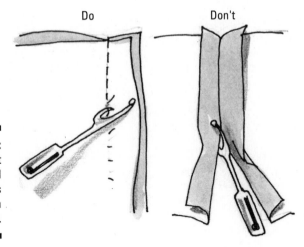

Figure 6-9:
Rip out
unwanted
stitches
using a
seam ripper.

This little tool is sharp enough to cut fabric. Don't push the ripper and cut through a whole line of stitching at once or you may cut a slit in the fabric, right next to the seamline — an almost impossible place to fix.

If you prefer to rip out stitches without the aid of a seam ripper, follow these steps:

1. **Loosen the stitches enough to have about a 2-inch thread tail.**

2. **Holding the project in one hand, jerk the thread tail back toward the stitching line, against the stitches, with your other hand.**

   This action breaks four to six stitches at once.

3. **Turn the project over and pull out the bobbin thread tail.**

4. **Jerk on that bobbin thread tail, pulling against the stitches and breaking another four to six stitches.**

5. **Keep pulling the top thread and then the bobbin thread until you have unsewn as much stitching as needed.**

Shaping Up Those Curved Seams

Have you ever heard someone say, "The devil's in the details"? When it comes to sewing, nothing is truer. Sewing would be wonderful (but very boring) if all the seams were straight. No such luck. In this section, you see how to take curved seams and whip them into shape by using your sewing machine and scissors. You use these techniques time and time again in many aspects of sewing, so mark this spot in the book with a sticky note and refer to it often.

. . . with your sewing machine

Staystitching is a technique that you can use on a single layer of fabric inside the seam allowance to *stay* or prevent curved fabric edges from stretching out of shape while you work on a project.

Staystitch neckline curves, armhole curves, and those edges cut on the bias (see Chapter 4 to read more about the bias).

To staystitch an edge, use a regular straight stitch and sew a row of stitching ½ inch from the raw edge, as shown in Figure 6-10. If you're not sure whether to staystitch an area, see your pattern guide sheet for a recommendation.

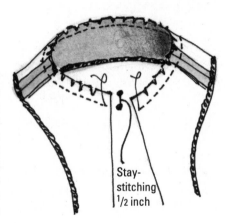

Figure 6-10: Staystitch to keep the fabric from stretching out as you handle the project.

Stay-stitching ¹/₂ inch

Understitching is a line of stitching found *under* or on the inside of a project close to the seamline. You understitch collars and facings so that they stay in shape and conform to the opening you sew them into. You can't see understitching, but without it, armhole and neckline facings pull out of their openings and collar seams roll and look . . . well . . . tacky.

You finish curved seams, like those on an armhole or neckline, with another piece of fabric called a *facing*. After you sew the facing to the neckline or armhole, you press the seam allowance to one side, toward the facing. After you press, understitch the seam allowance to compress the bulk created by the extra thickness of the seam allowance, to conform to the curve's shape.

You can understitch with a straight stitch, but the stitch doesn't really compress all that bulk. Using the three-step zigzag stitch really flattens the seam allowance and gives you beautifully finished edges.

To understitch, do the following:

1. **After sewing the seam in question, press the entire seam allowance to one side.**

   For a neckline or armhole that has a facing stitched to the opening, press the seam allowance toward the facing.

2. **Set your machine like this:**

   - **Stitch:** Three-step zigzag
   - **Length:** 1 to 1.5 mm/20 to 24 spi
   - **Width:** 4 to 5 mm
   - **Foot:** All-purpose

3. **Place the fabric right side up under the presser foot so that the crack of the seam allowance is to one side of the needle or the other, as shown in Figure 6-11.**

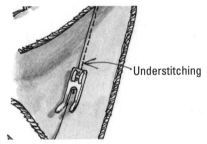

Figure 6-11: Under-stitching keeps your facings in line.

Understitching

Which side? The side where you pressed the seam allowance. When the right side of the project is up and you press the seam to the right, the needle should be to the right side of the seamline. When you press to the left, the needle should be to the left side of the seamline.

4. **Sew; guide the needle so that when it travels over to the left side of the stitch it comes to within ¹⁄₁₆ inch of the seamline.**

As you sew, grasp the facing and seam allowance in your right hand with your thumb under the facing. By periodically peeking under the fabric, check that you're pushing the seam allowance toward the facing side of the seam. This way, you catch all the bulk of the seam allowance in the understitching.

Edgestitching is *topstitching* (stitching sewn on the top or right side of the fabric) that is very close to the finished edge. You find edgestitching on the edge of collars, cuffs, pockets, waistbands, front shirt plackets, and other edges where you want a crisp, tailored look. Even though you can edgestitch with an all-purpose presser foot, sewing in a straight line is tricky because you sew so close to the fabric's edge.

This technique uses the blind hem foot (see Chapter 1) as a guide, enabling you to edgestitch quickly, accurately, and professionally:

1. **Set your machine like this:**

   - **Stitch:** Straight

   - **Length:** 2 to 3 mm/9 to 13 spi

   - **Width:** 0 mm

   - **Foot:** Blind hem or edgestitch

   - **Optional:** Near left needle position (check your operating manual)

2. **Place the guide in the foot along the finished edge and sew, as shown in Figure 6-12.**

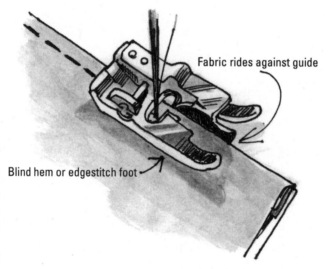

Fabric rides against guide

Blind hem or edgestitch foot

Figure 6-12: The right foot makes even edge-stitching a snap.

Instead of backstitching, pull the threads to the back and tie them off (see "Tying off threads" earlier in this chapter for more information).

If you don't have a blind hem foot and a variable needle position, place the fabric under the foot so that when the needle is in the fabric, the edge of the fabric is about ⅟₁₆ inch from the needle. Notice where the edge of the fabric is in relationship to the foot (this spot could be at the edge of the needle hole, where you see a line in the foot, or where the foot changes direction). Sewing slowly, guide the edge of the fabric by that spot on the foot.

. . . *with your scissors*

Clipping a seam to the staystitching or seamline releases the seam allowance on an inside curve, making it flexible enough to spread open. This way, after you stitch the armhole or neckline facing, for example, the facing turns smoothly to the inside of the garment. If you didn't clip the seam, when you turn the facing to the inside of the armhole or neck edge, the seam would be stiff and bunchy and the facings would pop out of the opening and bind.

When clipping, use very sharp scissor tips. Cut clips in the fabric perpendicular to the seamline and to within $\frac{1}{16}$ inch of the staystitching or seamline, as shown in Figure 6-13. Rather than holding the seam allowance closed and clipping both seam allowances simultaneously, clip each seam allowance separately, alternating the clips across the seamline from one another. This surefire clipping technique pads the seam allowance, creating the smoothest curved seam ever.

Notching a seam to the staystitching or seamline is just the opposite of clipping. You notch a seam to reduce the bulk in the seam allowance of an outside curve, such as the outside edge of a collar or princess seam line (refer to Figure 6-13).

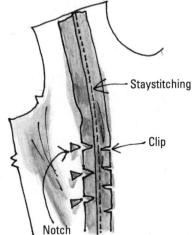

Staystitching

Clip

Notch

Figure 6-13:
Clipping and
notching
a seam.

Notch a seam allowance by cutting away little triangular-shaped pieces of fabric. Rather than holding the seam allowance closed and notching both seam allowances simultaneously, use your scissor tips to cut one notch out of a seam allowance separately, alternating notches across the seamline from one another. Cut away each notch to within $\frac{1}{8}$ inch of the seamline.

Cut away small notches from small curves that are spaced about ¼ to ½ inch apart. Cut away larger notches from larger curves spaced from about ½ to ¾ inch apart.

After some experience, you find that cutting away more notches is usually better than cutting fewer, bigger ones. This way, when you stitch, notch, turn, and press an affected area, the seam allowance fits and presses smoothly — no unwanted lumps or bumps.

When notching an edge, don't cut through the stitching at the seamline.

My favorite way to notch an edge on light- to mid-weight woven fabric is by using my pinking shears. I trim or grade the seam with the pinking shears, cutting to within ⅛ inch of the stitching line. Pinking automatically notches the edge, so I'm on to the next step in no time.

Don't be confused between notches that are match points marked on the pattern paper and notches that you cut out of the seam allowance at an outside curve. (See Chapter 4 for more on notches and match points.) Even though the word is the same, it represents two different sewing concepts.

Trimming seams eliminates bulk from the seam allowances that you stitch and then turn right side out so that the seamline is on the edge. Trim as close to the stitching line as possible, leaving enough seam allowance so that the stitches don't pull off the fabric (see Figure 6-14).

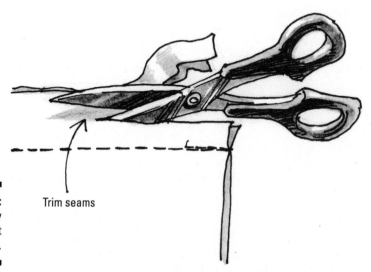

Figure 6-14:
Trim away
the bulk at
the seams.

Trim seams

Chapter 7

Hems and A-Ha's

• •

In This Chapter

▶ Making your mark on hems

▶ Working with a hem allowance

▶ Polishing the raw edges of a hem

▶ Invisible hemming by hand and machine

▶ Hemming tricks for knit fabrics

• •

*H*ave you ever bought a pair of pants and left them hanging in the closet until the dust settled on the hanger before shortening them? Have your kids outgrown their clothes before you could get to the hemming? If this sounds familiar, this chapter's for you. The following tips, tricks, and techniques are my favorites for hemming and may keep you from procrastinating the next time a new outfit needs hemming or rehemming.

But, first, what are hems and why do you need them? A hem is a turned-up edge that you stitch in place at the bottom of skirts, pants, shorts, sleeves, and drapery panels. Besides making the edges neat, hems add weight to an edge, so the garment or drapery hangs better with a hem than without one.

Marking a Hem

Before you can sew the hem, you need to mark it. To get a hem an even distance from the floor, you also need a helper. (My husband, although reluctant, became really good at being the helper after he understood what he had to do.) You have two roles to fill when marking hems: The hem-ee and the hemmer.

If you're the hem-ee

As the hem-ee, you wear the garment, so the hemmer marks the hem to fit you. Here's what you do:

1. **Try on the garment, wearing the same underwear and shoes that you'll wear when fashioning the garment out of the house.**

   Because most people are lopsided, put the garment on with the right side out — or the hemmer measures the hem to fit the wrong side of your body.

2. **Stand on a hard floor, table, or stool.**

   Carpet can distort the measurements.

3. **Stand up straight with your hands down at your sides and don't lock your knees.**

   I locked my knees once and passed out!

If you're the hemmer

As the hemmer, your job is to measure and mark the hem of the garment worn by the hem-ee. Here's what you do:

1. **Find a pleasing hem length by temporarily pinning up the hemline.**

   When hemming a skirt or dress, you don't have to pin all the way around, just about 12 inches or so in the front to make sure you have the right length.

   For slacks, temporarily pin up the hemlines so that the creases break slightly at the top of the shoe. You can hem pants to whatever length you prefer, so if you have a favorite pair of pants, notice the hem and compare. Pin both hems, making them even at the heel and creases. Now, skip ahead to the section "Finishing the Raw Edges of the Hem" later in this chapter.

   By temporarily pinning up a section of the garment at the proper length, you create a *hem fold*. This fold allows you to measure the hem for the rest of the garment more accurately.

2. **Using a yardstick, measure the distance from the floor to the hem fold and tightly wrap a thin rubber band around the yardstick the proper distance from the floor.**

3. **Pin through a single thickness at the hem fold by using two pins and pinning parallel to the floor. Remove the rest of the pins so that the hemline hangs free.**

4. **Using the rubber band on the yardstick as a guide, pin-mark the hemline even with the rubber band, pinning all the way around the garment.**

   Place pins about every 2 to 3 inches, pinning parallel to the floor. Pin-mark a few inches, move, and then measure and pin-mark again until you mark the entire hemline.

   Move around the hem-ee rather than the other way around. This way, the hem-ee doesn't shift weight and distort the hemline.

Deciding on the Hem Allowance

After you measure and mark the hemline, decide how deep you want the *hem allowance* — the distance from the folded hemline to the finished edge of the hem. Hem allowances range from ¼ to 3 inches depending on the type of garment and the fabric.

When you sew a project, look for the hem allowance marked on the pattern. If you're preparing to alter a ready-made garment and are clueless about the best hem allowance for your project, refer to Table 7-1 for some general guidelines.

Table 7-1	Recommended Hem Depths
Garment	*Recommended Hem Allowances*
T-shirts, sleeves	⅝ to 1¼ inches
Shorts, slacks	1¼ to 1½ inches
Jackets	1½ to 2 inches
Straight skirts and coats	2 to 3 inches

Finishing the Raw Edges of the Hem

After you measure and mark the hemline and determine the proper hem allowance, even up the hem allowance and finish the hem edge.

Quick-fix hemming with Res-Q-Tape

You're getting ready for work and reach in the closet for the only suit that isn't at the cleaners. With one leg in the trousers, you slip and catch your big toe in the hem and rip it out. You really don't know one end of the needle from the other, so you grab the Res-Q-Tape. You fix the hem and walk out the door in five minutes.

Res-Q-Tape is a very sticky, double-faced tape that doesn't harm fabric. Find it on the notion wall of your local fabric store or through your favorite sewing mail-order source.

Why is it called Res-Q-Tape? Because it's the quick-fix superhero: It holds up strapless dresses, fixes gaposis, keeps shoulder pads in place, attaches fake mustaches or side burns, and holds spaghetti straps on padded hangers. It holds plaques on trophies and secures car trim. It holds ties and scarves in place, secures bra straps, keeps leather belt ends from flapping, and tapes up loose lining.

Don't iron over Res-Q-Tape or it melts. Res-Q-Tape isn't washable or dry-cleanable, so before cleaning, use one of the hemming techniques found in this chapter to repair a loose hem.

Even up the hem allowance by measuring from the hemline to the raw edge. Say that you need the hem allowance to be 2½ inches. On your project, the hem depth varies from 2½ to 3 inches, so measure down from the hemline 2½ inches and mark around the hem edge by using a fabric marker. Trim off the excess fabric so that the hem allowance measures an even 2½ inches all the way around.

You finish the hem edge of each fabric type differently:

- ✔ Knits that don't run don't need finished hem edges, although they may look better. If you choose not to finish the hem edge, skip ahead to the section "Hemming Things Up" later in this chapter.

- ✔ You hem knits that curl, such as T-shirt knits and fleeces, with twin needles, so skip ahead to the section "Hemming Knits" later in this chapter.

- ✔ Finish the raw hem edges on woven fabrics so that they don't ravel by using one of the methods shown in Figure 7-1:

    • Sandwiching the raw hem edge inside a length of bias tape and topstitching the tape to the edge

    • Sewing on hemming lace by pinning and topstitching it ¼ inch from the hem edge

    • Overcasting the edge with a three-step zigzag stitch

    • Serge-finishing the edge using a three-thread overlock

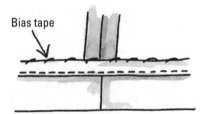
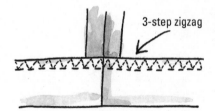

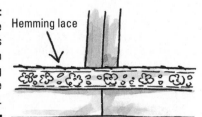
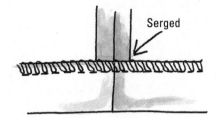

Figure 7-1:
Finish the
raw edges
of woven
hems using
one of these
methods.

If you have a sewing machine that has only a straight and zigzag stitch, finish the hem edge by sewing on hem tape or hem lace, as follows:

1. **Pin the hem tape to the hem edge.**

   Place the hem tape or lace on the right side of the fabric, overlapping the raw hem edge about ¼ inch. Pin-baste the tape to the hem edge. (After you really know what you're doing, you can sew on the tape or lace without basting.)

2. **Set your machine like this:**
   - **Stitch:** Straight
   - **Length:** Appropriate for the fabric
   - **Width:** 0 mm
   - **Foot:** All-purpose

3. **Sewing with the right side of the fabric up, stitch the hem tape or lace in place without stretching it.**

Hemming Things Up

After you mark the hem, even up the hem allowance, and finish the raw edge, you're ready to pin up the hem and either fuse or sew.

If you're not following pattern instructions or are re-hemming, refer to Table 7-1 to find the right hem depth for your project.

No-sew hemming

Fuse up a quick, permanent hem using paper-backed fusible web (available through you local fabric store).

A fused hem is almost impossible to change because adhesive residue sticks all over the place when you try to un-fuse it. If you foresee a chance that you may change the hem later on, skip ahead to the sections "Hand blind hemming" and "Machine blind hemming" later in this chapter.

1. **Measure, mark, and finish the hem as described in the previous sections of this chapter.**

2. **Fold up and pin the hem, placing the pins at the hemline.**

3. **Press the hem edge without pressing over the pins, pressing firmly enough so that you see the hem fold when you're done.**

4. **Place the project on the ironing board with the inside facing you.**

5. **Remove the pins and open up the hem.**

6. **Fuse the paper-backed fusible web to the wrong side of the hem edge following the manufacturer's instructions.**

   You place the exposed fusible side against the fabric and the paper-side up against the iron.

7. **Let the release paper cool and remove it.**

8. **Fuse up the hem as shown in Figure 7-2, following the manufacturer's instructions.**

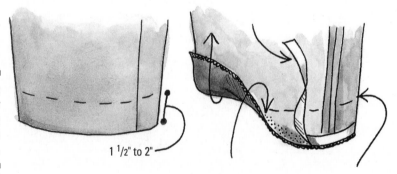

Figure 7-2: No-sew hemming with fusible web.

1 1/2" to 2"

Pinning up the hem for hand or machine hemming

Pin up a hem the same way for both hand and machine blind hemming. Pin through both fabric layers, ¼ to ⅜ inch from and perpendicular to the finished edge, as shown in Figure 7-3.

Figure 7-3: Pin the hem the same way, whether blind hemming by hand or machine.

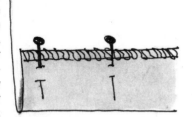

Hand blind hemming

If you don't have a blind hem stitch on your machine, or until you master blind hemming by machine, stitch your hems this way by hand:

1. **Thread the needle with one 15- to 18-inch length of thread, one shade darker than the fabric.**

   If the thread is much longer, it tangles and wears out before you use it all.

2. **Lay the hem across your lap so that the inside of the garment is up and the hem fold is away from and perpendicular to your body. Fold the hem allowance back to where the pins enter the fabric so the finished edge is away from you.**

   Approximately ¼ to ⅜ inch of the hem allowance is showing.

3. **Take the first stitch on the single layer of the hem allowance, poking the point of the needle down into the fabric and then bringing it up no farther than ⅛ inch from where it entered (see Figure 7-4).**

4. **Stitching from left to right (if you're right-handed) or right to left (if you're left-handed), take another stitch, picking up one fine thread (at the edge of the fold and where the pins enter the fabric) from the garment side of the project.**

You want to make the stitches as invisible as possible on the right side of the project, so take the finest stitch you can on the garment side of the project. Continue stitching, taking one stitch on the hem allowance and then taking the next stitch on the garment where the hem is folded back to the pins. Continue until you stitch the hem.

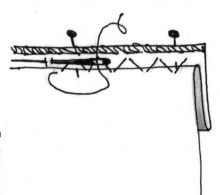

Figure 7-4:
Hand blind
hemming.

Machine blind hemming

After you use your sewing machine to blind hem, I bet you don't go back to doing it by hand. This is what you do:

1. **Set your machine like this:**

    • **Stitch:** Blind hem

    • **Length:** 2 to 2.5 mm/10 to 12 spi

    • **Width:** 2 to 2.5 mm

    • **Foot:** Blind hem

2. **Fold the hem allowance back to where the pins enter the fabric and place it under the blind hem foot.**

    The right side of the project is against the feed dogs, the wrong side is up, and the hem fold snuggles up against the guide in the foot.

3. **Make the first few stitches on the hem allowance; the zigzag bites into the fold as shown in Figure 7-5.**

    You want to create invisible stitches here (just like with hand blind hemming), so if the stitch grabs too much of the hem fold, you've made it too wide. Use a narrower stitch width.

4. **Remove the project, pull the threads to one side of the fabric, and tie them off.**

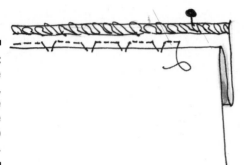

Figure 7-5:
Machine
blind hem,
letting the
stitch bite
barely into
the hem fold.

5. **Gently press the hem allowance from the wrong side of the project, applying more iron pressure on the hem fold than on the top of the hem allowance.**

Hemming Pegged or Straight Hems

Whether making pants or rehemming ready-made pants, you taper the hem allowance so that it conforms to the shape of the pant leg. If you don't taper the hem allowance, the hem edge is shorter than the leg circumference. What happens? The hemming stitches pull at the fabric, so the pant leg puckers at the top of the hem allowance. Yuck. This is how you taper a hem allowance:

1. **Measure, mark, and finish the hem edge, leaving about a 1½- to 2-inch hem allowance.**

2. **Starting at the bottom, rip out each inseam (the seam on the inside of the legs) and each outseam (the seam on the outside of the legs)** *only* **up to the hem fold.**

3. **Restitch the inseam and the outseam, sewing from the new hemline fold out to the finished edge.**

   Tapering these seams from the hemline fold out to the finished edge ensures that they fit comfortably into the circumference of the opening.

Hemming Knits

Knits stretch. Because of this tendency, traditional hand and machine blind hemming techniques often don't hold up to a lot of wear. Commercial hemming techniques keep your knits looking good for a long time. You can duplicate these techniques by hemming with elastic thread in the bobbin or by using your twin needles.

Hemming with elastic thread in the bobbin

Here's a really easy hemming technique adapted from a commercial method used in swimsuit construction. Follow these steps to create a hem that stretches with your knit fabric:

1. **Mark, press, and pin up the hem as described in the preceding sections.**

2. **Set your machine like this:**
   - **Stitch:** Straight
   - **Length:** 3 to 4 mm /6 to 9 spi
   - **Width:** 0
   - **Foot:** Embroidery
   - **Thread:** Top, matching to the fabric. Bobbin: Elastic thread threaded in the case, bypassing the tension

3. **Wind the bobbin with elastic thread.**
   - Place the bobbin on the bobbin winder and the tube of elastic thread on your lap.
   - Loosely tie the elastic thread onto the bobbin.
   - Wind the bobbin slowly, guiding the elastic thread onto the bobbin evenly.

   - Even if your machine has a self-winding bobbin, wind the bobbin by hand. Don't stretch the elastic thread while winding. If you do, the elastic thread loses its elasticity while placed on the bobbin and the zip is zapped.

4. **Thread the bobbin case by bypassing the bobbin tension.**

   If you have a removable bobbin case, place the bobbin in the case, threading the elastic thread end up through the large hole in the top.

   If you have a stationary bobbin case, set the bobbin in the case without threading the tension.

   Some brands have a special tension bypass hole, so refer to your operating manual or ask your dealer if your model has this feature and how to thread it.

5. **With the right side of the project up, place the presser foot so it rests on a double layer of fabric (the hem allowance and the garment) and sew.**

   Sewing straight and even is easier when the foot rests completely on a double layer of fabric.

6. After sewing around the hem, pull the threads to the wrong side and tie them off securely, as shown in Figure 7-6 (see Chapter 6 for the best way to tie off threads).

7. Carefully trim away the excess hem allowance above the stitch.

Figure 7-6: Rehemming a knit shirt with elastic thread in the bobbin.

Twin needle hemming

Twin needles are sized in two ways: by the distance the needles are from one another and by the needle size and point type. For example, a 4.0 - #80/12 Universal twin needle means

✔ You have 2 needles that are 4 millimeters apart.

✔ Each needle is a size 80 (European sizing) or 12 (American sizing).

✔ Each needle has a Universal point.

Only sewing machines with top- or front-loading bobbins (a category that includes most machines) can use twin needles. If your bobbin goes in the side, the needles sit in the machine sideways and don't work. If you can't use twin needles in your machine, fuse the hem by using fusible web (see "No-sew hemming" earlier in this chapter and follow the manufacturer's instructions on the package).

Follow these steps to hem knits:

1. **Mark, press, and pin up the hem as I describe in previous sections.**

2. **Set your machine like this:**

   - **Stitch:** Straight
   - **Length:** 3 to 4 mm/6 to 9 spi
   - **Width:** 0 mm
   - **Foot:** Embroidery
   - **Needle:** 4.0-80/12 Universal twin

   If you notice that all your stitches are not the same length (you have several normal length stitches and then a long one), try a stretch twin needle.

3. **Thread your twin needle by following the instructions in your operating manual.**

4. **With the right side of the project up, place the hem so that the presser foot rests on a double layer of fabric (the hem allowance and the garment) and sew.**

   Sewing straight and even is easier when the foot rests completely on a double layer of fabric.

5. **After sewing around the hem, pull the threads to the wrong side and tie them off securely (see Chapter 6).**

6. **Carefully trim away the excess hem allowance above the stitch as shown in Figure 7-7.**

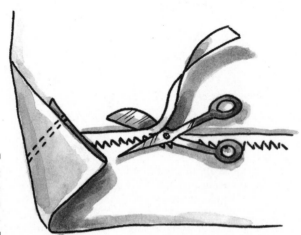

Figure 7-7:
Trim off the excess hem allowance.

Part III
Fashion Fundamentals

The 5th Wave   By Rich Tennant

Can't you wait until after the reception to examine the stitching?

In this part . . .

*W*hen the pattern guide sheet of your fashion project tells you to "sew in the zipper," you may be left scratching your head. How in the world are you supposed to do that? Your first step is to turn to Chapter 9 in this part. There you find step-by-step instructions on how to sew in a zipper. I also give you the skinny on sewing darts, tucks, pleats, sleeves, pockets, and other sewing delights! And to help you firm up your fashion fundamentals, I include a stylish clothing project that shows you, step-by-step, how to sew the perfect little black dress.

Chapter 8

Shaping Things Up

Darts, gathering, tucks, pleats, and elastic enable you to give form to otherwise lifeless pieces of fabric. You can use these structural elements separately or together to turn a potato sack into a creation that conforms to all sorts of contours not only in clothing, but also in almost anything made of fabric.

Darting Around

Darts are little wedges of fabric that you pinch out and stitch to shape pattern pieces at the waistline, back waist, shoulder, bustline, and hips, as shown in Figure 8-1.

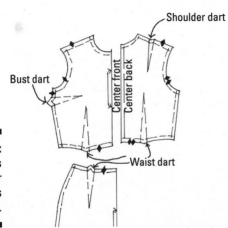

Shoulder dart

Bust dart

Center front

Center back

Waist dart

Figure 8-1:
Darts
help your
projects
take shape.

Paper patterns mark darts with stitching lines and sometimes a foldline that converges to the point of the dart. (See Chapter 4 for more information on how to decipher the markings on patterns.)

Making the dart

To construct perfect darts every time, just follow these steps:

1. **Mark the dart with pins or a fabric marker. (See Chapter 4 for more about marking elements from a pattern.)**

2. **Fold the dart, right sides together, matching at the foldline and pinning perpendicular to the stitching line, at the dots marked on the pattern piece.**

3. **Place a strip of invisible tape the length of the dart, next to the stitching line, as shown in Figure 8-2.**

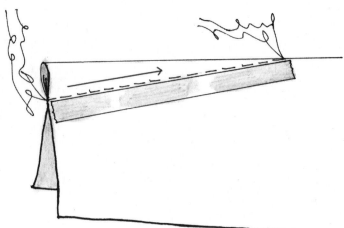

Figure 8-2:
Use tape as a stitching template and sew from the wide end to the point of the dart.

The tape forms a stitching template that helps to keep your sewing straight.

4. **Starting at the wide end of the dart, lower the presser foot and sew next to the tape for a perfectly straight dart.**

Pull out the pins as you sew.

Finishing the dart

After sewing your dart, press it so that the dart forms a clean, smooth line in the fabric. Just follow these easy steps:

1. **Remove the tape and press the dart flat and together.**

   Place the dart on the ironing board with the wrong side of the fabric up. Place one edge of the iron over the stitching line with the rest of the iron over the fold of the dart; press the dart flat from the stitching line out to the fold. Sewers refer to this procedure as *pressing the dart flat and together.* By pressing over the seamline, you set the stitches so that they blend well into the fabric.

2. **Tie off the thread tails at the point of the dart (see Chapter 6 for the how-to's on tying off threads).**

3. **Press the dart to one side, as shown in Figure 8-3.**

   Press horizontal darts so that the bulk of the dart is down. Press vertical darts so that the bulk of the dart is toward the center of the garment.

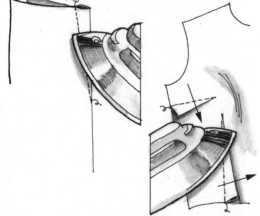

Figure 8-3: Press darts flat and together and then to one side.

Gathering No Moss

Gathering adds softness and shape to a project. Picture a gently gathered waistline and puffed sleeve in a child's dress, soft gathers above a shirt cuff, or a skirt gathered onto a waistband. All these examples use gathers as a way to fit a larger fabric piece, such as a skirt, into another, smaller fabric piece like a waistband or dress bodice. In this section, I show you three methods for gathering fabric. The method you use depends on the type of fabric you're working with.

Gathering with two threads

The two-thread method works best for creating fine, controlled gathers on lightweight fabrics, such as batiste, challis, charmeuse, gauze, gingham, georgette, lace, silk broadcloth, and voile. (See Chapter 2 for more information on fabrics.) Just follow these steps:

1. **Set your machine like this:**

   - **Stitch:** Straight

   - **Length:** 2.5 to 3 mm/9 to 13 spi

   - **Width:** 0 mm

   - **Foot:** All-purpose or embroidery

   - **Upper tension:** Loosen slightly

2. **Thread your needle with the thread you used for sewing your project together; thread your bobbin with a contrasting thread color.**

   Using a different thread color in the bobbin makes these stitches easier to find when you're ready to pull up the gathers.

3. **Sew a row of gathering stitches ½ inch from the raw edge, leaving at least a 2-inch thread tail at the beginning and end.**

   Do not backstitch at the beginning or end.

   The gathering stitches for a seam sewn together at the ⅝-inch seamline are just inside the seam allowance and don't show on the outside of the project.

4. **Sew a second row of gathering stitches ⅜ inch from the raw edge, leaving at least a 2-inch thread tail at the beginning and end, as shown in Figure 8-4.**

   Be careful not to cross the stitching lines.

5. **Pull up the gathers by pulling on the contrasting bobbin threads.**

Working from the ends toward the center, hold the bobbin threads taut in one hand while sliding the fabric along the stitches with the other. Adjust the gathers as needed for the fullness you desire. Remember to put your upper tension back to the normal setting for regular sewing.

Not only are the gathers even, but using two threads also gives you a back-up thread if the first one breaks.

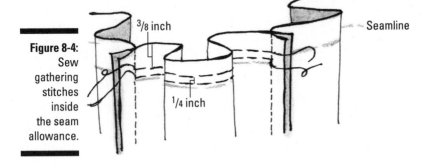

Figure 8-4: Sew gathering stitches inside the seam allowance.

Gathering over a cord

You can use gathering over a cord as a terrific way to gather mid- to heavyweight fabrics, such as chambray, chintz, corduroy, lightweight denim, linen and wool suiting, oxford, pique, poplin, and seersucker. (See Chapter 2 for more information on fabrics.) The cord technique also works well when you gather yards of fabric all at once when sewing ruffles. Just follow these steps:

1. **Set your machine like this:**

   - **Stitch:** Zigzag

   - **Length:** 2.5 to 3 mm/9 to 13 spi

   - **Width:** 3 to 4 mm

   - **Foot:** Embroidery

2. **Cut a long strand of *pearl cotton* (a twisted embroidery floss available through your local fabric or craft store) or dental floss, or reel off three or four strands of any thread long enough to accommodate the area you want to gather. For example, if you're gathering 10 inches, the cord should be 12 to 14 inches long.**

   If you're using thread, slightly twist the strands together — making a sort of cord — before sewing over it.

3. **Place the fabric under the needle with the wrong side up. Leaving the foot up, pierce the fabric with the needle ½ inch from the raw edge.**

4. **Center the cord under the foot, and lower the presser foot.**

5. **Zigzag over the cord, as shown in Figure 8-5.**

   The zigzag stitches create a channel for the cord to slide through.

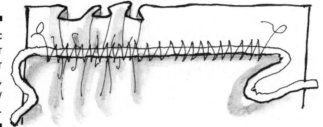

Figure 8-5:
Zigzag over cord for fast, strong, and easy gathering.

6. **Pull up the gathers by sliding the fabric down the cord.**

   You can easily adjust the gathers, and the cord doesn't break when working the stitches up and down for dense gathering.

Tackling Tucks

Tucks are stitched folds that run the full length of the garment. You usually use tucks to decorate or embellish a project, but occasionally you use tucks for fitting detail.

Knowing how to sew three types of tucks should take care of most of your tucking needs. The three most common tucks are plain, pin, and shell.

You often find plain tucks on either side of a blouse or shirt (on the front of a tuxedo shirt, for example). They come in two varieties:

   ✔ **Blind tucks:** The stitching line is right next to the fold of the next tuck, which hides the tuck's stitching.

   ✔ **Spaced tucks:** Space between the fold of the tuck and the stitching line highlights the stitching.

You make both types of plain tucks in the same way. Just follow these steps:

1. **Using a fabric marker, mark the tuck stitching lines at the dots on the paper pattern, transferring them to the fabric. (Chapter 4 tells you all about working with patterns.)**

2. **Fold the tuck, wrong sides together, matching and pinning the fabric together at the dots on the stitching lines.**

3. **Sew the tuck by lowering the presser foot and sewing on the stitching line.**

To help you keep the width of your tucks even, guide the edge of the fold along the lines marked on the needle plate of your sewing machine. For example, to sew a ½-inch-wide tuck, guide the tuck fold along the ½-inch line on the needle plate.

You Can't Beat Pleats

Pleats are folds in the fabric that control fullness. You find pleats in all sorts of places, including the following:

- ✔ Around a whole garment, like on a pleated skirt

- ✔ In sections, such as at the waistline of a pair of trousers

- ✔ As a single pleat, like a kick pleat in the back of a skirt

You make most pleats by folding a continuous piece of fabric and then stitching the folds to hold them in place. The pattern guide sheet explains how to fold and construct pleats for a particular project; refer to the pattern often as you sew your pleats.

To make a pleat, mark it as you would a dart or other symbol found on the pattern tissue (see marking instructions in Chapter 4). Fold the pleat on the foldline and stitch the pleat on the stitching line.

Types of pleats

When you look through pattern catalogs and fashion magazines (and probably your own closet), you see a variety of pleats. Become familiar with the different types of pleats (Figure 8-6) and where you find them on clothing:

- ✔ **Knife pleats:** These pleats have one foldline and one placement line and are pleated in one direction. You often find several knife pleats clustered together on each side of a garment, where one cluster faces one direction and the other cluster faces the opposite direction — like at the top of a pair of trousers.

- ✔ **Box pleats:** These pleats have two foldlines and two placement lines. The folds of each pleat face away from each other, and the backside of the folds may or may not meet. You most commonly see box pleats down the center front of a dress or skirt.

✔ **Inverted pleats:** You find two foldlines in these pleats, but they come together at a common placement line.

✔ **Kick pleats:** These pleats have one foldline and one placement line, and you usually find them at the hem edge at the center back of a slim skirt. Besides adding a style, kick pleats give the skirt enough room for comfortable walking.

✔ **Accordion pleats:** Sorry — you can't make these pleats at home. Accordion pleats look like the bellows of an accordion, providing a kicky, flared effect. Commercial pleaters permanently set these pleats into the fabric using a combination of heat and steam. You can purchase accordion pleated fabric by the yard.

Figure 8-6:
Look for (from left to right) knife pleats, box pleats, inverted pleats, kick pleats, and accordion pleats in garments.

Making a pleat

Regardless of the type of pleat you make, with the exception of the accordion pleat, you make all pleats just about the same. After you know how to make a knife pleat, you have the basic skills you need to make the others.

You often find simple knife pleats in trousers. To create a knife pleat, follow these steps:

1. **Mark the pleats at the dots as directed on your project's pattern guide sheet. Check out Figure 8-7 for an illustration.**

2. **Fold and pin the pleat, bringing the foldline over to meet the placement line.**

3. **Stitch the pleat on the stitching line, as shown in Figure 8-8.**

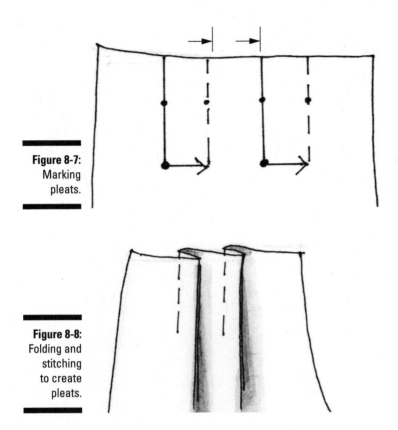

Figure 8-7:
Marking
pleats.

Figure 8-8:
Folding and
stitching
to create
pleats.

Getting Elastic

Besides adding shape and form to a project, elastic usually makes a garment more comfortable to wear.

Elastic comes in a variety of configurations, each of which may be appropriate for a different use. Refer to Chapter 2 for more information on the different types of elastic and which type may be appropriate for your project.

In this section, I tell you how to use elastic thread to create a gentle control called *shirring.* You also discover the easy way to put elastic through a casing. And, if you want to know how to sew elastic to an edge, I show you two techniques — one using a sewing machine and one using a serger.

For shirr

Shirring sort of resembles scrunched gathering. (See "Gathering No Moss," earlier in this chapter, for more information on gathering.) However, although gathering and shirring are both means for controlling fullness, they do have their differences. You usually set gathering in a seam — as in a gathered ruffle or a gathered skirt — that goes on a waistband. Shirring involves several equidistant rows of gathering that aren't covered up at a seam. Rows of shirring help shape garments at the waist or wrist, for example.

The best fabrics for shirring are soft, lightweight wovens that have been preshrunk, such as batiste, charmeuse, and calico. The best-knit fabrics for shirring are tricot, cotton T-shirt knits, and interlocks.

You shirr fabric using regular thread on the top and bobbin. However, my favorite way (and the easiest to fit) is to shirr using elastic thread in the bobbin.

You need the following magic ingredients for shirring success:

- **Quality elastic thread:** You can get elastic thread at your local sewing machine dealer. It has a stretchy core wrapped in cotton and is a little beefier than what you typically find on the notion wall at the fabric store.
- **Paper adding-machine tape:** Your local office supply store should stock this tape. I have a roll that I keep with my sewing stuff because it comes in handy for other sewing jobs.

Armed with the proper tools, follow these steps to shirr:

1. **Set your machine like this:**
    - **Stitch:** Straight stitch
    - **Length:** 3 to 4 mm/6 to 9 spi
    - **Width:** 0 mm
    - **Foot:** Embroidery
    - **Upper tension:** Tighten slightly

2. **Wind the bobbin with elastic thread.**

    Place the bobbin on the bobbin winder and place the tube of elastic thread on your lap. Loosely tie the elastic thread onto the bobbin and then wind the bobbin slowly, guiding the elastic thread onto the bobbin evenly.

Even if your machine has a self-winding bobbin, wind the bobbin by hand. Self-winding bobbins work only when the thread is through the eye of the needle and the needle moves up and down while the bobbin winds. The needle action tears up the thread (and would probably put your sewing machine into the hospital, too).

Don't pull on the elastic thread while winding it. If you do, the elastic thread stays stretched out and relaxes while resting on the bobbin, and then it won't shirr the fabric.

3. **Thread the bobbin case as you would with a normal sewing thread, pulling the thread through and snapping it into the bobbin tension.**

The weight of the fabric determines how much the fabric shirrs, so you need to perform a test to see how your fabric behaves. Cut a strip of fabric 10 inches long and about 6 inches wide and then do the following steps on your test strip before shirring the real deal.

4. **Place a strip of adding machine tape under the fabric; place the fabric and tape under the presser foot with the right side of the fabric up.**

The tape prevents the fabric from shirring before you want it to. After you remove the tape, the fabric shirrs beautifully.

5. **With the right side of the fabric up and the adding machine tape under the fabric, sew the first row of shirring across the top of the strip.**

6. **When you reach the end of the fabric, pull out enough thread so that you leave at least 1 inch of elastic thread at the end of the first row of stitching.**

Doing so ensures that the elastic thread doesn't pull out of the stitching when you catch it in a seam.

7. **Sew a second row next to the first, sewing a presser foot distance away.**

8. **Repeat Steps 5, 6, and 7 until you shirr the desired amount of fabric.**

9. **Tear off the adding machine tape from behind the stitches, as shown in Figure 8-9.**

The fabric shirrs as the elastic thread relaxes. If the 10-inch test fabric strip shirrs to 5 inches, you know to use a 2:1 ratio when shirring a dress bodice, a cuff on a sleeve, or a waistline.

When you shirr at the wrist of a sleeve or at a waistline, remember to catch each row of shirring in the seams at both ends. This way you secure the elastic threads in the seam, and they don't pull out.

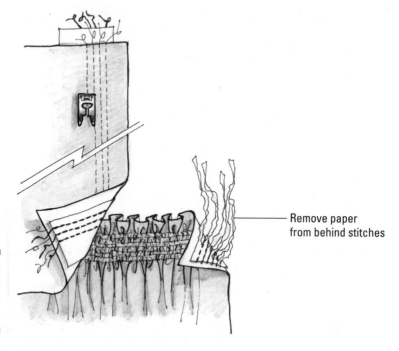

Remove paper
from behind stitches

Figure 8-9:
Sewing and
finishing
shirrs.

Elastic in a casing

A *casing* is a fabric tunnel that holds a drawstring or elastic at waistlines, wrists, and ankles to shape a garment. Traditionally, you create a casing in one of the two following ways:

✔ By folding down and stitching a casing, using fabric at the top of a waist-line. You often see and use this method for the waistband on a pair of pull-on shorts.

✔ By sewing another strip of fabric to the wrong side of the fabric. This method is popular at the waistlines of dresses and at the back of jackets.

In this section, you make a casing by using the fold-down method. Pattern instructions often tell you to create the casing and then thread the elastic through the casing with a large safety pin or *bodkin* (a little tool that pinches together over the end of the elastic like a pair of tweezers with teeth).

I've made hundreds of casings. I can't tell you how many times I've gotten to within 2 inches of the end and given the elastic one last tug, just to have the safety pin or bodkin pull off the end before the elastic was all the way through the casing. If that didn't happen, the safety pin or bodkin got hung up in the seam allowances. By the time the elastic was through the casing, I felt like I had acute arthritis in both hands. Painful and frustrating!

So, with help from my friend Karyl Garbow, I devised the following technique for creating elastic casings. Our technique takes about as long as the conventional method, but you don't lose the elastic or stress your hands. The trick is to start with a length of elastic that's longer than the circumference it's going in. Manufacturers often package elastic in several-yard lengths, so you get enough elastic for several treatments.

Try this fold-down method at the wrist or ankle of a pair of pants or a top. You can also use this method for the waistline of pull-on shorts, pants, and skirts:

1. **Set your machine like this:**
   - **Stitch:** Three-step zigzag
   - **Length:** 1 to 1.5 mm/25 spi or fine
   - **Width:** 4 to 5 mm
   - **Foot:** All-purpose

   If you're using a serger, use the following settings:
   - **Stitch:** Three-thread overlock
   - **Length:** 3 mm
   - **Width:** 5 mm
   - **Foot:** Standard

2. **Overcast the raw edge of the casing so that the fabric doesn't ravel.**

   To *overcast,* guide the fabric so that the stitches catch the fabric on the left and sew just off the edge at the right.

3. **Fold down the casing toward the inside of the project the width of the elastic plus ⅝ inch. Press the casing into place.**

4. **Set your machine like this:**
   - **Stitch:** Straight
   - **Length:** 2.5 to 3 mm/10 to 12 spi
   - **Width:** 0 mm
   - **Foot:** All-purpose or edgestitch
   - **Needle position:** Left (optional)

5. **Edgestitch around the top of the casing, sewing ⅛ inch from the folded edge. (See Chapter 6 for more on edgestitching.)**

   The edgestitch foot has a guide in it that keeps your sewing straight. It's not a standard foot, so ask your dealer whether they make one for your machine.

6. **Leaving the elastic in one long strip, place and pin the elastic into the casing, snuggling it up against the edgestitched fold, as shown in Figure 8-10.**

   Pin parallel to and just under the elastic. A lot of elastic hangs off either end of the casing, which you cut to fit later.

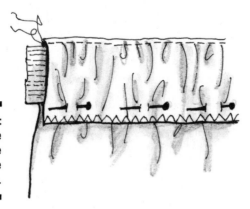

Figure 8-10:
Pin the casing close to the elastic.

7. **Anchor one loose end of the elastic with a pin. Using your all-purpose foot, stitch under (but not through!) the elastic, as shown in Figure 8-11.**

   Instead of stitching the casing down all the way around, leave a 2-inch opening in the casing for the elastic ends to pull through.

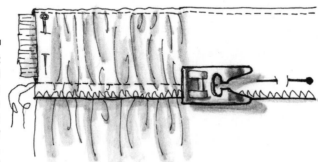

Figure 8-11:
Be careful not to stitch through the elastic when you sew the casing.

8. **Pull the elastic taut through the opening in the casing until it fits comfortably around your waist.**

9. **Pin the elastic ends together.**

   Don't cut off the elastic until you check that it stretches enough to fit over your hips. Nothing is worse than sewing in the elastic and then discovering that you can't pull up your pants.

10. **Cut the elastic to fit, adding a 1-inch overlap at both ends.**

11. **Overlap one end of the elastic over the other 1 inch and sew a square to really secure the ends.**

    Join the elastic at the overlap by straight stitching across the top, down the side, across the bottom, and then up.

When you work with a shorter piece of elastic or replace worn out elastic, thread the elastic through the casing. Instead of using a safety pin or bodkin, which can sometimes pull off the end or get hung up on the seam allowances, cut a small slit in the elastic and thread a bobby pin through it. The bobby pin has smooth ends and is narrow enough to easily slide through almost any casing, as shown in Figure 8-12.

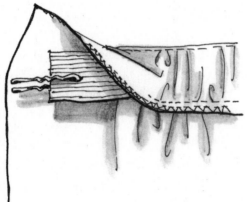

Figure 8-12:
Use a bobby pin to pull elastic through a casing.

Elastic on an edge

Elastic sewn into ready-made clothing is stitched on an edge of an opening and then flipped over and topstitched. You can very easily duplicate this factory technique with your sewing machine or serger.

Use the following technique to apply elastic to just about any edge where you need it, including waistbands, sleeves, and pant legs:

1. **Set your machine like this:**

   • **Stitch:** Overlock

   • **Length:** Longest (as described in your operating manual)

   • **Width:** 5 mm

   • **Foot:** All-purpose

If you're using a serger, use these settings:

- **Stitch:** 3-thread overlock
- **Length:** 3 to 3.5 mm (8 to 9 spi)
- **Width:** 5 mm
- **Foot:** Standard

2. **Using your fabric marker, mark off the edge of the fabric at the garment opening into eight equal parts.**

Chapter 1 tells you more about markers. Eighths, rather than quarters, are easier to work with.

3. **Stretch the elastic around your waist (or wherever you plan to sew the elastic) until it fits comfortably.**

Remember that you need about one inch of extra length to overlap each end of the elastic.

4. **Using your fabric marker, mark off the elastic into eighths.**

5. **Pin the elastic into the opening, matching the marks on the elastic with the marks on the garment opening.**

When you put elastic into a waistband or leg opening, leave one of the side seams open — you can easily sew in the elastic and adjust the fit at a seam.

6. **Sew the first couple of stitches to anchor the elastic to the casing.**

7. **Stop and reposition your hands, grabbing the fabric and elastic in front of and behind the presser foot.**

Stretch the elastic to fit the fabric, sewing from pin to pin so that the fabric and the elastic edges match up. Stitches should catch with the fabric and elastic on the left side of the stitch and then swing just off the edges on the right side of the stitch, as shown in Figure 8-13.

Remove the pins as you get to them so that you don't sew over them and break a needle.

When serging, serge from pin to pin, removing pins before getting to them and guiding the elastic so that the knife slightly trims away the excess fabric.

8. **Change the settings on your machine as follows:**

- **Stitch:** Straight
- **Length:** 3 to 3.5 mm/8 to 9 spi
- **Width:** 0 mm
- **Foot:** Embroidery
- **Bobbin:** Thread with elastic thread (see the section "For shirr" earlier in this chapter)

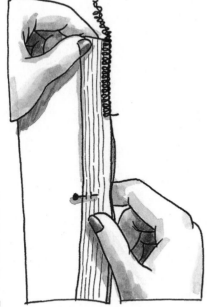

Figure 8-13:
Stretch the
elastic as
you sew
from pin
to pin.

9. **Flip the elastic over so that the *overcasting stitches* (those stitches that you used to sew the elastic to the edge) are to the wrong side of the project and then topstitch the elastic.**

   With the right side up, guide the edge of the casing, following a line on your needle plate so that the topstitching just catches the bottom edge of the elastic, as shown in Figure 8-14.

Figure 8-14:
Topstitch the
bottom edge
of the elastic
using elastic
thread in the
bobbin.

10. **Now that you've stitched the elastic into place, sew up the side seam, catching the elastic ends in the seamline.**

Most sergers have a special elastic applicator foot that you purchase separately. The serger combined with the elastic applicator foot makes quick work of elastic application. Thread the elastic through the slot in the foot and then adjust the tautness of the elastic by tightening or loosening the adjustment screw on the foot.

Chapter 9

Zippers and Company

. . . .

In This Chapter

▶ The four-minute zipper — really!

▶ The buttonhole nitty-gritty

. . . .

I remember searching through catalogs for patterns without zippers or buttonholes early in my sewing career. After a while, though, I didn't have many choices, and I was bored by the styles that fit the bill. I realized I had to overcome my fear if I wanted to make anything with pizzazz. I took a deep breath, chose patterns with zippers and buttonholes, and in the process picked up some cool shortcuts.

After you read this chapter, you'll no longer be zapped by zippers or baffled by buttonholes!

Yes, Virginia, There Are Easy Ways to Put in Zippers

Pattern guide sheet instructions often assume that you have some knowledge of sewing, and they've been recommending the same zipper application techniques for decades. In my search for an easier way, I ran across some great factory methods that I share with you in this section.

At first glance, these techniques may look complicated, but they overcome the typical roadblocks most folks have when sewing in zippers. So follow along with me step-by-step, and you can have a really professional-looking project with a zipper you love to use.

You can use several methods to sew in zippers. You sew the two most common methods in one of two ways:

- ✔ **Centered application:** Center the zipper teeth at the seamline, such as down the center back of a dress.

- ✔ **Lapped application:** A flap of fabric overlaps the zipper teeth. You find lapped zipper applications on the side seams of skirts, pants, and pillows.

Breaking a few rules

Regardless of whether you sew a centered or a lapped zipper, follow these tips. You may have a hard time believing some of them, but these tips can save you a lot of frustration — take my word for it:

- ✔ **Use a longer zipper than necessary:** How much longer doesn't really matter — just go longer. This way, the *zipper pull* (the part you tug on to open and close the zipper) is out of the presser foot's way when you sew the top of the zipper. The result? Nice, even stitching at the top of the zipper. After you finish sewing on the waistband or facing, you simply cut the zipper tape to fit.

- ✔ **Use ½-inch tape — like Scotch Magic Mending Tape — and baste in the zipper across the back without using pins:** The tape holds everything flat and in place, and sewing through it doesn't damage the needle or the fabric.

- ✔ **Use ½-inch tape on the right side of the project as a topstitching guide when sewing in the zipper:** This way, the stitching lines are parallel, and the zipper application looks as good as in ready-made clothing. (Who cares whether the zipper looks good from the wrong side, anyway?)

Putting in centered zippers

Sewing in a centered zipper is as easy as following these steps:

1. **Before taking the paper pattern off the fabric, use the points of your scissors to clip into both layers of the seam allowance ¼ inch to mark the bottom of the zipper placement.**

2. **Remove the pattern paper from the fabric and then place and pin the seam, right sides together.**

   Put two pins parallel and close together in the seamline, and at the zipper placement marks you clipped in Step 1, as a reminder to stop sewing when you get to them.

3. **Starting from the bottom of the seamline and using a 2.5 to 3 mm (10 to 12 spi) stitch length, sew the ⅝-inch seam.**

   Stop and securely backstitch at the bottom of the zipper placement clip and double pins.

4. **Remove the work, cutting the threads off at the fabric.**

5. **Set your machine like this:**
   - **Stitch:** Straight
   - **Length:** 4 to 6 mm/4 spi
   - **Width:** 0 mm
   - **Foot:** All-purpose

6. **Starting at the backstitching, baste the remainder of the seam together at the ⅝-inch seamline, leaving generous thread tails (see Figure 9-1).**

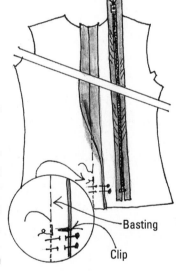

Figure 9-1:
Position the bottom of the zipper at the clip you find at the bottom of the seam allowance.

Basting

Clip

7. **Remove the pins, press the seam flat and together, and then press the seam open (see Chapter 5 for the best way to press seams open).**

8. **Match the bottom of the zipper with the clips in the seam allowance, centering the zipper teeth over the seamline.**

9. **Using the ½-inch Scotch Magic Mending Tape, tape across the zipper every inch or so.**

   The zipper pull should be up on the zipper tape, out of the way (see Figure 9-2).

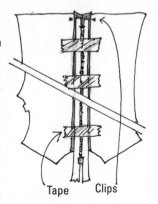

Figure 9-2:
Tape the
zipper over
the seam
allowance
with the
zipper
pull out of
the way.

Tape   Clips

10. **On the right side of the fabric, place a strip of ½-inch tape over the basted seamline, centering the seamline under the tape.**

    This tape is your stitching guide or template.

11. **Set your machine like this:**

    • **Stitch:** Straight

    • **Length:** Appropriate for the fabric

    • **Width:** 0 mm

    • **Foot:** Zipper

12. **Move your zipper foot so that the toe of the foot is to one side of the needle.**

    A zipper foot has one toe (rather than two toes like the all-purpose foot) so that you can move it from one side of the needle to the other for easy zipper application. Moving the toe in this step prevents the foot from riding over the zipper teeth (see your operating manual and Figure 9-3).

13. **Starting from the bottom of the zipper, stitch next to the tape, sewing across the bottom and then up one side of the zipper on the right side of the fabric (refer to Figure 9-3).**

    Don't backstitch; you pull the threads through to the wrong side and tie them off later.

14. **Sew in the other side of the zipper, guiding next to the tape template.**

    Move the toe of the foot to the other side of the needle. Sew next to the tape, starting back at the bottom and sewing up the other side of the zipper.

15. **Pull off the tape from both sides of the project.**

    Remove the basting stitches by pulling on the bobbin thread.

16. **Tug the zipper pull to the bottom of the zipper.**

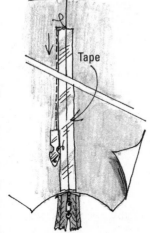

Figure 9-3:
Sew from
the bottom
up, next to
the tape on
the right
side of the
garment.

17. **Place, pin, and stitch the facing or waistband, intersecting the seam at the ⅝-inch seamline, and securely backstitch over the zipper coil at the top of the zipper (see Figure 9-4).**

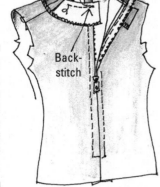

Figure 9-4:
Backstitch
over the
zipper coil
before
cutting off
the zipper
tape.

Backstitching prevents the zipper pull from coming off the track so that you can safely cut off the zipper tape. When you sew the rest of the project together, the intersecting seam at the top of the zipper tape that crosses over the teeth or coil prevents the pull from coming off the track.

If you cut off the excess zipper tape without backstitching over the zipper teeth or coil first, the pull zips off the zipper tape, and you have to rip out and replace the zipper.

18. **Cut off excess zipper tape.**

Putting in lapped zippers

You can sew in a lapped zipper easily by following these steps:

1. **Follow Steps 1 through 6 for a centered zipper application (see the previous section).**

2. **Set your machine like this:**

   - **Stitch:** Straight
   - **Length:** Appropriate for the fabric
   - **Width:** 0 mm
   - **Foot:** Zipper

3. **Position the zipper in the seam so that the bottom of the zipper is even with the clip marks in the seam allowance, as shown in Figure 9-5.**

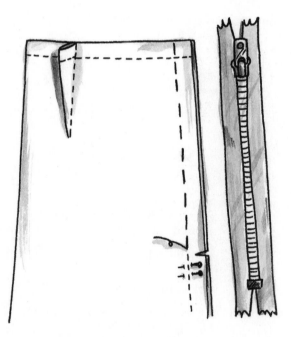

Figure 9-5:
Buy a zipper longer than the seam it's going in to.

Match the bottom of the zipper with the clips in the seam allowance. Position the zipper face down so that the right-hand edge of the zipper tape is on the right-hand side of the seam allowance. Center the zipper teeth over the seamline. You sew this side of the zipper only to the seam allowance. Remember to keep the zipper pull up on the zipper tape, out of the way.

4. **Move your zipper foot so that the toe is to the right-hand side of the needle and sew the zipper to the seam allowance, as shown in Figure 9-6.**

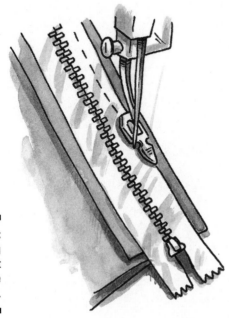

Figure 9-6:
Sew along the right side of the coils.

Moving the toe prevents the foot from riding over the zipper teeth — see your operating manual.

5. **Move the zipper foot so that the toe is to the left-hand side of the needle; form a fold in the seam allowance by turning the zipper face up so that the edge of the fold is close to the zipper teeth or coil.**

6. **Stitch over the fold, sewing through all thicknesses as shown in Figure 9-7.**

7. **Tape-baste across the back of the zipper.**

From the wrong side of the project, spread the zippered seam as flat as possible and gently press. Tape-baste across the seam allowance and zipper, placing the tape every inch or so. Flip the project over. (Refer to Step 9 and Figure 9-2).

8. **Tape the stitching template onto the right side of the project, as shown in Figure 9-8.**

Place a strip of ½-inch tape so that the edge of the tape is even with the seamline.

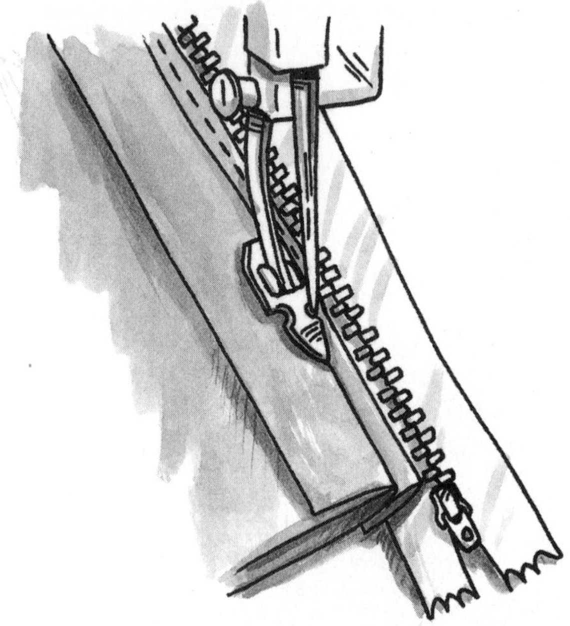

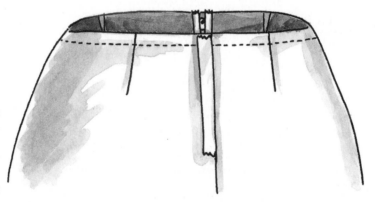

Figure 9-7:
Turn the zipper face up so the edge of the fold is close to the zipper teeth or coil.

Figure 9-8:
Use tape as a zipper template.

9. **Sew in the zipper from the right side of the project, guiding next to the tape template as shown in Figure 9-9.**

   Move the toe of the foot to the right-hand side of the needle. Sew next to the tape, sewing across the bottom, pivoting at the corner, and then up the right-hand side of the zipper.

10. **Finish the lapped zipper application by following Steps 15 through 18 in the section "Putting in centered zippers" earlier in the chapter.**

   The intersecting stitches used to sew on the waistband prevent the zipper from coming off the track, even after you cut off the zipper tape. Check out Figure 9-10 to see the finished product.

Figure 9-9:
Stitch next
to the tape
on the right
side of the
garment.

Figure 9-10:
Sew the
waistband
onto the
waistline,
and then
cut off the
excess
zipper tape.

Buttonhole Basics

What comes first, the button or buttonhole? To make the buttonholes, you need to know the size of the buttons, so you have to have the buttons before you can make the buttonholes.

Buy buttons in the size that the back of the pattern envelope recommends and sew the buttonholes in the same direction the pattern recommends — if the buttonholes on the pattern are horizontal, make them that way. Following the pattern instruction ensures that the buttons are in the best proportion to the garment and give you the best fit and look.

Sport snaps (the buttonhole alternative)

Sport snaps, which hold up to a good deal of wear and tear, were available only to clothing manufacturers — until now. Several companies make and sell commercial-grade sport snaps. These snaps are quite tailored and often make a wonderful alternative to buttons and buttonholes.

Snaps, from the very simple sew-on type to the heavy-duty sport snap, have two sides — a ball and a socket. Instead of sewing them onto a project as you do with traditional snaps, you attach sport snaps to the fabric in two ways:

✔ By poking a hole for post-style snaps

✔ By pushing prongs through the fabric for prong-style snaps

Sport snaps range from about ¼ inch (size 12) to about ¾ inch (size 27). When shopping for snaps, consider the project and where you plan to place the snaps before buying the first thing you see. For instance, you probably don't want a size 27 snap at the crotch of a pair of toddler's overalls. The snap is just too big and bulky.

Don't mix snap parts from different brands. Manufacturers make snap parts to function in harmony and don't guarantee their product if you use a wrong part or tool.

Each brand of sport snap has its own method of application, so make sure that you have the proper snap-setter tool(s) for the brand. Read the instructions for application thoroughly before putting them on your project. Doing so assures you snapping success. As with buttonholes, apply a test snap, using the same fabric, number of layers, and interfacing, before putting sport snaps on your finished project.

Sizing buttonholes

Even two buttons that measure ½ inch may not fit through the same buttonhole. The difference is in the shape: Thicker buttons need longer buttonholes than flatter ones. For example, a ½-inch, half-round, ball button needs a longer buttonhole than a ½-inch, flat, four-hole button. The fastest and easiest way to determine how long to make buttonholes is to do the following:

1. **Cut a strip of paper about 5 to 8 inches long.**

   Cut a longer strip when working with larger buttons.

2. **Fold the paper strip and snug one edge of the button, at its widest diameter, against the fold in the paper strip.**

3. **Pin-mark the edge of the button on the other end of the paper strip.**

4. **Pull the button out of the paper strip, flatten the paper strip, and then measure the length from the fold to the pin as shown in Figure 9-11.**

   The buttonhole must be this length for the button to easily slip through it.

Double-check that the buttonhole is just the right length for your button by test-stitching it on an interfaced fabric scrap. You can adjust the buttonhole length to the right size before putting it in your project for good.

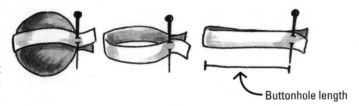

Buttonhole length

Marking buttonholes

You should position buttonholes ½ inch from the finished edge. To prevent sewing the buttonhole too close to the edge, stick a strip of ½-inch-wide Scotch Magic Mending Tape the length of the opening, placing one straight edge even with the finished edge.

Using your seam gauge, stick another strip of tape parallel to and a button-hole-length away from the first. Place a third strip of tape perpendicular to the long tapes and ¼ inch from the marked buttonhole. All this taping shown in Figure 9-12 gives you a guide that keeps buttonholes straight and even.

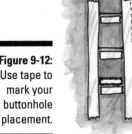

Sewing sensational buttonholes

You can probably make buttonholes by hand, but unless you have the prac-ticed hand of a master tailor, your buttonholes just don't look right. The sewing machine companies have done a wonderful job of making buttonholes easier to create, and each brand and model has a special way of making them. In this section, I show you how to make a buttonhole *manually* (meaning that you manually turn the fabric around to complete both sides of the buttonhole) in 11 easy steps. This method works on even the most basic zigzag machine and buttonholes look great every time.

Some machines make buttonholes in one step; others make them in two, three, or four steps. Most machine brands have a pretty darn good patented method of buttonhole-making, so read your operating manual to determine how the process works with your make and model and for instructions for making an *automatic* buttonhole (meaning that you make the buttonhole without turning the fabric).

On a scrap of your fabric, mark and stitch a test buttonhole or two, using your buttonhole foot and the same thread and interfacing that you use in the project. This way, you know that the buttonhole is long enough to fit the button, and that you've adjusted the stitch length properly for the fabric.

Buttonholes consist of two long sides made with short, narrow zigzag stitches called *satin stitches,* and with wider zigzag stitches, called *bartacks,* on the ends. Follow these steps to make a buttonhole:

1. **Set your machine like this:**

    • **Stitch:** Zigzag or buttonhole

    • **Length:** 0.5 to 0.8 mm/60 spi or fine setting

    • **Width:** 2 to 2.5 mm

    • **Foot:** Buttonhole

    • **Needle position:** Left (read your operating manual)

2. **Place the fabric under the foot so that the finished edge of the project is even with the back edge of the presser foot and the needle starts sewing at the edge of the tape.**

    The short length of tape must be at the side edge of the foot so that the needle doesn't stitch through it.

3. **Sew down the left side of the buttonhole, stopping at the tape and with the needle in the right side of the stitch.**

4. **Lift the presser foot, pivot the fabric 180 degrees, and lower the foot.**

5. **Lift the needle all the way out of the fabric.**

6. **Move the stitch width to 4.5 or 5 mm.**

7. **Holding back on the fabric slightly so that it can't move, take four or five stitches, creating the bartack.**

    Stop with the needle out of the fabric.

8. **Set the stitch width back to where you had it in Step 1 and then sew the other side of the buttonhole.**

    Stop — with the needle out of the fabric — when the needle reaches the edge of the tape.

9. **Move the width to where it was for the first bartack (4.5 to 5 mm).**

    Holding back on the fabric slightly so that it doesn't move, take four or five stitches, creating the bartack. Stop with the needle out of the fabric.

10. **Set the width to 0 mm and stitch up and down a few stitches, holding back on the fabric and stitching in place.**

    Doing so creates a machine-made knot.

11. **Pull threads to the back of the fabric, tie them off, and then cut off the threads.**

Cutting open buttonholes

I open buttonholes two ways: By using the seam ripper or by using a buttonhole cutter and block. If you plan on making a large number of buttonholes, buy a cutter and block. This tool saves you time and cuts open buttonholes very accurately.

Prevent your buttonholes from coming undone before their time. Put a drop of seam sealant, such as FrayCheck, on the knot on the backside of the buttonhole by dipping the point of the pin in the liquid and dotting it on the thread. Before cutting the buttonhole open, dribble a thin bead of FrayCheck on the cutting space between the two sides of the buttonhole. Let the FrayCheck dry and then cut open the buttonholes.

Using a ripper

Carefully cut open your buttonholes with a ripper by following these steps:

1. **Score the cutting space between the two rows of stitching by running the backside of the ripper blade between the two rows of buttonhole stitches.**

    Doing so separates the threads, allowing you to more easily cut the buttonhole open without cutting the buttonhole stitches.

2. **Place a pin at the inside edge of one of the bartacks.**

    The pin acts like a brake and prevents you from cutting open the buttonhole past the bartack.

3. **Starting at the inside edge of the opposite bartack, push the point of the ripper down through the fabric, bringing the point up and through the cutting space in front of the pin, using the same motion you use when pinning.**

4. **With the point of the ripper up through the cutting space, push hard, cutting the fabric between the sides of the buttonhole.**

Using a cutter and block

These little tools are really great. You can find them through your local sewing machine dealer or mail-order source.

Follow these steps to cut open your buttonholes using a cutter and block:

1. **Center the buttonhole over the little wood block.**

2. **Center the cutter blade over the cutting space in the buttonhole.**

3. **Push down firmly on the cutter, cutting through the fabric to the wood block.**

   Tada! You're done.

Marking the button placement

You can mark the button placement before removing the paper pattern piece, but I like marking the button placement after I make and cut open the button-holes because the mark is more accurate.

Follow these steps to mark the button placement:

1. **Hold the project so that the buttonholes and button opening are wrong sides together.**

   If the project has an overlapping front placket (like the front of a dress shirt), hold it as though the front placket is buttoned.

2. **Mark the end of the cutting space at the bartack.**

   From the button side of the opening, push a pin straight through the project so that it goes in at the buttonhole opening, right next to the bartack. Using a fabric marker, mark the button placement at the pin.

   - For horizontal buttonholes, mark button placement nearest the finished edge.

   - For vertical buttonholes, mark button placement so that all the buttons place either at the top or at the bottom of the bartack.

3. **Before sewing on the button by hand or machine (see Chapter 5), double-check that the button is three-fourths to a full button-diameter's distance from the finished edge and then adjust the placement as needed.**

Remove buttons from the card the easy way: On the back side of the card, slide a pin under the fine wire that holds the buttons on the card. Pull the button off the front. The pin prevents the wire from pulling through the card. The pin often ends up bent — if it bends, throw it away.

Chapter 10

Sleeves: The Long and the Short of It

Sleeves are easy to put in when you know how. In this chapter, I show you the easiest methods, first by not putting in a sleeve at all, but by facing or binding off a sleeveless armhole. Facing the armhole gives you practice staystitching, seaming, trimming, notching, pressing, and understitching. (If these terms are new to you, read Chapters 5 and 6.) The wonderful technique I show you for binding off an edge is a factory method that you don't usually find in traditional pattern guide sheet instructions. You'll love it.

Next, I tackle sleeves, starting with the raglan sleeve. Raglan is not the best style for sloping shoulders, but you'll appreciate the easy sew and good looks when you use the right shoulder pad underneath. I save set-in sleeves for last. You actually sew these sleeves into an armhole. The easiest set-in sleeves I talk about are either gathered or set in flat, before you sew up the side seam. I finish up the chapter showing you another factory technique for setting in sleeves in the round. After a little practice, you get perfect results every time with this set-in sleeve.

Sleeveless Armhole Facings and Bindings

Have you ever cut off the sleeves of a T-shirt or sweatshirt to make it sleeveless? Cutting off the sleeves does give you extra room and ventilation, but after a while, the armhole stretches out, never to be the same size again. Because your only sacrifice is a T-shirt or a sweatshirt, you'd say no big deal. But for your other clothes, the armholes are finished with either a facing or binding that keeps those armholes in shape and looking good for the life of the garment. By the way, if you want to bind off the armholes in that T-shirt or sweatshirt, use the following techniques to give your old favorites staying power.

Facing sleeveless armholes

A *facing* is a piece of fabric that you reinforce with a piece of interfacing (see Chapter 2 for more on interfacings and how to use them). You stitch a facing to an opening and turn it back toward the inside of the project to finish off the opening. You can attach facings not only to armholes but also to other areas, such as necklines and, sometimes, hem edges.

Follow these easy steps for the best-finished armholes in town:

1. **Cut out and interface the armhole facing using fusible interfacing as shown on your pattern guide sheet instructions.**

2. **After placing the right sides together and matching the notches, pin and sew the facing together, backstitching at the top and bottom of the seam.**

3. **Place the facing in the armhole, right sides together and matching the notches.**

   Double notches are at the back of the armhole; single notches are at the front of the armhole. The seam allowances have different curves, so if you mistakenly place the left facing into the right armhole, the pieces don't match.

4. **Starting at the underarm seam, sew the facing on the armhole at the ⅝-inch seamline.**

   Backstitch at the end of the seam.

5. **Clip the seam allowance at the inside curves to within ⅛-inch of the seamline, as shown in Figure 10-1.**

   Armholes and armhole facings are inside curves, so clip into the seam allowance by using your scissor tips, clipping almost to the stitching line at the front and back of the armhole (see your pattern guide sheet and Chapter 6 for info on clipping seams). Clipping releases the seam allowance so that it doesn't bunch up when you turn and press the facing to the inside of the garment.

6. **Trim the facing seam allowance to ½ inch.**

   Trimming one seam allowance narrower than another is called *grading the seam*. The facing falls automatically toward the narrower seam allowance, making it easier to turn and press the facing.

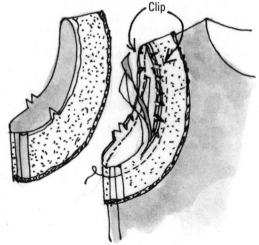

Figure 10-1:
Clip into
the seam
allowance
around the
armhole
and facing.

7. **From the wrong side of the fabric, press the seam allowance toward the facing.**

8. **Understitch the facing seam, sewing ¹⁄₁₆ inch away from the seamline on the facing side of the seam allowance, as shown in Figure 10-2 (see Chapter 6 for more information on understitching).**

   Understitching helps the facing turn toward the inside of the garment and stay there.

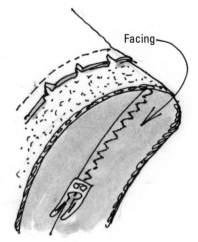

Figure 10-2:
Understitch
the facing
seam.

9. **Press the facing toward the inside of the garment and tack down the facing by stitching-in-the-ditch (see Figure 10-3 for an illustration and check out Chapter 5 for more stitching-in-the-ditch info).**

Sewing from the right side of the garment, center the crack of the seam under the needle. Sew, guiding the stitches so that they bury themselves in the crack of the seam. Don't backstitch; simply pull the threads to the facing side and tie them off (see Chapter 6 for the best way to tie off threads).

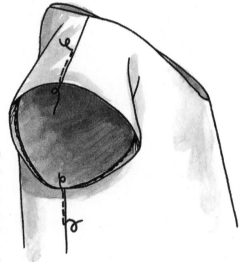

Figure 10-3:
Secure the armhole facing by stitching-in-the-ditch.

Binding sleeveless armholes

You can use binding as a particularly clean way to finish an edge on an armhole, neckline, or other hem edge. You sew a doubled band to the wrong side of the garment and then bring the folded edge of the binding over the seam allowance toward the right side of the garment and edgestitch it in place. This commercial binding method ensures a sensational ready-to-wear look on any bound edge.

This technique works best on light- to mid-weight fabrics.

Choosing the binding fabric

Binding comes in strips of

✔ Bias-cut woven fabric

✔ Knit fabric cut across the grain

✔ Fold-over braid, trim, or bias tape

Which one to choose? Look at the fabric you're working with and match the trim with the fabric by color, fiber content (see Chapter 2 for more on fibers), and *hand* (the drapeability of the trim after you put it on the edge of the project). Also read the back of the pattern envelope to see what the pattern company recommends. Both bias-cut woven fabric and knit fabric cut across the grain stretch a little bit, so they shape smoothly to a curved edge, such as an armhole or neckline. (Check out Chapter 4 to understand more about bias and grainlines.)

Cutting the binding

When cutting your own binding, cut woven fabric on the bias; if you're using knit fabric, cut across the grain. Cut the fabric into a strip four times the finished width, plus another ½ inch for the seam allowances (two ¼-inch seam allowances = ½ inch).

So, for a ½-inch finished binding width, you start with a strip that's 2½ inches wide. I always cut a little longer binding than I need so that I don't run out.

Sewing the binding

Follow these steps to construct the binding that goes around the edge of the armhole:

1. **Trim the garment armhole seam allowance to ¼ inch.**

   If you're working with a knit fabric, trim the seam allowance using regular scissors or shears. If you're working on a woven fabric and have pinking shears, use them for trimming because pinkers automatically notch the seam allowance for you, making the seam allowance easier to work with (see Chapter 6 for more information on notching seams).

2. **Staystitch around the trimmed armhole under the arm from notch to notch. (Chapter 6 tells you more about staystitching.)**

3. **Fold and press the binding in half the long way so that the *wrong* sides of the fabric are together.**

4. **Open the binding strip, fold down the short end ½ inch, and press, as shown in Figure 10-4.**

   This end overlaps the binding at the other end, giving the opening a nice, finished look.

5. **Fold and press the binding strip back to its original position, as shown in Figure 10-4.**

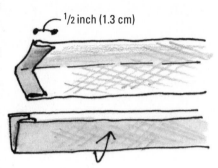

Figure 10-4:
Fold down
the short
end ½ inch,
and then
press the
binding strip
back to its
original
position.

6. **Starting slightly to the backside of the underarm seam (and with the short hemmed end first), pin the binding to the *wrong side* of the garment so that all the raw edges are even, as shown in Figure 10-5.**

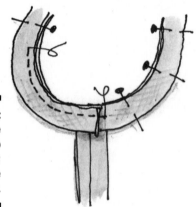

Figure 10-5:
Pin the
binding to
the *wrong
side* of the
garment.

7. **When you get back to where you started pinning on the binding, overlap the binding end over the folded end at the opening by about ½ inch and then cut off the excess from the binding strip.**

    This way, the binding ends up long enough.

8. **Set your machine like this:**

    • **Stitch:** Straight

    • **Length:** 2.5 to 3.5 mm/10 to 12 spi

    • **Width:** 0 mm

    • **Foot:** All-purpose

9. Sew the binding to the armhole using a ¼-inch seam allowance, backstitching at the end of the seam.

10. With the wrong side of the garment up, press the seam allowance toward the binding side.

11. Fold, pin, and press the band in shape around the opening, as shown in Figure 10-6.

    Fold the edge of the band over the opening, toward the right side of the project, so that the edge of the band covers the seam allowance and the previous stitching line.

12. Edgestitch the band to the opening, guiding ⅛ inch from the folded edge of the band. (See Chapter 6 for more on edgestitching.)

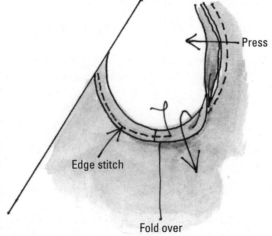

Figure 10-6:
Fold the edge of the band over the opening and edgestitch.

Press

Edge stitch

Fold over

Rarin' to Sew Raglan Sleeves

You find raglan sleeves on garment tops — from sweatshirts to cashmere sweater sets. What makes them different from traditional set-in sleeves? The seams on the front run from the neck edge diagonally across to the underarm and up the back to the neckline, making them a lot easier to sew than set-in sleeves.

Because the raglan sleeve covers the shoulder, either a seam or a dart shapes the top of the sleeve so that it fits smoothly at the shoulder line. The most common way to shape a raglan sleeve is with a dart.

Just follow these steps to sew in a raglan sleeve:

1. **Sew and then press the shoulder dart.**

   Placing the right sides together, pin the shoulder dart as shown in your pattern guide sheet. Sew the dart, starting from the wide end and stitching to the point (see Chapter 8 for more information on sewing darts).

2. **Pin the sleeve to the garment.**

   Match the notches and pin the right sides together.

3. **Sew the sleeve to the garment at the ⅝-inch seamline.**

4. **Sew the garment side seams, right sides together at the ⅝-inch seamline, backstitching on both ends of the seam.**

5. **Trim the seam allowance to ⅜ inch from notch to notch *at the underarm seams only.***

   This approach keeps the underarm seam from bunching up (and cutting off the circulation under your arm).

6. **Press the front and back shoulder seams open, from the notches up to the neckline. (See Chapter 5 for more tips and tricks for perfect pressing.)**

Big News about Set-In Sleeves and Armholes

Set-in sleeves have a seam that goes all the way around your arm where your arm connects to your torso. Instead of going diagonally across your body from the neckline, as with raglan sleeves, a set-in sleeve starts at the underarm (or armpit), travels up, runs over your shoulder, and then goes straight back down again to the underarm.

So here's the big news: Set-in sleeves are bigger than the armholes they go into, so you can comfortably move your arms around. This extra fabric in the sleeves causes a lot of sewers major sleeve-setting difficulties. So how do you get the sleeve in there — shrink it? Yes and no. In this section, I share some tricks with you to help make set-in sleeves less mysterious.

Setting sleeves in flat

Setting sleeves in flat means that the side seams of the shirt or bodice are open (not sewn yet), and the sleeves are not sewn into a tube. Even if the pattern says to sew the underarm sleeve seam first, try this simple flat method. By sewing with the sleeve against the feed dogs of your sewing machine (rather than the other way around), the excess sleeve fabric works itself into the armhole seam almost automatically. Follow these steps to relieve your sleeve-sewing worries:

1. **Sew and press the shoulder seam of the shirt (as the pattern instructions tell you to) and then open the shirt flat so that the right side of the fabric is up.**

2. **Pin the sleeve to the shirt, right sides together, matching the front and back notches and centering the sleeve cap at the shoulder seam.**

3. **Sewing with the sleeve side down against the feed dogs, stitch the sleeve into the shirt at the ⅝-inch seamline.**

The feed dogs on your sewing machine feed the underlayer of fabric a little faster than the top layer of fabric, which is directly under the presser foot. Use this fact to your advantage when sewing in a sleeve. Sewing with the sleeve side down allows the feed dogs to ease in just enough fullness of the sleeve so that it fits perfectly into the armhole.

4. **Trim the seam allowance to ⅜ inch under the arm from notch to notch only.**

5. **Overcast the edges of both seam allowances together by using the three-step zigzag on your sewing machine or serging them together (see Chapter 6 for the details of overcasting).**

6. **Pin and sew the garment side seam and underarm at the ⅝-inch seamline, sewing the entire side seam and underarm sleeve seam in one step.**

Start sewing the seam from the hem edge and up through the underarm seam, as shown in Figure 10-7.

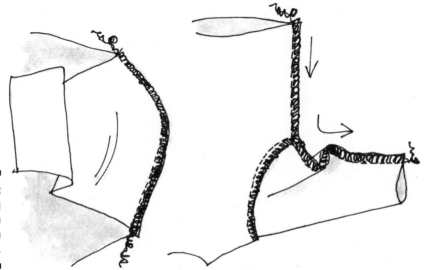

Figure 10-7: Start sewing the seam at the hem edge.

Setting gathered sleeves in the round

Setting sleeves in the round means that you sew together the side seams of the shirt or bodice and then stitch together the sleeves at the underarm seams. This technique gives you a better fit, and I recommend it for gathered, fitted, or tailored sleeves.

The easiest set-in sleeve to sew is the gathered sleeve. Because you sew the gathering stitches at the sleeve cap from dot to dot or from notch to notch, the fullness at the sleeve cinches in enough to comfortably fit the armhole (review the tricks of two-thread gathering in Chapter 8).

The information in this section may look more involved than what you see in the pattern guide sheet instructions, but by providing you with these easy steps, I assure you success:

1. **Using a fabric marker, transfer the dots on the armhole and sleeve seamlines from the paper pattern pieces to the fabric. Also mark the top of the sleeve cap.**

   These dots are additional match points and also tell you where to sew the gathering stitches on the sleeve cap (for example, pattern guide sheet instructions may direct you to gather "from dot to dot").

   If you don't find a dot at the top of the sleeve cap pattern, just mark one there or make a tiny clip into the seam allowance. This way, when you put in the sleeve, the mark at the top of the sleeve cap matches up with the shoulder seam.

2. **Place, pin, and sew the garment, right sides together, at the side seams.**

3. **Place, pin, and sew the sleeve, right sides together, at the underarm seam, following your pattern guide sheet instructions.**

4. **Press the seam open or to one side (see Chapter 5 for more on pressing seams).**

5. **Sewing with the right side of the sleeve up, stitch two rows of gathering stitches on the sleeve cap, sewing from notch to notch as shown in Figure 10-8.**

   Sew the gathering stitches so that the row of stitching closest to the seamline is ½ inch from the raw edge, and the second row is ¼ inch from the raw edge.

6. **Pin the sleeve into the armhole, right sides together, pinning at the notches, dots, and underarm seams.**

7. **Pull on the bobbin threads, working the gathers down the stitches until the fullness of the gathered sleeve fits the armhole, as shown in Figure 10-9.**

Figure 10-8:
Press the seam open and sew gathering stitches.

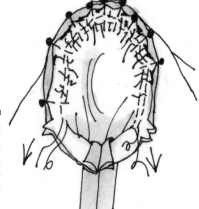

Figure 10-9:
Pull on the bobbin threads to gather the sleeve.

Gather half the sleeve at a time. Gather the back half of the sleeve from the back notches to the dots and then from the dots to the top of the sleeve cap. For the front half of the sleeve, gather from the front notches to the dots and then from the dots up to the top of the sleeve.

By gathering the sleeve section by section, you can distribute the fullness evenly, working from one small area to the next.

Double notches are at the back of the armhole and sleeve; single notches are at the front of the armhole and sleeve. The seam allowances have different curves, so if you get the left sleeve into the right armhole, the pieces don't match, and the garment really feels funny when you wear it (ask me how I know this).

8. **Stitch the sleeve to the armhole at the ⅝-inch seamline, backstitching at the end of the seam.**

   With the sleeve side up, start sewing at the underarm seam, guiding your needle just to the left of the first row of gathering stitches.

9. **Starting at the notches, clip into the seam allowance, clipping to within ⅛ inch of the seamline at the inside curves.**

10. **Trim the seam allowance to ⅜ inch from notch to notch, cutting away the excess seam allowance from both the garment and the sleeve at the underarm seam *only*.**

    This way, the sleeve fits comfortably and you don't cut off the circulation under your arms.

11. **Overcast the trimmed underarm seams together from notch to notch.**

    Overcast the raw edges together by using a three-step zigzag stitch with your sewing machine or 3-thread overlock with your serger (see Chapter 6 for more on overcasting). Tie off threads at either end of the overcast edges.

12. **Press the armhole seam flat and together all the way around, pressing from the seamline out to the raw edge. Gently press the seam back together.**

    If you have a pressing ham, press the armhole seam over the curves of the ham. This handy tool helps to comfortably shape the sleeve into the armhole.

Using easestitch-plus to sew traditional set-in sleeves

Traditional set-in sleeves are the most challenging because you have to make the circumference of the sleeve smaller to fit into the armhole opening *without* gathering the sleeve to fit. You can accomplish this feat by *easestitching*. Easestitching differs from gathering because you don't see a visible line of gathering.

In this section, I show you a more extreme version called *easestitch-plus,* in which you manipulate the fabric to get it to shrink enough so that the sleeve fits the armhole.

Here's how to use the easiest technique to get your sleeves ready to set into the armholes:

1. **Set your machine like this:**

   - **Stitch:** Straight

   - **Length:** 2.5 mm (12 spi) for fine fabrics to 3.5 mm (10 spi) for mid-weight to heavy fabrics

   - **Width:** 0

   - **Foot:** All-purpose

   - **Upper Tension:** Tighten slightly

   - **Needle Position (optional):** Far right

2. **Position the fabric under the needle so that the wrong side faces up and the needle starts at one of the notches on the sleeve.**

   You do easestitching inside the seam allowance, so guide the sleeve so that you sew ½ inch from the raw edge.

3. **Lower the presser foot, and as you begin sewing, hold your index finger firmly behind the foot so that the fabric bunches and piles up behind it, as shown in Figure 10-10.**

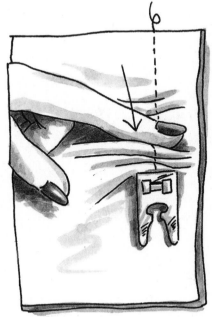

Figure 10-10:
Hold your finger firmly behind the presser foot so the fabric bunches up.

Let the fabric pile up until you can't hold it any longer. Release the fabric and then repeat the process until you easestitch the sleeve seam from notch to notch. This technique eases in the fabric automatically without stitching in unwanted tucks or gathers.

Use this easestitch-plus technique not only for set-in sleeves, but also to ease in the edge of a flared hem (see Chapter 7 to read more about hemming).

4. **Follow Steps 5 through 9 in the section "Setting gathered sleeves in the round" earlier in this chapter to finish setting in the sleeve and pressing it into shape.**

You start creating this casual, elegant look by turning a square of home-decor fabric into a tablecloth (see Chapter 14). Make the complementary napkins (Chapter 14), and finish this cozy setting by fashioning a French Country Cornice (Chapter 17) out of the same fabrics.

Product accessories featured on this page are from Southern Living At HOME®.

Brighten up your breakfast nook with an easy cornice, drapes (Chapter 16), and a reversible table runner (Chapter 13).

You can change the look and feel of a room just by adding chair back covers (Chapter 18) and changing the tablecloth (Chapter 14). Product accessories featured on this page are from Southern Living At HOME®.

Pillows give new life to your living room. Choose mod square pillows or elegant-but-easy napkin pillow covers. Chapter 15 shows you how to make both.

The little black dress never looked so good. Make your own version of this show-stopper using the instructions in Chapter 12.

Don't be a stuffed shirt — sew one!
Check out Chapter 15 to turn a
shirt into a pillow, complete
with secret hiding places
for the remote control
or a favorite toy. Get
cozy under this simple
fleece throw, which
you can find in
Chapter 17.

Place mats aren't just for the table anymore. You need only four mats to make this great vest and six for the jacket. (See Chapter 4.)

Redo a room in a weekend! Use sheets to make a duvet and contrasting fabric to create a dust ruffle (both Chapter 17). Top off the window with shirred and flipped panels (Chapter 16). You can even fancy up your sheets by adding lace (Chapter 17).

Chapter 11

A Pocket Full of Ideas

*I*n this chapter, I tell you how to sew pockets using the shortcuts that professionals use. I also include a really great project that lets you use the power of pockets to conceal even the worst of shirt disasters — with a pocket collage!

A Little Pocket Primer

Pockets are little pouches sewn on or into pants, shirts, and other garments (even decorative home interior items, such as pillows — see Chapter 15), all for the express purpose of holding pennies and other portable paraphernalia (or just to look clever, as in the case of accessories for your living areas).

✔ *Inseam* or *set-in pockets* are stitched in a seam.

✔ *Patch pockets* attach like a patch to the surface of the fabric.

Stitching All-in-One Inseam Pockets

The easiest inseam pocket to make is one in which you cut out a pattern that includes the pocket, pocket lining, and the garment itself all in one piece. Even though your pattern may call for you to cut and sew pocket-lining pieces to the garment separately, the construction steps are the same:

1. **Mark the pocket opening on your fabric.**

   The pocket openings are usually marked with dots on the seamline on the pattern paper. Using your fabric marker, mark the pocket placement by transferring those dots onto your fabric (see Chapter 4 for information on marking your fabric).

2. **Stay the pocket opening, as shown in Figure 11-1.**

Staying an area means stabilizing it so that it doesn't stretch out. For example, staystitching prevents a curved edge from stretching out of shape while you work on the project (see Chapter 6 for more on staystitching). To stay the pocket, use a strip of twill tape.

Cut a piece of ¼- or ½-inch wide twill tape 2 inches longer than the length of the pocket opening. Place the tape on the wrong side of the front pocket seamline, centering it next to the marks for the pocket opening. Stitch it to the front pocket fabric only. This tape acts as a pocket stay and makes the pocket opening stay in shape, even when you hang your hands in your pockets for hours at a time.

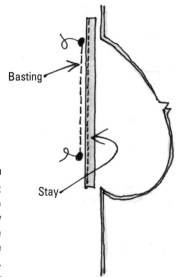

Figure 11-1:
Use a strip
of narrow
twill tape
to stay the
pocket.

3. **Set your machine like this:**
   - **Stitch:** Straight
   - **Length:** 3.5 to 5 mm/5 to 9 spi
   - **Width:** 0 mm
   - **Foot:** All-purpose
   - **Upper tension:** Loosened
   - **Bobbin thread:** Contrasting color to needle thread

4. **Pin and baste the pocket opening shut (see Chapter 5 for more information on basting).**

   Pin the garment and front and back pocket pieces, right sides together. Baste the pocket closed, basting the pocket opening from dot to dot, as shown in Figure 11-1. This way, after you stitch and press the pocket, you can pull out the basting stitches and expect a perfectly formed pocket opening!

5. **Set your machine like this:**

   - **Stitch:** Straight
   - **Length:** 2.5 to 3 mm/10 to 12 spi
   - **Width:** 0 mm
   - **Foot:** All-purpose
   - **Upper tension:** Normal
   - **Bobbin thread:** Matching color to the needle thread

6. **Pin the garment, right sides together, and then sew up the side seam, starting from the bottom of the project and pivoting at the pocket opening dots, as shown in Figure 11-2.**

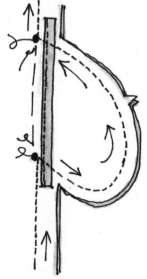

Figure 11-2: Start sewing at the bottom of the pocket and work up, pivoting at the openings.

7. **Clip from the raw edge to the dots at the top and bottom of the back pocket seam allowance, as shown in Figure 11-3.**

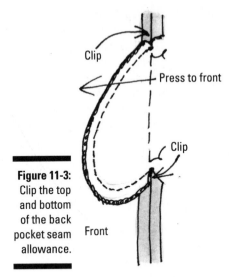

Figure 11-3:
Clip the top and bottom of the back pocket seam allowance.

When you press open the clipped seam allowance, the pocket falls toward the front of the garment. Why is this a good thing? When you wear the garment, you push the pocket toward the front of the garment. By clipping the seam allowance, you don't pull the side seam out of whack.

8. **Press the pocket seams flat and together from the wrong side of the garment.**

9. **Again from the wrong side, press the side seams open by pressing the pocket toward the front of the garment.**

10. **Remove the basting stitches by simply pulling out the contrasting bobbin thread.**

   Cool, huh?

Putting Together Patch Pockets

In this section, you cut, shape, and stitch an unlined patch pocket with square corners and an unlined patch pocket with curved corners. You also unravel the mysteries of creating patch pockets with self-lining and with a separate lining. Finally, you discover the most professional pocket-application technique ever.

But how do you know what pocket style is best to make? Here's my formula: For round body types, select a pocket and garment style that has square and rectangular lines. For thin and angular figures, choose pocket and garment styles that are curved and rounded. By using an opposite-shaped pocket, you de-emphasize figure characteristics.

Pocket placement is also an important consideration. If you're very busty, placing a curved pocket over the bust is a bad choice. You may want to omit the pocket altogether. For those of us with generous backsides, don't even think about sewing curved patch pockets in that area of the physique . . . they just emphasize the obvious.

Unlined patch pockets with square corners

I like sewing this pocket on shirts, even when the pattern doesn't call for one. This cornering technique works really well, so you can have the squarest corners going. Just follow these steps:

1. **Cut out the square-corner pocket by following the pattern guide sheet instructions or by using one of the pocket patterns found in this chapter (see the section "Using the Pocket Patterns" later in this chapter).**

2. **Using your sewing machine, overcast the top edge of the pocket facing (see Chapter 6 for more information on finishing raw edges).**

3. **Press the pocket side seams toward the wrong side of the pocket.**

4. **Fold up and press a triangle the width of the seam allowance at both pocket corners, as shown in Figure 11-4.**

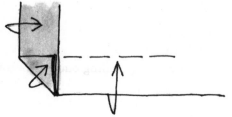

Figure 11-4: Fold up and press a triangle at both pocket corners.

5. **Fold up and press the bottom of the pocket on the seamline, enclosing the triangle in the seam allowance, as shown in Figure 11-5.**

You have just *mitered* a corner.

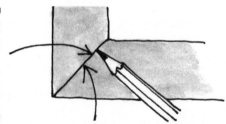

Figure 11-5: Fold to enclose the triangle in the seam allowance.

6. **Using your fabric marker, mark the angle of the miter so that the ink of the marker touches both fabric edges on the angle.**

7. **Unfold one pocket corner.**

   When connected, the marked lines make a large triangle in the corner, which becomes the *stitching line* of the miter.

8. **Fold the triangle in half so that the side and bottom pocket seams are right sides together; stitch the miter on the marked line.**

9. **Turn the corner right side out and check that the miter is at a right angle.**

10. **Turn the pocket corner wrong side out again, trimming the seam allowance to ¼ inch and tapering it at the corner, as shown in Figure 11-6.**

    Repeat for the other corner of the pocket. Press the corner seams open.

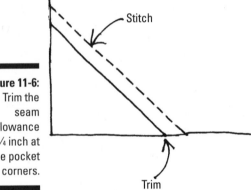

Figure 11-6:
Trim the seam allowance to ¼ inch at the pocket corners.

11. **Fold the pocket facing on the foldline toward the right side of the pocket. Sew the seams at both sides of the pocket, as shown in Figure 11-7.**

    Backstitch at the top and bottom of both seams.

12. **Trim away the excess seam allowance at the corners.**

13. **Turn the pocket right side out and press, as shown in Figure 11-8.**

    Now your pocket is ready to be attached to your project.

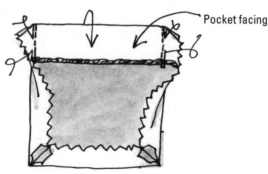

Figure 11-7: Fold the pocket facing toward the right side before sewing the seams.

Pocket facing

Figure 11-8: Press the pocket before attaching it to your project.

Unlined patch pockets with curved corners

The biggest challenge with a curved corner pocket is making both curves the same shape. Follow these steps and see how easy the job becomes when you use the right tools:

1. **Cut out the curved-corner pocket by following the pattern guide sheet instructions or by using one of the pocket patterns found in this chapter (see Figure 11-13).**

2. **Using your sewing machine or serger, overcast the top edge of the pocket facing (see Chapter 6 for more information on finishing raw edges).**

3. **Set your machine like this:**

   - **Stitch:** Straight
   - **Length:** 3.5 to 4 mm/6 to 7 spi
   - **Width:** 0 mm
   - **Foot:** All-purpose

4. **Easestitch-plus to shape the curved corners, as shown in Figure 11-9. (Check out Chapter 10 for more about easestitch-plus.)**

Sewing with the wrong side of the fabric up, easestitch-plus from about 1½ inches above the curve to 1½ inches to the other side of the curve, sewing ¼ inch from the raw edge. Repeat for the other corner.

Using your sewing machine, easestitch-plus by guiding the fabric so that the needle sews ¼ inch from the raw edge. (You use the same technique to ready sleeves for an armhole.) While you sew, hold the fabric very firmly behind the foot so that it bunches and piles up.

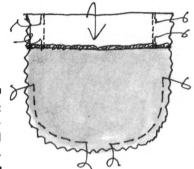

Figure 11-9:
Easestitch-plus around the pocket.

5. **Press and shape the corners of the pocket around a pocket former.**

Making sure that both pocket corners come out in exactly the same shape is a challenge — to say the least. My favorite tool for this task is a *pocket former,* a flat 4-inch aluminum square that has different curves on each corner. (Check it out in Figure 11-10.) You can find pocket formers at your local fabric store or sewing supply mail-order company.

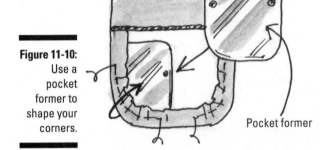

Figure 11-10:
Use a pocket former to shape your corners.

Pocket former

If you can't locate a pocket former, make one out of a piece of cardboard. Cut a 4-inch x 4-inch square of cardboard. (Cardboard found on the back of writing tablets or cut from a manila folder works well.) Set a small saltshaker or bottle of paper correction fluid in the corner and then trace around the bottom curve of the container with a pencil, creating a smooth curve at the corner. Trim the corner by following your pencil line. This pattern is your pocket former.

With the wrong side of the pocket up, snug the gentlest curve of the pocket former into one of the corners and gently steam-press the seam allowance up to the seamline, shaping the curve of the pocket corner around the curve of the pocket former.

6. **Fold down, pin, and stitch the pocket facing.**

   Fold the pocket facing on the foldline, putting the right sides together. Sew the seams at both sides of the pocket. Backstitch at the top and bottom of both seams. Trim away the excess seam allowance at the corners (you can read more about trimming corners in Chapter 6).

7. **Turn the pocket right side out and press.**

   Now your pocket is ready to join up with a project.

Lined patch pockets

Sometimes you want to add more oomph to the pocket so that it can hold more of whatever you put in it or to give the pocket a smoother-looking finish. You can get this result by lining the pocket. The decision usually depends on the fabric, the style of the pocket, and the type of project.

If you want to make a self-lined pocket, make sure that you have a lightweight fabric, like cotton oxford — wool coating is way too heavy for a self-lining.

Follow these steps to create a lined pocket:

1. **Prepare the pocket pattern by folding down the facing portion of the pattern along the fold line at the top of the pocket pattern.**

2. **Prepare the fabric for layout and cutting in one of two ways:**

   • **For self-lined pockets:** Fold the fabric into a double layer so that the right sides are together and the fold is perpendicular to the lengthwise grain (see Chapter 4 for more about grainlines). Lay out the pocket pattern on the fabric and cut out the pocket so that the top of the pattern is on the fold.

   • **For pockets with a separate lining:** Following the pattern guide sheet instructions, cut two separate pocket pieces — one out of the project fabric and one out of the lining fabric.

3. **Pin the pocket and lining together, with right sides together.**

4. **Set your machine like this:**

   - **Stitch:** Straight
   - **Length:** 2.5 to 3 mm/10 to 12 spi
   - **Width:** 0 mm
   - **Foot:** All-purpose

5. **Stitch around the sides of the pocket, sewing ⅝ inch from the raw edge and backstitching at the end(s) of the seamline.**

   If you have a pocket former and are sewing a curved-corner pocket, use your fabric marker and trace the curve of the pocket former onto the fabric at the seamline of both corners. Stitch over the traced lines, and the corners turn out to be the same shape.

6. **Trim away the excess seam allowance at the corners.**

   If the pocket has curved corners, notch the curves with your pinking shears or scissors (read up on notching outside curves in Chapter 6).

7. **Slash the center back of the lining, cutting the slit on the bias, as shown in Figure 11-11.**

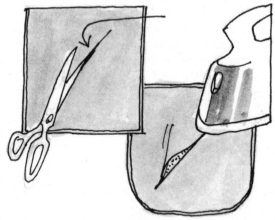

Figure 11-11:
Slash on the bias to prevent raveling when you turn the pocket right side out.

   Slashing means cutting into a piece of fabric either in the center of it or from an edge to the center of it. You cut a slash on the bias so that the fabric doesn't ravel when you pull the pocket right side out through the slash.

8. **Turn the pocket right side out through the slash.**

In this commercial patch pocket technique, instead of turning the pocket through a seamline, you turn the pocket right side out through the slash.

9. **Using the tip of your blunt-end scissors, push out the corners and curves of the pocket.**

Because the slash is in the center of the lining, a point turner tool works more easily into the curves and corners, helping to create a really good-looking pocket.

10. **Press the pocket so that the seamline is on the outside edge of the pocket.**

If leaving the slash open bothers you, slip a lightweight strip of fusible interfacing under the slit and fuse it shut by following the manufacturer's instructions (see Chapter 2 for more information on fusible interfacing).

Now you have a well-made pocket ready to attach to your next project.

Attaching patch pockets

Attach your pocket the easy way by edgestitching it in place by following these steps:

1. **Pin your already-made pocket to the project by following your pattern guide instructions.**

Patch pockets are usually intended to hold something, so instead of placing them so that you have to stitch them flat as a pancake to the project, position them so that they have a little slack at the top, as shown in Figure 11-12.

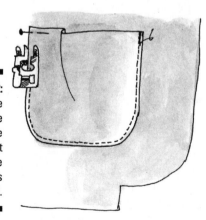

Figure 11-12: Leave a little slack at the top of the pocket to make sure it's functional.

2. **Set your machine like this:**

   - **Stitch:** Straight
   - **Length:** Appropriate for the fabric
   - **Width:** 0 mm
   - **Foot:** Edgestitch or blind hem
   - **Needle position:** (Optional) Adjust the needle position so that you sew ⅛ inch from the edge of the pocket

3. **Edgestitch around the pocket (read more about edgestitching in Chapter 6).**

   Guide the edge of the pocket along the blade in the foot, backstitching at the top of the pocket. If you topstitched this pocket and don't see it getting a lot of tough wear and tear, don't backstitch. Instead, pull the threads to the back and tie them off (see Chapter 6 for more information on backstitching and tying off threads).

Using the Pocket Patterns

Sometimes I just want to put a pocket on a project, and the pocket's not part of the original pattern. Instead of rifling through other patterns or buying another pattern to find just the right pocket, I dig into my reserve of pocket patterns when the inspiration strikes. In this section I show you how to make three different pocket patterns.

For instance, you can make three different pocket patterns from the shirt pocket pattern in Figure 11-13: Rectangular, rounded, and chevron.

1. **Find a piece of pattern tracing material or leftover pattern tissue that's at least the length of the pocket patterns in Figure 11-13. Fold it in half the long way.**

2. **Place the pocket pattern under the pattern paper, lining up the pattern on the fold of the pattern paper.**

3. **Trace off the desired pocket by following the key in Figure 11-13.**

4. **Cut out your pocket pattern on the cutting line and open up the pattern flat.**

   Voilà! A pocket pattern you can use over and over again.

While you're at it, why not trace off all three styles? You can have a ready pocket pattern resource for any shape when you need it! After you trace off these pocket patterns, safely store them between the pages of this chapter!

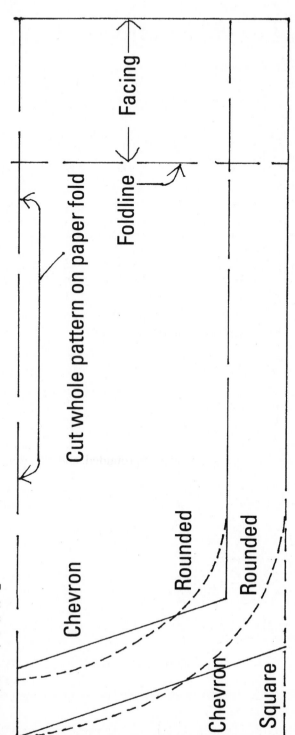

Figure 11-13:
Use this guide to pattern your pocket in a rectangular, rounded, or chevron shape.

Making a Cool Pocket Collage Shirt

My husband ruined three shirts in one week with the same leaky pen. Go figure. So instead of throwing them away (the shirts, not my husband and his leaky pen), I artfully stitched on pocket collages, covering the ink stains on the front of his (now *my*) favorite shirts. Check out Figure 11-14 to see the results.

This is how you stitch on pocket collages:

1. **Dig through your fabric stash for fabric that matches the color or design of your injured garment.**

   One of my husband's stained shirts is white with blue and black stripes. So I looked for fabrics with black, white, and blue in them.

2. **Trace off the pocket patterns and cut out the pockets.**

   Using the pocket patterns in Figure 11-13, cut out three different pocket styles from three coordinating fabrics.

3. **Make the unlined pockets by following the steps in the section "Putting Together Patch Pockets" earlier in this chapter.**

4. **Pin each pocket to the front of the shirt, creatively arranging three pockets to cover the stains.**

5. **Edgestitch each pocket to the front of the shirt. (You can read more about edgestitching in Chapter 6.)**

Figure 11-14:
Sew on a pocket collage to cover up a stain on your favorite shirt.

Moving a Pocket and Making a Stain-Covering Appliqué

I once stained a brand-new, day-old shirt with iced tea and couldn't get out the stain. Instead of throwing away my new shirt, I stitched new life into it by following these easy steps:

1. **Using your seam ripper, remove the existing breast pocket by cutting through the stitches (see Chapter 6 for ripping instructions). Set the pocket aside.**

   You sew it on in Step 6.

2. **Cut out an 18-inch square of contrasting fabric (I used a patchwork fabric of red, white, and blue). Chop that square into two triangles, cutting the square apart from the upper-left corner to the lower-right corner.**

3. **Turn under and press the outside edges of each triangle ⅝ inch, following the instructions for making a square pocket in the section "Unlined patch pockets with square corners" earlier in this chapter.**

4. **Place and pin a triangle on the right side of the shirt front so that you position the longest side of the triangle ¾ inch from the finished edge. Repeat for the left side of the shirt front.**

   If your shirt has a strip of fabric where the buttonholes and the buttons are stitched (this area is called a *placket*), snug the long edge of the triangle up to the long edge of the placket.

5. **Edgestitch around the three edges of the triangle, sewing on the right side of the shirt front (see Chapter 6 for more details on edgestitching). Instead of backstitching, pull the threads to the wrong side of the project and tie them off.**

   Repeat for the left side of the shirt front.

6. **Place, pin, and sew the pocket you ripped off the shirt in Step 1, wherever you want it, edgestitching it in place.**

   I put mine near the lower edge of the shirt, halfway between the shirt opening and the side seam. This way, the pocket is in the perfect position for keys.

Chapter 12

Making the Little Black Dress

In This Chapter

▶ Picking out your supplies

▶ Taking the preparatory steps

▶ Shaping, basting, and fitting

▶ Seaming and zippering

▶ Hemming, pressing, and wearing!

*W*elcome to the Grand Finale of Parts I, II, and III. I have written this chapter like one big project with cross-references to the appropriate sections of this book, and it gives you all the steps you need for sewing success. Use this chapter along with a pattern guide sheet as you sew. Keep it handy so that whenever you run into a step in your pattern guide sheet that confuses you, you can look in the index of the book or find the cross-references in this chapter that clear things up.

I rarely make a dress like this from beginning to end in one sitting, so I divide this project into natural stopping points. Now you can complete a section and then tackle the next one at another time. To make this project, you need the following materials in addition to your Sewing Survival Kit (see Chapter 1).

✔ Dress pattern

✔ Fabric (refer to the back of your pattern envelope for specific yardage requirements)

✔ Notions/findings (zipper and thread)

✔ Interfacing

If you have a bulletin board or wall in front of your sewing machine, post the pattern guide sheet and check off each step as you complete it. If you don't have a place to post the guide sheet, fold it to the step you want to work on, and then place it to the right-hand side of your sewing machine for handy reference.

Selecting the Pattern, Fabric, and Notions

Before you choose a pattern, review the information on choosing the right patterns in Chapter 4. After you finish your research, browse through your favorite pattern catalog at the local fabric store. The pattern I chose for the dress you see in the color section is about as basic as you can get, creating an elegant finished product that you can make without frustration.

Note: The pattern I use in this chapter has three-quarter length sleeves, which work with most figures, but you may choose to make your dress with short sleeves or even no sleeves. For these pattern variations, refer to the pattern guide sheet instructions and Chapter 10.

The easiest way to select a fabric for this project is to decide what time of the year you plan to wear the dress and how you want to take care of it. In the spring and summer, the most comfortable fabrics are cotton, linen, or silk (as well as the blended versions of these fabrics). In the fall and winter, the more comfortable fabric is a wool or wool-blend.

Also review the information in Chapter 2 on "Choosing the Right Fabric for Your Project," and then check the back of the pattern envelope to see what type of fabric it recommends. If you have any questions about this, ask a sales associate at your local fabric store to help you.

You also need to buy *notions* or *findings* for your project that include thread, a zipper, and interfacing. Refer to the back of the pattern envelope, as well as Chapters 2 and 3, to review what's best for your dress.

After you get home from the fabric store, preshrink all the washable fabrics and findings. This way, if your material isn't stitched up right away, you don't have to wonder if the fabric is needle-ready. Review the ins and outs of preshrinking almost everything in sight in Chapter 2.

Laying Out, Cutting, and Marking Your Fabric

I figure if I can lay out, cut, and mark the pattern pieces, as well as apply the interfacing on a project in one session, I've accomplished a lot. Follow these steps to get a running start:

1. **Find the pattern pieces you need.**

   Open your pattern envelope, find the pattern view you want in the pattern guide sheet, locate your pattern pieces, and separate them from those you don't use for this project.

2. **Lay out and pin your pattern to the fabric.**

   Lay out the tissue pattern pieces on the fabric as shown on your pattern guide sheet. (For more on pattern layout, see Chapter 4 for all the details.) When you lay out the pattern on the fabric it looks something like Figure 12-1.

Figure 12-1: Place the pattern pieces on the fabric in the same direction.

For more on pinning and cutting out your fabric, see Chapter 4.

3. **Cut out the fabric, following the cutting line printed on the pattern tissue.**

   Sharp shears make the cleanest cuts, so make sure your shears are in good shape before you start. Also, try not to lift the fabric up off the table while cutting. The flatter the fabric, the more accurate the cut.

As you remove the pattern tissue from the fabric, fold the tissue so the pattern piece name and pattern number are showing, and then place them in a gallon-sized zip-lock bag that you tape to the right-hand side of your sewing machine. This way, when you need to find a pattern piece for one reason or another (and I know you will), you can easily put your hands on it.

Putting Your Dress Together

The fun begins as your project starts to take shape. After I finish the edges, sew the darts, put in the zipper, and baste the seams together, I usually start dreaming about where I can wear my new creation and who I may see. I imagine the compliments, the accolades, the personal recognition . . . and then I snap out of it and get busy. After all, my public awaits!

After you accomplish everything in this section, you can try on your dress and do a little daydreaming of your own.

Marking the pattern pieces and shaping the curves

Without bust and back waist darts, a dress hangs on you like a flour sack. Follow these steps to turn those flat, lifeless pieces of fabric into parts of a shapely dress you love to wear:

1. **Use your dressmaker's chalk and/or pins to mark the bust and back waist darts.**

   Check out the information in Chapter 4 for all the marking details. Review Chapter 8 for more on sewing the perfect dart.

2. **Set your machine like this:**
   - **Stitch:** Straight
   - **Length:** 2.5 to 3 mm/10 to 12 spi
   - **Width:** 0 mm
   - **Foot:** All-purpose

3. **Sew the bust and back waist darts, as shown in Figure 12-2, following the instructions on the pattern guide sheet.**

   Turn to Chapter 8 for all the details on darts.

4. **Using a press cloth, press the darts — press the bust darts down and press the back waist darts toward the center back.**

   Look for more on perfect pressing in Chapter 5.

   Don't use a too-hot iron for your fabric. *Do* use a press cloth. Some black fabric is tricky to work with because, if pressed with a too-hot iron and/or without a press cloth, it can shine and the seam allowances create *shadows* on either side of the seamline. If you're not sure about the iron's heat setting and what it does to your fabric, use a press cloth and test-press a fabric scrap.

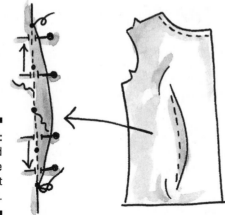

Figure 12-2:
Mark and
sew the
back waist
darts.

Staystitching and finishing the seams

I used to omit staystitching because I didn't understand what it accomplishes. But here's what I discovered: Besides keeping the fabric from stretching out of shape, staystitching prevents the fabric from raveling to the seamline when you clip the seam.

Follow these steps to staystitch your dress:

1. **Staystitch the front and back neck edges, as shown in Figure 12-3.**

   Staystitching prevents the curves on the back and neck from stretching out of shape. You can see more on staystitching in Chapter 6.

2. **Using your sewing machine, your serger, or pinking shears, finish all the raw edges except the hem edges.**

   You finish the hem edges after you fit the hems on both the sleeves and the bottom of the dress.

   For more on edge finishing, review the information in Chapter 6.

Figure 12-3:
Staystitch
the neck
edge first.

Inserting the Zipper and Sewing the Seams

After you install the zipper and sew the seams together, you get to practice pressing your seams during this session.

Follow these steps to sew in the zipper and seam your dress:

1. **Sew in the lapped zipper at the center back of the dress. The finished product looks like Figure 12-4.**

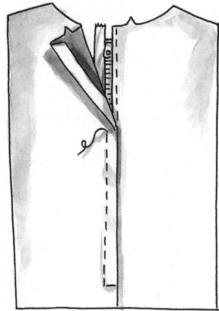

Figure 12-4: Sew a lapped zipper in the back of your dress.

Look for the best way to put in a lapped zipper in Chapter 9.

2. **With the right sides together, place and pin the dress together at the shoulder and side seams.**

3. **Set your machine like this:**
   - **Stitch:** Straight
   - **Length:** 3.5 to 4 mm/6 to 8 spi
   - **Width:** 0 mm

- **Upper tension:** Loosened slightly
- **Bobbin Thread:** Contrasting color to needle thread
- **Foot:** All-purpose

4. Baste the dress together at the ⅝-inch seamlines.

Refer to Chapter 5 for more on basting.

5. Try on your dress to check the fit.

This dress fits fairly close to the body, so use easy-to-pull-out basting stitches to adjust the fit before permanently stitching the seams together. Review your pattern guide sheet instructions for more on adjusting the fit.

6. Set your machine like this:

- **Stitch:** Straight
- **Length:** 2.5 to 3 mm/10 to 12 spi
- **Width:** 0 mm
- **Foot:** All-purpose

7. Sew the shoulder seams together, and then sew the side seams together, as shown in Figure 12-5.

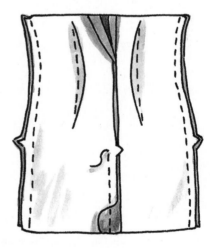

Figure 12-5:
Sewing shoulder and side seams.

Check out Chapter 6 for the best way to sew seams.

8. Pull out the basting stitches, pulling on the contrasting bobbin thread (see Chapter 5 for more on removing basting stitches).

9. Carefully press the seams open.

Turn to Chapter 5 for pressing tips and techniques.

Facing the Neckline

Facing a neckline is a way of finishing it so it fits smoothly around your neck and is comfortable to wear.

Follow these steps to face the neckline of your dress:

1. **Fuse interfacing on the neck facing pattern pieces following the manufacture's instructions.**

   See Chapter 2 for more on selecting and using interfacing.

2. **Place, pin, and sew the front and back neck facing pieces, right sides together, following your pattern guide sheet instructions.**

3. **Finish the raw, outside edge of the facing.**

   You can overcast, serge, or turn the edge under and edgestitch. Which technique you use depends on your sewing equipment. See Chapter 6 for more on finishing raw edges.

4. **Placing the right sides together, pin the neckline facing to the dress neckline, matching the notches and facing seams with the dress shoulder seams.**

   Both ends of the facing extend past the back opening edges. Turn both ends under to be finished later.

5. **Sew the neckline facing to the dress neckline as shown in Figure 12-6a.**

Figure 12-6: Facing the neckline.

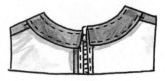

a.   b.   c.

6. **Trim the facing seam and clip the curves to the staystitching line.**

7. **Press the neckline facing, pressing the seam allowance away from the garment and toward the facing.**

   See the information in Chapter 10 for more on sewing, clipping, and trimming a facing.

8. **Understitch the seam allowance toward the facing as shown in Figure 12-6b.**

This prevents the facing from rolling out of the neck opening. Again, see the information in Chapter 10 for more on understitching a facing.

9. **Turn the facing to the inside of the garment, turning under and slip-stitching the center back edges to either side of the zipper; press as shown in Figure 12-6c.**

   See Chapter 5 for more on this slipstitching technique.

10. **Sew on a hook and eye at the top of the zipper following the pattern directions.**

11. **Tack down the facing to the dress at the shoulder seams.**

   You can do this by stitching-in-the-ditch (see Chapter 5 for more on this technique).

Setting In the Sleeves

Refer to Chapter 10 for more information about setting in a sleeve the easy way. Here's an overview of how you get the job done:

1. **Place, pin, and stitch each underarm sleeve seam together as shown in Figure 12-7.**

Figure 12-7: Stitch the underarm seam together and then press the seam open.

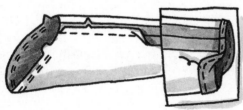

2. **Press the seams open.**

3. **Sew in both set-in sleeves, using easestitch-plus to shrink the sleeve to fit the armhole, as shown in Figure 12-8. Press.**

When you set in a sleeve, you end up shrinking the larger sleeve cap into the smaller armhole so you can move your arms around when you wear the dress. If you need more information on accomplishing this mission, check out the techniques in Chapter 10.

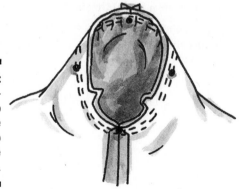

Figure 12-8:
Easestitch-
plus to
ready the
sleeve cap
for the
armhole.

Hemming Your Dress

Consider hemming the last sewing session and the home stretch. For the best-looking, invisible hems, review all the information on hemming in Chapter 7.

Use the following steps to hem your dress:

1. **Try on your dress and grab a helper to measure and mark the sleeve and dress hems for you.**

2. **Measure and mark the sleeve hems using the guidelines on the tissue pattern piece.**

   Try on the dress and have your helper pin up the sleeve to where you feel comfortable. If needed, have your helper adjust the sleeve length by lengthening or shortening the finished hemline.

   You can do this step without a helper, but you end up trying on the dress several times before getting it right.

3. **Have your helper measure and mark the finished dress hemline.**

   Adjust the hem length to your liking. For more information on what the *hemmer* (your helper) and the *hem-ee* (you) do when hemming, see Chapter 7.

4. **Even up the cut hem edges, creating an even hem allowance.**

5. **Finish off the hem edges of the sleeves and the dress (look for edge finishing techniques in Chapter 6).**

6. **Pin up the hem allowances in preparation for hemming.**

   If your little black dress has a slit at the center back, narrowly hem and slipstitch the slit opening, as shown in Figure 12-9, and then pin and blind hem around the rest of the hem edge.

Figure 12-9:
Hem and slipstitch the slit opening before you finish the hem.

7. **Machine or hand-blind hem the sleeve and dress hems (see Chapter 7).**

8. **Carefully steam press the hems from the wrong side of the fabric using a press cloth.**

   To easily press your sleeve hems, use a sleeve roll (review the information in Chapter 1 for more on pressing with a sleeve roll). If you don't have a sleeve roll, roll up and rubber band a magazine and wrap it with a clean dishtowel — preferably one without a texture. Slip the roll inside the sleeve and press away.

Now that your little black dress is complete, you're set for the next dinner out, school play, or power lunch.

Part IV
Sewing for the Home

The 5th Wave   By Rich Tennant

"One thing I learned banging out license plates at the State Penn for six years is always use a complementary color to border your designs and establish an overall sense of depth."

In this part . . .

1 know that playing favorites is wrong, but I just can't help it — this part of the book holds probably the coolest set of chapters you'll ever read! In this part, I show you how you can create new looks for just about any room in your house. After you read the chapters in this part, you no longer have to settle for store-bought napkins, tablecloths or runners, duvet covers, pillows, window treatments, or slipcovers. You can make your own — in hours! — with the exact colors and fabrics that fit your own decor best.

Chapter 13

Home Decor Sewing: The Cure for Decoraphobia

Wouldn't you love for your home to look like those you see on TV or in a model home? Never fear . . . your decorating coach is here. In this chapter, I cover the all-important home decorating basics.

First, I give you some strategies for conquering decoraphobia — the fear of decorating. You figure out how to uncover your home's complexion, choose a color scheme that works, use color to create flow from one room into the next, and discover the how to's of safely putting stripes, plaids, and prints all in the same room — maybe even on the same project. Really!

Conquering Decoraphobia

Decoraphobia, noun. 1. A paralyzing malady that leads people to live in a bland, colorless environment; 2. The fear of working with an interior designer; 3. The fear of choosing the wrong interior colors; 4. The fear of stepping foot into a fabric store; 5. The fear of working with home decor fabrics; 6. The fear of making a big mistake for the entire world to see.

Ever bought a piece of clothing on sale and gotten it home only to find out you picked the wrong color or size? You can return that little mistake to the store, no harm done. But a decorating mistake in your family room haunts your days and nights until you can afford to change it. Decoraphobia sets in and some folks never, *ever* get over their fear of decorating.

Avoiding costly mistakes (and acute decoraphobia) requires simple planning strategies. You need to

- Understand how color works
- Figure out your home's complexion
- Decorate with the right fabrics

Understanding color

You can find out a lot more about color than meets the eye. One important factor is that every color has either a blue base or a yellow base. Picture a Red Delicious apple. Compare it to a Beefsteak tomato. Both are red, but when you put them side-by-side, your eyes tell you that they clash. The apple has a blue color base, making it a cool red. The tomato has a yellow color base and is considered a warm red.

Every color — even blue or yellow — has a warm and a cool version. Now that you know that, start noticing how home decor fabrics are grouped together in the store. The store usually displays collections in groups according to their color bases. Look through decorating magazines and try to identify the warm environments and the cool ones. After a little practice, and reading more about the color cues in "Unmasking your home's complexion" later on in the chapter, you can get the hang of this.

When you put both blue-based colors and yellow-based colors in the same room, they clash — just like the apple and the tomato. Your yellow-based sofa looks dirty against the blue-based pillows thrown on top of it. So before hiking off to the paint or fabric store, determine the color base of your home — what I call your home's *complexion* — and then work with the right blue-base or yellow-base colors throughout your home.

Unmasking your home's complexion

Most of us don't have the budget to decorate from scratch, so work with what you have. Look at the largest surfaces — the ones that are more difficult and expensive to change — such as the flooring, countertops, sinks, kitchen appliances, and kitchen and bathroom cabinets. The color of these surfaces determines the complexion of your home.

Your home complexion is blue-based, or cool, if your

- ✔ Carpet and tile colors are blue, gray, white, or black
- ✔ Cabinetry is whitewashed, pickled, maple, or cherry
- ✔ Countertops are blue, black, gray, or white
- ✔ Sinks and kitchen appliances are blue, white, black, or stainless steel

Imagine a crisp white sail against the big, blue sea. When selecting print, striped, or plaid fabrics for a cool-complexioned room, choose those with a white background (like the sail).

Your room has a yellow-based, or warm, complexion if your

- ✔ Carpet and tile colors are coffee, mustard, off-white, beige, or terra cotta
- ✔ Cabinets are natural oak, pine, or birch
- ✔ Countertops are brown or tan
- ✔ Sinks and kitchen appliances are almond, tan, or off-white

When selecting print, striped, or plaid fabrics for a warm-complexioned room, choose those with an off-white background (like Grandma's lace tablecloth).

When you use one color base throughout your entire home, your colors work together from room to room, and the wrong color bases that you need to live with for a while aren't as noticeable.

Determining your color odds

When selecting the color scheme for your home, think odd — odd numbers, that is. Start your color scheme using three colors: Use two dominant colors in equal amounts and one accent color. As you gain experience, you can add more colors, but remember that an odd number looks best.

Say you want to redo your bedroom and master bath using the color scheme in the fabric on your bedspread — blue and white with lemon yellow accents. Your carpet and ceiling are white (the first dominant color), so paint the walls blue (the second dominant color). Find blue and white throw pillows for the bed. Add one lovely round yellow pillow as the accent. The lamps on the night tables are blue and white, so you can add yellow tassels as the accent. The draperies match the bedspread, so you can add yellow tassel tiebacks. Place a yellow tulip arrangement in a blue vase on the dresser.

Reverse the colors to keep the scheme flowing through the whole house. Make the accent color in your bedroom the dominant color in your bathroom, for example.

Stumped because you don't have a color scheme? Find something you love — a dish, a scarf, a piece of clothing, a throw pillow, maybe even a picture in a magazine. If it has nothing to do with home decor, that's okay — you're looking for the colors you like and nothing else. Go to the paint store with your treasure and find paint chips that match these same three colors. Now you have your color scheme!

Remember to carry your paint chips with you. This way, you buy things that work with your color scheme (even when you're tempted to buy something cute you find for cheap). If it doesn't fit the scheme, don't buy it.

Homing in on home decor fabric

All fabrics are not created equal. The best fabrics for home decor projects are home decor fabrics, for a number of reasons:

- ✔ Many home decor fabrics are heavier and more durable than dressmaking fabrics.

- ✔ They run 54 to 60 inches wide (9 to 15 inches wider than dressmaking fabrics) — a real advantage for your home decor projects because you get better coverage with a yard of wider home decor fabric than with narrower dressmaking fabric.

- ✔ Home decor fabrics are often chemically treated to resist stains and sun damage. Due to the extra width and chemical treatment, decor fabrics are generally more expensive than dressmaking fabrics. Expect to pay from $12 to $40 per yard.

Always check the bolt end or hang tag of your home decor fabrics for proper cleaning and care instructions, which differ widely from fabric to fabric.

Most home decor fabrics also have a color strip or color bars printed on the *selvages* (the finished edges on the long sides of the fabric). You just have to match the color bars when seaming one panel to the next, and the design matches perfectly at the seamline.

Tackling Trim

Decorator trim is the icing on your home decorating cake and comes in three basic styles — braid, cord, and fringe. In this chapter, I show you some cool ways to use each one.

Braving braid basics

Braid is a flat home decor trim with two finished edges. The two most common types of braid are

- ✔ **Gimp:** This flat braid is usually glued to furniture to conceal upholstery tacks (see Figure 13-1). You can also stitch gimp to the edge of decorator cord-edge trim (see the following section for the details on cord).

- ✔ **Mandarin:** A dressier, ½-inch dimensional gimp (meaning that it has a texture), this braid is great for outlining pillows, place mats, and other home decor projects. You can also use mandarin braid in crafting by gluing it to handmade boxes and decorating lampshades.

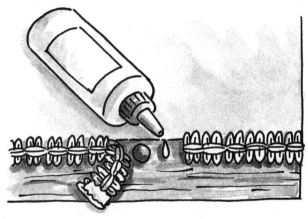

Figure 13-1: Use gimp to cover a join where the upholstery attaches to the furniture frame.

Conquering cord

Cord is a round, twisted strand of fibers that looks like rope. Cord can be anywhere from ⅛ inch to 1 inch around and is made out of cotton, shiny rayon, spun satiny rayon, or a combination of fibers, each with a unique texture. See what the different cords look like in Figure 13-2.

Figure 13-2: Cable cord, filler cord, and chair tie.

The most common kinds of cord include the following:

- ✔ **Cable cord:** A twisted cotton or cotton/polyester cord used as a filling for fabric-covered piping (see the following section for more information on piping). Preshrink the cable cord before you use it in a project. Cable cord is also a key ingredient of *piping* (or *welting*). You make piping by covering the cable cord with a strip of fabric called a *casing.* The casing has a ¼-inch to ½-inch seam allowance so that you can sew it into the seam at the edge of a pillow, slipcover, or sofa cushion cover. Piping gives a crisp, tailored finish to the edge.

- ✔ **Filler cord:** You use this web-covered, cotton-filled cord inside piping. Filler is softer and fatter than cable cord because of the loose cotton filling. You can find filler cord in diameters up to 1¾ inches thick.

Because of loose construction, you can't wash filler cord or it turns into a lumpy mess. That means you don't preshrink filler cord before covering it, and you should dry-clean projects made with this cord instead of washing them.

- ✔ **Cord-edge trim:** A twisted cord with a lip edge of flat gimp sewn to it, cord-edge trim is pretty by itself. You don't have to cover it with a casing like cable or filler cord. The lip edge makes it easy to insert the trim at a seam in a pillow or at the edge of a window cornice, swag, or jabot (see Chapter 16 for more information on window treatments).

Cord-edge trim is a dry-clean only trim. So even though you may use it with a washable fabric, dry clean your project to properly care for it.

- ✔ **Chair tie:** A twisted decorator cord 27 to 30 inches long with tassels on both ends, Chair ties are traditionally used to attach cushions to chairs. Chair ties also make nice drapery tiebacks.

- ✔ **Tassel tieback:** This twisted decorator cord is shaped into a three-sectioned loop. A color-coordinating ring cinches the loop so that the tassel hangs in the center loop. The side loops encircle a drapery and hold it back by looping over the hardware attached to the wall.

Figuring out fringe

Fringe is a decorative edging made of packed yarns that hang from a band, kind of like a hula skirt. Decorator fringes are a lot of fun to work with and add richness and value to your home decor projects.

Look for these common types of fringe when you want to add a little flair to a project:

✔ **Ball fringe:** This decorative fringe is constructed with a gimp edge and cotton pompoms. Use it to trim whimsical home decor projects, children's rooms, and costumes.

✔ **Boucle fringe:** A fringe constructed with permanently kinked, nubby yarns called *boucle yarns*. Boucle fringe can be short, long, looped, or bullion.

✔ **Bullion fringe:** Sewers use this long fringe with twisted, looped ends on pillows, upholstery, and slipcovers. It even makes nice doll hair.

✔ **Butterfly fringe:** This fringe has cut edges on two sides connected by an open threaded area. When you fold butterfly fringe in half the long way and stitch it to a project, you create a double-thick row of fringe.

✔ **Chainette fringe:** Constructed of many short or long chainette ends, this fringe is great for garment sewing, window treatments, and table toppers (see Chapter 14 for the instructions for making a table topper).

✔ **Moss fringe:** This short, cut fringe looks like a brush after you sew it into a pillow or slipcover and remove the chainstitch from the edges.

As tempted as you may be to remove the chainstitch from the fringe before sewing it into your project — don't do it. If you do, this trim is almost impossible to work with because the little fringe fibers are tough to keep out of the seam. The chainstitch keeps the fringe flat for easy sewing and prevents you from accidentally stitching the fringe ends into the seam.

✔ **Tassel fringe:** This fringe has many tiny tassels attached to a length of gimp.

Attaching decorator trims: A primer

Here are some sewing guidelines to keep in mind as you sew home decor trims onto your projects:

✔ Use a size 14/90 to 16/100 Universal point or sharp needle in your sewing machine. Home decor fabrics can get very thick under the presser foot and need a sharp, heavy needle.

✔ Use a little longer stitch length (6 to 8 spi) than for garment sewing. Again, the longer stitch length makes sewing the extra thicknesses created by the fabric and trim a lot easier.

✔ In certain cases, when the fabric moves sluggishly under the presser foot, lighten up the foot pressure (see your operating manual for instructions). A *wedge* is also helpful when sewing up and over uneven thicknesses.

When sewing uneven thicknesses (such as when hemming jeans by sewing up and over the thick jean seams and then back down to the level hem allowance), use a wedge under the heel to level the presser foot when approaching and coming off the heavy seams. You can find wedges through your local sewing machine dealer, fabric store, or sewing mail-order source. Look for them by the brand names of Jean-A-Ma-Jig or Hump-Jumper.

If you don't want to buy a wedge, make one by cutting out a 6-inch square of denim. Fold it in half and then in half again until you have four layers of fabric. Continue folding this denim square until the wedge is thick enough to keep the foot level when it rests on the wedge and the thick seam.

✏ Prevent unnecessary needle breakage by sewing slowly over thick areas.

✏ Start sewing a trim at the center of any side of a pillow or cushion unless the project instructions say explicitly to do otherwise.

✏ Fabric and trim must be equal lengths; don't pull or stretch the trim to fit an edge or the edge puckers, and no amount of pressing can straighten it out.

✏ When making pillows and slipcovers or covering cushions, sew the trim to the top pillow piece first. Sew the back pillow piece to the trimmed front fabric piece afterward. This way, if you get any stitch distortion, it shows on the back, rather than the front, of the project.

Attaching Piping, Cording, and Fringe

Call me crazy, but I love sewing piping, cording, or fringe in a seam. I like the way these trims set off style lines in a garment. I love seeing trim at the edge of a pillow or cushion because it says *quality*.

Making your own piping

If you're lucky enough to find piping to match your project, buy it. If not, this section tells you how to make your own piping to match your project.

You make piping by covering a cable or filler cord with a strip of fabric called a *casing*. ("Conquering cord," found earlier in this chapter, tells you more about cable and filler cord.) The casing has a ¼-inch to ½-inch seam allowance so that you can sew the casing into the seam at the edge of a pillow, slipcover, or sofa cushion cover.

To make your own piping, just follow these steps:

1. **Measure the perimeter of the area you want to pipe and add 2 inches or so for overlap and seaming for each length of piping you want to insert.**

For example, if you want to pipe the edge of a pillow that has a perimeter of 30 inches, you need 32 inches of piping. If a seat cushion has two seams that you want to pipe, and each seam measures 40 inches around the perimeter, you need to make 84 inches of piping.

2. **Preshrink your cable cord (see Chapter 2 for more information on preshrinking) and cut it to the measurement you determined in Step 1.**

   You can also use filler cord, but remember not to preshrink it.

   Prevent the cable or filler cord from uncontrolled fraying by taping around the end of the cord with masking tape before cutting through it. Leave the tape on while you make the project.

3. **Determine how wide to cut the fabric casing that covers the cording.**

   - Wrap your tape measure snugly around the cording. This length is the circumference of the cord.

   - Add an inch (for seam allowances) to the circumference measurement.

4. **Cut a fabric strip long enough to cover the length of the cable or filler cord.**

   If you can't cut one strip of fabric long enough to cover the entire length of the cord, cut as many small strips as you need and sew them together with a ½-inch seam allowance.

   You cover cable or filler cord with either a straight- or bias-cut fabric casing, depending on the shape of the seam you put it in.

   - If you want to sew the piping to straight seams (such as the edges of a rectangular slipcover or square pillow), cut the fabric into strips either across the grain or on the lengthwise grain (see Chapter 4 for more information on grainlines).

   - If you want to sew the piping to a curved edge, like a round pillow, cut the fabric strips on the bias (the next section tells you exactly how to do this).

Cutting bias strips for covering cable cord

Cut bias fabric strips the easy way following these steps:

1. **Fold down a corner of the fabric so that the cut edge is parallel to, and even with, the selvage and then press a crease in the fold, as shown in Figure 13-3.**

2. **Open up the fold; the foldline marks the cutting line.**

3. **Using the foldline as a starting point, measure the width of the strip desired and mark off more strips, using a straight edge and pencil or dressmakers chalk.**

Figure 13-3:
Find the
bias.

4. **Cut the fabric strips along the marks you made in Step 3 and as shown in Figure 13-4.**

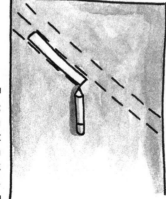

Figure 13-4:
Use a
straight
edge when
you mark
cutting lines.

5. **Place the short ends of the two fabric strips right sides together and seam them using a ½-inch seam allowance. Figure 13-5 shows you how.**

   Repeat this step with each strip, creating a long chain, until you have a fabric strip of the proper length.

6. **Press open the seams.**

7. **Set your machine like this:**

   - **Stitch:** Straight
   - **Length:** 3 mm/9 spi
   - **Width:** 0 mm
   - **Foot:** Zipper or piping

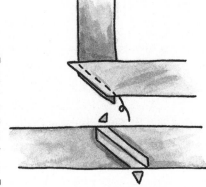

Figure 13-5:
Seam bias-cut fabric strips to create a casing for piping.

If you sew on a lot of piping, buy a piping foot. The underside of the foot has a deep groove that automatically guides over the cording for straight sewing and even piping application. I like and use the *Pearls and Piping Foot* a lot. Creative Feet manufactures it, and they design it to fit any brand or sewing machine model. Call CJ Enterprises at 800-776-6938 for more information (or see the appendix).

8. **Starting at one end, sandwich the cord in the casing — like you would put a hot dog in a bun.**

   The cord nestles into the wrong side of the fabric; the right side faces out.

9. **Working at a slow and steady pace, sew the strip closed along the length of the cord (as shown in Figure 13-6).**

   Use your hands to guide the fabric and cording together as you sew.

   Don't pin the casing around the length of the cable cord before sewing. Pinning takes forever, and you'll never want to look at another piece of piping as long as you live.

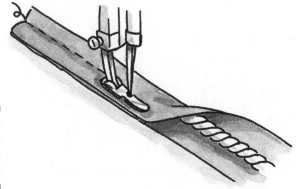

Figure 13-6:
Sew the cording into the fabric.

Attaching piping and fringe

Piping and fringe add pizzazz to your home decor projects. Both trims have a lip edge that is sandwiched between two seams to hold it in place, but because fringe has a braid as its lip edge, you can also sew it to the surface of a project as a decorative treatment where the braid shows.

When attaching piping, fringe, or other decorator trim to a pillow or cushion, attach the trim to the front piece first and then sew the back to the front.

When you reach the starting point of the fringe, overlap the two ends of the fringe. If you're using moss or brush fringe, just butt the fringe ends together at the join so that you don't make it so thick.

1. **Starting anywhere but at a corner, pin the piping or fringe to the right side of the fabric so that the lip edges of the piping or fringe and the fabric are almost even.**

   Keep the trim in one long length until you're absolutely sure that you have enough to go around the project.

   Don't stretch the trim to fit the edge or the seamline ends up puckered.

2. **Set your sewing machine like this:**
   - **Stitch:** Straight
   - **Length:** 3 mm/9 spi
   - **Width:** 0 mm
   - **Foot:** Zipper or piping

3. **Sew on the trim at the ½-inch seamline, as shown in Figure 13-7, pulling out the pins as you get to them. Stop sewing about 2 inches before the end of the trim.**

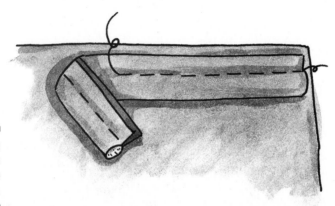

Figure 13-7:
Sew the trim onto the fabric.

If you're sewing trim to a straight edge, skip to Step 6 under "Joining piping ends in a casing."

4. **When you reach a corner, clip the seam allowance of the lip edge up to, but not through, the stitching line (see more about clipping into seam allowances in Chapter 6).**

   This allows the lip edge of the trim to easily bend around the corner without buckling.

5. **Sew around the corner.**

   • **If you're using piping:** Stop sewing with the needle in the fabric, raise the foot and pivot slightly, nudging your index finger into the corner of the piping so that it bends around your finger and away from the needle.

   • **If you're using fringe:** Stop sewing with the needle in the fabric, and raise the foot and pivot the fabric, pulling the fringe around the corner so the lip edge is even with the raw fabric edge.

   Lower the presser foot and continue stitching. You may have to stitch a gentle curve rather than a sharp corner to accommodate the bulk of the piping or fringe.

Follow the steps in the next section to finish attaching the piping or fringe.

Joining fringe and piping

In this section, you see how easy it is to join a trim the right way for a professional-looking project.

Joining fringe ends

Fringe is the easiest trim to join. When you reach the starting point around a pillow, tablecloth, or cushion, butt the fringe ends together at the join and simply pin and sew the fringe in place, sewing ½-inch from the raw edge.

Joining piping ends in a casing

This join is a little trickier than the one you use for fringe, and I've tried a lot of different techniques. The following process works and looks best, time after time:

1. **Follow Steps 1 to 3 from "Attaching piping and fringe" above.**

2. **Open the casing about 1 inch on both ends by ripping out the stitching that holds the fabric casing around the cable or filler cord.**

3. **Cut one end of the cable cord so that it butts the other end, and then tape the ends of the cable cord together.**

4. **Turn under one short end of the casing, overlapping the folded end over the flat end. Pin the casing at the overlap.**

5. **Finish stitching on the rest of the piping so that you secure it around the perimeter of the project.**

6. **Pin the piped seam allowance to the non-piped seam allowance with the right sides together and at the ½-inch seamline.**

7. **Place the project under the presser foot so that the stitching from Steps 5 and 6 is where you can see it and start sewing.**

   The needle should fall just to the left of the stitching line. You want to sew close enough to the piping or fringe that the previous row of stitching doesn't show when you turn the project right side out.

Attaching and joining cord-edge trim

You attach cord-edge trim the same way you attach piping and fringe (see the preceding section). The difference is that when you reach the starting point to join the trim, you need to overlap the two ends of the cord rather than butting them together.

Follow these steps to make a clean join with your cord-edge trim:

1. **Using a tape measure and your scissors, cut the cord-edge trim 6 inches longer than the finished area it must go into.**

   The trim has a 3-inch tail on each end that can be overlapped and beautifully finished.

2. **Separate the lip edge from the tails with a seam ripper.**

3. **Separate the plies of the cord, wrapping masking tape around the end of each ply to prevent raveling.**

4. **Trim each lip to 1 inch, leaving enough to overlap on each end; tape each lip end with masking tape.**

5. **Arrange the plies of the decorative cord so that the right-side plies face up and the left-side plies face down, as shown in Figure 13-8.**

   Pull the right-side plies under the lips, twisting and arranging the cord until it returns to the original shape. Secure with tape.

6. **Repeat Step 5 for the left plies until the twisted plies look like one continuous decorative cord.**

7. **Set your sewing machine like this:**

   • **Stitch:** Straight

   • **Length:** 3 mm/9 spi

- **Width:** 0 mm
- **Foot:** Zipper or piping

8. **Stitch through all the layers to secure the cord-edge trim and loose plies to the fabric.**

Figure 13-8:
Attach the cord-edge trim by over-lapping and wrapping the loose plies at the ends.

Making a Pillow with Moss Edge or Bullion Fringe

You can get some experience sewing in fringe by making this great-looking pillow.

To make this pillow, you need the following supplies (in addition to the Sewing Survival Kit I tell you about in Chapter 1):

✔ One 16-inch pillow form

✔ ½ yard of 48-inch-wide to 54-inch-wide home decor fabric

✔ Thread that matches the fabric

✔ Two yards of moss edge or bullion fringe that matches the fabric

Just follow these steps to create the pillow:

1. **Cut two 16-inch squares from the home decor fabric and set it aside.**

2. **Pin the fringe to the outer edges of the pillow front.**

   Keep the finished band of the fringe in the seam allowance and the deco-rative fringe section toward the center of the pillow, butting the fringe ends against each other.

3. **Set your sewing machine like this:**
   - **Stitch:** Straight
   - **Length:** 3 mm/9 spi
   - **Width:** 0 mm
   - **Foot:** Zipper or piping

4. **Sew the fringe around the pillow front (see Figure 13-9) using a ½-inch seam allowance.**

Figure 13-9:
Sew fringe
to the
outside
edge of the
pillow fabric.

The fringe plies face toward the center of the pillow.

Refer to the sections "Attaching piping and fringe" and "Attaching and joining cord-edge trim" earlier in the chapter for more information on attaching trim.

5. **Pin the pillow back onto the pillow front, right sides together.**

6. **Stitch the pillow together, using a ½-inch seam allowance and leaving a 5-inch opening on one side to turn the pillow through (see Figure 13-10).**

Press the seams flat and together (see Chapter 5 for more information on pressing seams).

7. **On either side of the opening, clip into the seam allowance just shy of the seamline, as shown in Figure 13-11. Press the seam allowance toward the center of the pillow cover.**

8. **Trim out the fabric bulk at the corners without trimming away the edge of the trim. Turn the pillow cover right side out.**

9. **Stuff the pillow form into the pillow cover and hand slipstitch the opening to close it (see Chapter 5 for more information on hand slipstitching).**

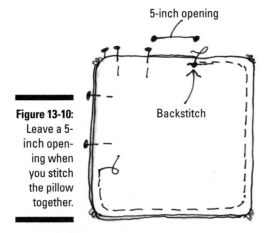

Figure 13-10:
Leave a 5-inch opening when you stitch the pillow together.

5-inch opening

Backstitch

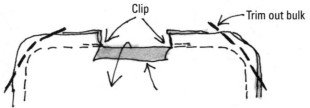

Figure 13-11:
Clip the seam allowance and press it back.

Clip

Trim out bulk

Attaching Tassels

Tassels are made of thread strands tied and banded at the top. You have a top loop on each tassel that can be as short as ½ inch or as long as 3 inches. You find this loop sandwiched in the seam of a table topper or a pillow and used on window treatments.

The method you use to attach tassels depends on the length of the tassels. You attach short-looped tassels (1 inch and under) by hand and long-looped tassels (over 1 inch) by machine.

Attaching short-looped tassels

Follow these steps to attach short-looped tassels:

1. **Thread and knot a hand needle with a doubled thread.**

   Poke the end of a long thread through the eye of the needle, pulling it so both thread ends are even; then, treating them as one, tie a knot (see Chapter 5).

2. **Place a drop of seam sealant on the knot and then pull the needle and thread up through the center of the tassel so that the knot snugs up inside the tassel.**

3. **Pass the needle and thread around and through the short loop several times.**

4. **Finish sewing on the tassel by sewing a knot (see Chapter 5 for the details on making knots).**

Attaching long-looped tassels

Follow these steps to attach long-looped tassels:

1. **Place the tassel on the right side of the fabric so that the head of the tassel is ½ inch outside the seamline and the tassel loop is inside the seam allowance.**

   You position the tassel itself toward the center of the project.

2. **Machine stitch, catching the long loop in the stitching at the seamline.**

Making a Reversible Table Runner

Try your hand at sewing tassels by making this easy table runner. You can create this pretty runner to *run* either the width or the length of a table — use it in place of place mats or a tablecloth.

To make the runner, you need the following supplies (in addition to the tools in the Sewing Survival Kit that I tell you about in Chapter 1):

- ✔ ½ yard of 60-inch-wide home decor fabric
- ✔ ½ yard of 60-inch-wide complementary home decor fabric
- ✔ Thread that matches the fabric
- ✔ Two decorator tassels (optional)
- ✔ One yardstick

Follow these steps to make your runner:

1. **Take one piece of the 18-x-60-inch fabric and, using your dressmaker's chalk, mark the midpoint of the short ends.**

2. **At the marks, fold the fabric toward the center as though you were making a paper airplane, as shown in Figure 13-12.**

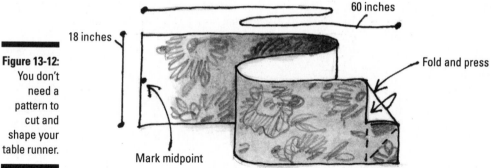

60 inches

18 inches

Fold and press

Mark midpoint

You should have a point at each end. Press each fold.

For an, easy, more-tailored runner like the one shown in the color section, don't cut the points on the ends — just leave the fabric pieces in a rectangle shape and omit the tassels.

3. **Cut your table runner along each of the foldlines on both ends of the fabric.**

4. **Repeat Steps 1 through 3 for the other piece of fabric to create the reversible side of the runner.**

5. **If you want to use tassels, pin them to the right side of the tapestry fabric so that the loop is in the seam allowance and the top of the tassel is as close to the seamline as possible.**

   You need enough room for the presser foot to ride next to the tassel to sew the seam, so adjust the tassel placement as needed.

6. **Pin the contrasting fabric to the tapestry fabric, right sides together (see Figure 13-13).**

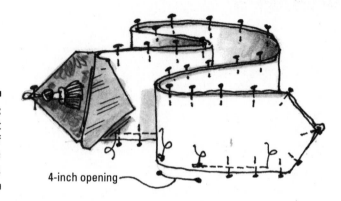

4-inch opening

7. **Starting on one long side and leaving about a 4-inch opening, sew all the way around the table runner using a ½-inch seam allowance (see Figure 13-14 for a complete illustration).**

Figure 13-14:
Sew the
runner
together;
trim away
the bulk at
the point;
notch the
corners; and
then press
the seams
open.

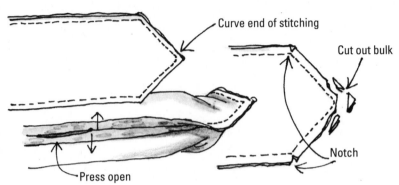

Curve end of stitching

Cut out bulk

Notch

Press open

Backstitch at each end of the stitching line.

8. **Trim excess fabric and tassel cord from around the points of the runner.**

9. **Press the seam flat and together (see Chapter 5 for more information on pressing).**

   At the opening, press the seam back toward the center of the runner on both edges (as if it were turned right side out). This technique makes the opening almost invisible and easier to close by hand.

10. **From the wrong side, press the seam allowance open over a seam roll or seam stick (if you have one), pressing as close to the points as possible.**

    If you don't have a seam roll, press the seam open as well as possible by using your iron and ironing board.

11. **Turn the runner right side out and press the edges.**

12. **Close the opening with hand slipstitches (see Chapter 5 for more information on hand slipstitching).**

Chapter 14

Quick-Change Table Toppers

. . . .

In This Chapter

▶ Picking the best fabrics for your table toppers

▶ Creating all sorts of napkins

▶ Cranking out a decorative tablecloth

. . . .

*O*ne of the fastest, easiest, and most colorful ways to cozy-up a room is by making table toppers. What's a table topper? Napkins and tablecloths that liven up any mealtime or add a little punch of color to that boring table in the corner of the family room or den.

I know what you're thinking . . . cloth napkins are only for special occasions. I say every day the family eats together *is* a special occasion and should be celebrated, and — who knows — table manners may even improve. So if you want to beautify any tabletop in your home, start by making the napkins and tablecloths in this chapter. I cover the fastest and easiest edge-finishing techniques so you can make your toppers and set your table with them — all in one afternoon.

Selecting Your Fabric for Table Toppers

Whether you want to make napkins, table runners, or a tablecloth, you should keep these things in mind when selecting fabric:

> ✔ Before buying a fabric simply because you like the color or design, consider the fiber content, the fabric finish, and what you want to make. Fabrics such as all-cotton or all-linen are absorbent but very wrinkle-prone, so you may want to choose fabrics blended with a little polyester. A fabric finish, such as Scotchgard, also repels stains and spills, so a fabric that has been Scotchgarded may not have the absorbency needed for napkins but works great as a tablecloth.

✔ Don't use fabrics that consist of more than 50 percent synthetic or man-made fiber. These fabrics aren't absorbent, and the stains and odors remain in the fabric even after repeated washings.

✔ Using fabrics with preprinted stripes, plaids, or checks helps you cut straight, and hemming is as easy as following the lines in the fabric.

✔ Don't use knits. Tightly woven fabrics work better and last longer as napkins and tablecloths.

✔ Look at the wrong side of the print. Does it limit your napkin-folding possibilities because of bad looks? If so, choose another fabric or use it for something other than a napkin, where the wrong side doesn't matter.

✔ If you want a light- to medium-weight fabric that works well for napkin-making, look for bandannas, broadcloth, calico prints, chambray, chintz, duck, gingham, kettle or weaver's cloth, light- to mid-weight linen and denim, muslin, percale, poplin, and seersucker.

✔ For heavier-weight fabrics better suited for tablecloths, look for damask, double-sided fabrics, linen, sailcloth, and terry cloth.

Making Napkins

Friends and family members usually expect handmade gifts from me — and I've made some really gorgeous things through the years. But the most appreciated gifts were also the simplest — cloth napkins that I made several years ago. I sewed 160 napkins (20 sets of eight) one holiday season. Cloth napkins are fast, easy to make, and good for our environment to boot.

I used fabric that coordinated with my friends' color schemes and lifestyles — Sally works with chimpanzees, so she got a jungle print. My classically-tailored pal, Carol, got the black and white stripes. I used a cheerful juvenile print for our son's day-care provider at the time.

Besides making the napkins that season, I went to garage sales and flea markets and bought wonderful baskets for pennies. When December arrived, I baked up loaves of my favorite pumpkin bread and included the recipe along with the napkins in the basket. What a hit!

Figuring out fabric yardage

Tables 14-1 and 14-2 tell you how much fabric you need to make napkins of various sizes, including a little extra for shrinkage and evening up the squares. The size of each unfinished napkin is shown in inches; the amount of fabric for each set of napkins is shown in yards.

Table 14-1	Yardage for 45-Inch Fabric			
Unfinished Napkin Size	*Six Napkins*	*Eight Napkins*	*Ten Napkins*	*Twelve Napkins*
15 inches	⅞	1⅜	1¾	1¾
18 inches	1⅝	2⅛	2⅝	3⅛
20 inches	1¾	2¼	2⅞	3½
22½ inches	2	2⅝	3¼	3⅞

Table 14-2	Yardage for 54- to 55-Inch Fabric			
Unfinished Napkin Size	*Six Napkins*	*Eight Napkins*	*Ten Napkins*	*Twelve Napkins*
15 inches	⅞	1⅜	1¾	1¾
18 inches	1⅛	1⅝	2⅛	2⅝
20 inches	1¾	2¼	2⅞	3⅜
24 inches	2⅛	2¾	3⅜	4⅛

Sewing basic table napkins

I discovered a fast, efficient way to make napkins while I was cranking out 160 of them for the holidays. These little beauties come together so quickly that you may be tempted to create a set for special dinner parties, family celebrations, or holidays. To make these napkins and the serged version in the next section, you need the following materials in addition to your Sewing Survival Kit (see Chapter 1):

✔ Napkin fabric (see Tables 14-1 and 14-2 for yardage)

✔ Thread that matches the napkin fabric

✔ Seam sealant (such as Fray Check)

Just follow these steps to have napkins in no time:

1. **Cut the napkin squares (see Tables 14-1 and 14-2 for suggested sizes).**

2. **Set your sewing machine like this:**

   • **Stitch:** Three-step zigzag

   • **Length:** 1 to 1.5 mm/24 to 30 spi

- **Width:** 5 mm
- **Foot:** All-purpose

If you're using a serger, set your serger like this:

- **Stitch:** Balanced three-thread overlock
- **Length:** 2 mm
- **Width:** 3 to 5 mm
- **Foot:** Standard

3. **Overcast the opposite edges of the fabric squares with your sewing machine or serger.**

    Place the raw edge under the foot so that the needle catches the fabric on the left and swings off the raw edge at the right (see Chapter 6 for more information on overcasting raw fabric edges).

4. **Overcast the other two opposite edges of each napkin.**

5. **Pin and press a ¼-inch hem on two opposite edges of the fabric square.**

    When you pin the hems this way, the corners turn out sharp and square.

6. **Set your machine like this:**

    - **Stitch:** Straight
    - **Length:** 3.5 mm/9 spi
    - **Width:** 0 mm
    - **Foot:** All-purpose

7. **With the wrong side of the fabric up, topstitch a ¼-inch hem, sewing the opposite hem edges (see Figure 14-1).**

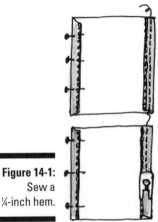

Figure 14-1:
Sew a
¼-inch hem.

8. **Continue sewing from one napkin to the next without cutting the threads in between, as shown in Figure 14-2.**

   By stringing the napkins together this way you can hem a lot of them at once.

9. **Cut the connecting threads between each napkin at the fabric.**

10. **Repeat Steps 7 and 8 for the opposite hem edges, backstitching at the end of each corner.**

11. **Cut the connecting threads between each napkin at the corners.**

    See Chapter 5 for more information on topstitching and backstitching.

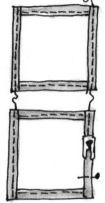

Figure 14-2:
Sew from one napkin to the next without stopping.

Serging napkins with narrow rolled edges

Have you ever noticed the neatly finished edges on restaurant napkins? If you have a serger, you can duplicate this finish and have a basket full of napkins done in no time. Read your operating manual to set your serger for a narrow rolled edge and then follow these guidelines:

1. **Set your serger like this:**

   - **Stitch:** 3-thread

   - **Length:** 1.0 to 1.5 mm

   - **Foot:** Narrow rolled edge

   - **Needle Plate:** Narrow rolled edge

   - **Lower Looper:** Tighten so that you see a straight line of stitching forming on the underside of the stitch

2. **Cut out your napkin squares using your favorite cutting tools (see Tables 14-1 and 14-2 for yardage requirements).**

   The narrow rolled edge takes up about a ¼-inch hem allowance all the way around, so remember to cut your napkins large enough so that they end up the desired finished size.

3. **Place all the napkin squares in your lap so that the right side of the fabric faces up.**

4. **Place the first napkin edge under the foot so that when you serge, you trim away about ⅛ inch.**

   This fabric placement ensures proper stitch formation and prevents the stitches from pulling off the edge of the fabric with repeated washings.

5. **Serge the first edge of the napkin and then, in a continuous step, butt the next napkin up to the first and finish one edge of the second napkin.**

   Continue in this way, butting one napkin up to the next, until you finish off one side of all the napkin squares in your lap. Your napkins resemble a kite tail connected with serged thread chains.

6. **Repeat Steps 3 through 5 for the opposite side of each napkin square.**

7. **Dot a drop of seam sealant (like Fray Check) at the base of the chain at each corner of the napkin squares.**

8. **After the seam sealant dries, cut apart the napkins, cutting the chains at the base of each corner as shown in Figure 14-3.**

9. **Serge the narrow rolled edges of the remaining opposite sides of each napkin, following Steps 3 through 8.**

TIP

Serging opposite edges makes the corners turn out square. To serge each napkin individually and create round corners, start by tracing around a dime at each corner. Trim off the excess fabric in the corners, cutting on the traced line. Starting in the center of one napkin edge, serge carefully, guiding the rolled edge toward and then around each corner.

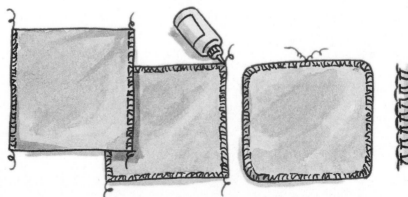

Figure 14-3:
Serge the edges, add seam sealant, and then cut apart your napkins.

Napkins as no-sew pillow covers

Make a quick-change pillow cover by covering a throw pillow with two napkins. Simply rubber-band the napkins together at the corners and pop in the pillow. Prevent the rubber bands from showing by covering them with ribbon or cord. Now you have a great way to change the look of a room and then change it back in an instant.

Making lapkins

You can create lapkins from napkins that you make or buy. I call them *lapkins* because the word rhymes with *napkins* (and because I didn't know what else to call them). Besides the name, lapkins are a cool thing because they do double duty. They not only go on your lap, but they also have stitch channels to hold the silverware in place, perfect for portable picnics, barbeques, and buffets.

To make these napkins you need the following materials in addition to your Sewing Survival Kit (see Chapter 1):

✔ Set of finished napkins

✔ Thread that matches the fabric

✔ Flatware to fit each lapkin

Just follow these steps to create lapkins from napkins:

1. **Fold a napkin in half, creating a triangle, and press.**

2. **Turn back one corner, pressing the crease at the bottom of the smaller triangle shown on the left in Figure 14-4.**

3. **Using your fabric marker, draw four lines perpendicular to the long fold, about 1½ inches apart (see Figure 14-4).**

   Center the four marked lines so that the slots are centered in the napkin triangle.

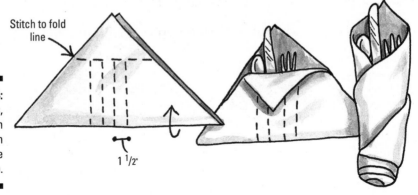

Figure 14-4:
Fold, press, and stitch a napkin to create a lapkin.

Stitch to fold line

1 1/2"

4. **Set your machine like this:**
   - **Stitch:** Straight
   - **Length:** 3 to 3.5 mm/7 to 9 spi
   - **Width:** 0 mm
   - **Foot:** All-purpose

5. **Straight stitch over the marked lines, sewing from the bottom fold up to the crease and backstitching at the top and bottom of each row.**

   This process creates the slots you slip the flatware into.

6. **Slip in the flatware, roll up the lapkin, and you're ready for a feast.**

Making fringed and stitched napkins

Impress even the pickiest guest eater with these napkins (see the beautiful setting shown in the color section). No extra trim to buy — simply pull out threads from the fabric edges, thereby creating fringe to match. (By the way, this fringing technique works on the edges of place mats, too.)

To make these napkins, you need the following materials in addition to your Sewing Survival Kit (see Chapter 1):

- ✔ Napkin fabric (see Tables 14-1 and 14-2 for yardage)
- ✔ Thread that matches the napkin fabric
- ✔ ½-inch transparent tape
- ✔ Size 26-tapestry needle

Follow these steps to make the fanciest napkins on your block:

1. **Cut a strip of fabric across the grain, perpendicular to the selvages, in the desired length.**

   For example, to make several 15-inch napkins, cut a 15-inch-wide strip of the fabric across the grain. After you fringe this longer strip, you cut it into squares.

2. **Cut off the finished selvage edges on both sides of the fabric strip.**

3. **Using the tape, mark the fringe depth (¾ to 1 inch) at the top and bottom of the fabric strip.**

   Doing so marks where the fringe stops.

4. **Using the tapestry needle, remove the crossgrain threads up to the edge of the tape.**

   Start at the top edge of the strip and work the point of the needle under one of the long threads in the strip. When you pull up on this one thread enough to create a loop, pull the thread out all the way across the fabric. You see a short length of fringe appearing on the long edge of the strip. Continue pulling out threads until you have fringe along both long edges of the strip. Stop when the fringe is at the edge of the tape.

5. **Cut the long fabric strip into napkin squares.**

   For example, if your fabric strip is 15 inches wide, cut the strip into 15-inch squares. Each square has two fringed edges and two fringeless edges (see Figure 14-5).

6. **Tape-mark the fringe depth on the nonfringed edges. Using the hand tapestry needle, remove the threads up to the edge of the tape as you did in Step 4.**

Figure 14-5:
Leave two edges of the napkin square fringeless before you tape-mark it.

7. **Set your machine like this:**

   - **Stitch:** Zigzag

   - **Length:** 2.5 to 3 mm/10 to 12 spi

   - **Width:** 3 mm

   - **Foot:** Embroidery

8. **Place the fabric under the needle so that the top edge of the fringe is halfway under the foot.**

   When the fabric moves under the foot, the needle catches halfway into the fringe and halfway into the fabric at the edge of the fringe.

9. **Lower the foot and sew around all the edges so that the stitches catch in the fabric on the left and zigzag into the fringe on the right (see Figure 14-6).**

   This stitching groups the fringe into neat tufts on the edge and prevents the fabric from fraying when you wash the napkins. When pivoting at each corner, stop with the needle in the left (fabric) side of the stitch, lift the foot, adjust the fabric, lower the foot, and proceed. This approach gives you an extra stitch at each corner for more security.

   Instead of backstitching to secure the ends when you finish sewing, pull the threads to one side of the fabric and tie them off (see Chapter 6 for instructions on tying off threads).

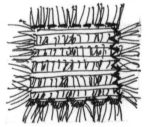

Figure 14-6:
Sew around all the edges of your napkin.

Turning Out a Tablecloth

After you sew this square tablecloth, simply place it on your table so that the points are centered on the sides and ends of the table — a process called *setting the square on point*. You can also use this tablecloth over another tablecloth to add color accents and dimension to your eating space. To make the tablecloth, you need the following materials in addition to your Sewing Survival Kit:

✔ Tablecloth fabric (see "Selecting Your Fabric for Table Toppers" earlier in this chapter for some suggestions). You need 1¼ yards of 45-inch-wide fabric for a 43-inch table square or 1½ yards of 54- to 55-inch-wide fabric for a 52-inch table square.

✔ Thread that matches the fabric.

✔ Four tassels (optional).

These few simple steps create a tablecloth you're proud to eat on:

1. **Cut the tablecloth fabric square.**

   For example, if you're working with 45-inch-wide fabric, cut a square 45 x 45 inches; if you're working with 54-inch fabric, cut a 54-inch square.

2. **Set your sewing machine like this:**

   - **Stitch:** Three-step zigzag
   - **Length:** 1.5 to 2 mm/13 to 15 spi
   - **Width:** 5 mm
   - **Foot:** All-purpose

   If you're using a serger, set your serger like this:

   - **Stitch:** Balanced three-thread overlock
   - **Length:** 2 mm
   - **Width:** 3 to 5 mm
   - **Foot:** Standard

3. **Finish the edges of the square.**

   Place the raw edge under the foot so that the needle catches the fabric on the left and swings off the raw edge at the right. After you finish the first edge, finish the edge on the opposite side. Do the same thing with the two remaining opposite edges.

4. **Pin and press a ½-inch hem on two opposite edges of the fabric square, as shown in Figure 14-7. Repeat for the other two sides.**

   Doing so ensures that the corners fold in correctly for secure hemming.

5. **(Optional) Slip in and pin four tassels — one at each corner, as shown in Figure 14-8.**

   For more on attaching long and short-looped tassels, see Chapter 13.

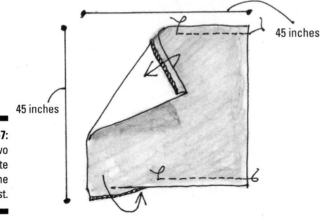

45 inches

45 inches

Figure 14-7:
Hem two
opposite
edges of the
square first.

Figure 14-8:
Add tassels
to each
corner
before
hemming the
other edges.

6. **Set your machine like this:**

   • **Stitch:** Straight

   • **Length:** 3.5 mm/7 spi

   • **Width:** 0 mm

   • **Foot:** All-purpose

7. **With the right side of the fabric up, topstitch around the hem edge, guiding the foot an even distance from the edge. Backstitch at the end of the topstitching.**

   If you would rather fringe the edges, refer to the fringing and stitching instructions in the section "Making fringed and stitched napkins" earlier in this chapter.

Romancing the Table (with Bows)

Add a little romance, color, and interest to any table by layering a square table topper made of lace or another contrasting fabric over a base table-cloth. Give your table further interest and dimension by cinching up the corners with small scarf rings called *Infinity Rings* (see the Appendix for more on Infinity Rings).

These three steps open the door to a perfect evening:

1. **Layer a square table topper over a small round table.**

2. **Cinch up the corners, using a small Infinity Ring to pull up a bow, as shown in Figure 14-9.**

3. **Light a candle and *voila* — romance.**

Figure 14-9:
Cinch up a romantic tablecloth using Infinity Rings.

Chapter 15

Praiseworthy Pillows

*P*illows prop us up when we read, cushion our falls, comfort weary heads, and plump up to pamper loved ones. Pillows are also perfect palettes for playing with shape, color, texture, and design. And you can easily put together a pillow project in one peaceful sitting. In this chapter, discover the secrets of making praiseworthy pillows perfect for most people (and their privileged pets).

Selecting Materials for Pillows

Achieving pillow perfection starts with using the right materials. Keep these tips in mind as you shop for materials for your pillows:

✔ **Fabrics:** For easy-care pillows, buy home decor fabrics that have a cotton fiber content of 50 percent or more. Also look for washable cotton/ polyester blends. Another fabric option (and a great shortcut) for making pillow covers is using fabric napkins (see if you can find the pillow covers made from napkins in the color pages of this book. Check out Chapter 14 to find out exactly how to make them).

If you use a cotton novelty print, corduroy, denim, duck, chintz, twill, or poplin to make your pillow, preshrink the fabric before making the pillow cover.

The amount of fabric you need depends on the size of the pillow you want to cover and the kind of pillow cover you want to make. To decide how much fabric you need, see the yardage instructions that I give throughout this chapter. Because pillow forms are soft and pliable, the pillow cover pieces you cut are cut the same size of the pillow form without seam allowances (so a cover made to fit a 16-inch pillow form is 16 inches square). When you add seam allowances to your pillow covers, they end up too big.

- ✔ **Thread:** Of course, you need thread to match your pillow fabric. Any all-purpose thread does the job.

- ✔ **Trims:** You have to use trims that are compatible with your fabric from a fiber and washability standpoint. When in doubt, show your fabric and trim choices to a sales associate at your local fabric store to confirm the care and use compatibility between your trims and fabrics.

Many home decor fabrics recommend *Dry Clean Only* care. If you choose such a fabric, make the pillow covers removable and have them dry cleaned to preserve their brand-new appearance. If you don't, fabrics can shrink, trims can disintegrate, and you spend all your time and creative energy for nothing.

- ✔ **Stuffing:** The easiest stuffing to work with is a pre-made pillow form. This timesaving fabric-covered pillow is a given size, shape, and density and pops into a decorative pillow cover. You can find pillow forms in many sizes (see the Cheat Sheet in the front of the book for more on pillow form sizes) and a variety of price ranges.

Don't Toss That! Stitching a Pillow with an Old Shirt

When our son grew out of his favorite flannel cowboy shirt it was still good enough for someone to wear, but I couldn't bring myself to give it away. I leafed through a mail-order catalog and saw clever pillow covers made from sweatshirts, sweaters, and blouses, so I thought, "Why not?" and made a pillow like the ones you see in the color pages of this book. You can help preserve the little kid in all of us or turn that lucky shirt into something that the recipient really treasures when you present it as a gift.

Although you can cut off the sleeves and shirttails to square up the shirt to fit the pillow cover, I keep them intact, turn them inside the shirt, and stuff them at the back of the pillow. The sleeves make wonderful hiding places for action figures, toy cars, special rocks, and the remote control.

To make this project, you need the following materials in addition to your Sewing Survival Kit (see Chapter 1):

✔ A flannel shirt, cotton blouse, or team jersey

✔ A throw pillow that coordinates with the shirt (Fold the shirt into a square until it looks the way you want it to show on the final pillow, measure it, and then use a pillow that measures the closest to that size.)

✔ Thread that matches the fabric

Follow these steps to make the pillow:

1. **Button up the front of the shirt.**

   If the shirt isn't a button-up style, skip to Step 4.

2. **Set your machine like this:**

   • **Stitch:** Straight

   • **Length:** 3 mm/9 spi

   • **Width:** 0 mm

   • **Foot:** All-purpose

3. **Sew the front opening of the shirt closed, sewing next to the buttons.**

   If the shirt already has a row of topstitching, just sew over it, and if the foot keeps running into the buttons, reposition the needle to the far right or far left, if you can. This way, just a skinny part of the foot rides next to and not over the buttons.

4. **Turn the sleeves inside out, pushing them back through the armholes, up to the shoulder seams, and out of the way. Pin them to the back of the shirt.**

5. **Pop in the fabric-covered pillow through the open, shirttail end.**

   Snug the pillow up to the neck and into the shoulders.

6. **Pin the shirttail shut, pinning next to the bottom of the pillow from side seam to side seam.**

   This pinning is the stitching line for the bottom of the pillow cover.

7. **Using a fabric marker or dressmaker's chalk, mark the stitching line on both the front and the back of the shirt. Remove the pins and the pillow form.**

8. **Turn the shirt inside out, placing right sides together and matching the marks made in Step 7. Pin the shirt together at the shirttail, pinning perpendicular to the marks from side seam to side seam.**

9. **Sew the shirttail closed, pulling out the pins as you get to them. Backstitch at the beginning and end of the seam.**

   Depending on how much of a shirttail your shirt has, you may want to trim it off, leaving about a ⅝-inch seam allowance.

10. **Turn the shirt right side out and pop in the pillow from the neckline end. Smooth the sleeves to the back of the pillow (see Figure 15-1).**

    You're done!

Figure 15-1:
Shirt pillows
are a great
way to
preserve
the kid in
all of us.

Making a Cover to Fit a Pillow Form

In this section, you see how easy making a pillow cover from start to finish can be. This pillow cover features an _envelope_ closure in the back that makes it very easy to sew and to take care of — when you want to wash the pillow cover, you just open the envelope and remove the pillow.

The amount of fabric you need for this project depends on the size of the pillow you want to cover. Measure your pillow form, or take it with you to the fabric store and ask the sales associate to cut enough yardage so that you can create three fabric squares exactly the size of your pillow form (see the next section for info on measuring your pillow form). You need three squares — one for the front of the pillow cover and two to make the back envelope closure with a little bit of fabric left over.

Measuring your pillow form and cutting the pillow front

Measure your premade pillow form from seam to seam across the middle before cutting the fabric for the pillow cover. Even though the package may say the pillow form is a 16-inch square, dimensions do vary.

After you measure your pillow form, cut one square the same size as the pillow form. For example, if you have a 16-inch pillow form, you cut one square of fabric 16 x 16 inches. This piece becomes the front of your pillow.

Signed and sealed: Making an envelope closure on the pillow back

The easiest way to close a pillow is by slipping the pillow form into the pillow cover through an envelope opening in the back. Here's how to do it:

1. **Measure and cut the back pillow cover pieces, shown in Figure 15-2.**

   Use two pieces of fabric to create this envelope closure. Cut two pieces of the pillow fabric that measure half the width of the pillow plus 4 inches by the length of the pillow.

   For example, for a 16-inch square pillow, cut two pieces of fabric 12 inches wide x 16 inches long.

2. **Finish one long edge of each back pillow piece.**

   See Chapter 6 for more about finishing edges.

3. **Fold, press, and topstitch a 2-inch hem on the long finished edge of each back pillow piece.**

   See Chapter 5 for more info on topstitched hems.

4. **Overlap the back pillow pieces 2 inches at the hemmed edges so the back envelope piece measures the same as the front pillow piece. Pin the back pillow pieces together at the top and bottom of the hemmed opening (see Figure 15-3 for an illustration).**

   For example, when you overlap the back pillow pieces for a 16-inch pillow, the finished size of the back is 16 inches square.

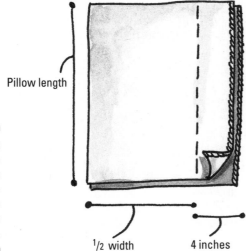

Pillow length

Figure 15-2: Cut two pillow backs half the width of the pillow plus 4 inches.

¹/₂ width   4 inches

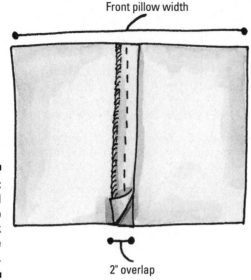

Front pillow width

2" overlap

Figure 15-3:
Pin and
overlap
the back
envelope
pieces.

Preparing the corners

Square pillows often end up with *bunny ears* or unintentionally exaggerated corners. Prevent this unfortunate outcome by following these steps:

1. **Pin the back and front pillow pieces together with the right sides joined.**

2. **Using a fabric marker and ruler, draw a line across the corner at the intersection of the ½-inch seam allowance.**

3. **Taper the lines out to the edge of the fabric to a point ¼ the length of the side of the pillow. Do this for each corner.**

Take your fabric marker or dressmaker's chalk and use the pocket former or a quarter as your template. Simply trace around one of the sharper curved edges of the tool to taper and smooth out all eight pillow cover corners, as shown in Figure 15-4. Remember to trace the same curve for each pillow corner so that all the corners match (see the corners on one of the striped pillows on the bed and the box-edged pillows on the sofa in the color section).

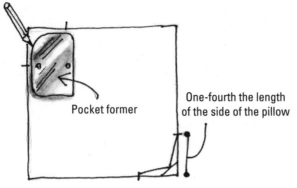

Figure 15-4:
Prevent
pillow
bunny ears
by gently
rounding the
corners of
your pillow
pieces.

Pocket former

One-fourth the length
of the side of the pillow

Sewing the pillow cover together

Follow these steps to put the pillow cover together:

1. **If you want cord edge trim, fringe, a ruffle, or piping sewn on the edge of the pillow, sew it on the front pillow piece.**

   Read more about cutting, sewing, and joining these trims in Chapter 13.

2. **Place and pin the pillow top and envelope back, right sides together, so that the envelope hems overlap each other by about 2 inches.**

   Make sure that the raw edges of the front and back pillow pieces are even around the perimeter of the pillow cover.

3. **Set your sewing machine like this:**
   - **Stitch:** Straight
   - **Length:** 2.5 to 3 mm/10 to 12 spi
   - **Width:** 0 mm
   - **Foot:** All-purpose

4. **Using a ½-inch seam allowance, sew the top and back pillow pieces together around all four edges, backstitching at the ends of the seam. Press the seams flat and together before turning the pillow cover.**

5. **Turn the pillow cover right side out through the envelope opening and pop in the pillow form.**

   Now lay your head on your sensational new pillow and take a nap.

No Sham Job Here: Crafting Your Own Flanged Pillow Sham

Your first question about this project may be, "What's a flange?" A *flange* is a flat border around the perimeter of the pillow cover. "What's a sham?" A *sham* is a removable pillow cover. (See the bedroom setting in the color pages of this book; the flanged pillow shams are on the bed, right up against the head-board. Also notice the flanged pillows that adorn the sofa: What do you think they are made from?)

Make shams not only for rectangular sleeping pillows, but also for large, square European-style bed pillows and floor pillows. (In Chapter 17, you find out how to make a bed skirt and a duvet cover. Put the finishing touches on that bedroom by making matching flanged pillow shams.)

The amount of fabric you need for this project depends on the size of the pillow you want to cover. Measure your pillow form, or take it with you to the store and ask the sales associate to cut enough yardage so that you can create three pieces of fabric exactly the size of your pillow form plus ½ yard — when making two shams, you need to double the yardage. You may have a little bit of fabric left over.

To make a beautiful pillow sham with a 3-inch flange, follow these steps:

1. **Measure your pillow and add 6 inches to the width and length measurements, as shown in Figure 15-5.**

   These measurements help you cut a piece of fabric the right size in the next step. For example, if you start with a 26-x-20-inch pillow, your measurements are 32 x 26 inches.

2. **Cut one piece of fabric the width and length that you calculate in Step 1. This is the front sham fabric piece.**

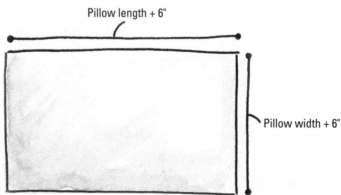

Pillow length + 6"

Figure 15-5: To make the front sham piece, add 6 inches to your pillow measurements.

Pillow width + 6"

3. **Measure half the pillow sham width you cut in Step 2 and add 4 inches.**

   This number gives you the measurement for the sham's back pieces. The back pieces form an envelope that allows you to take the pillow out and put it back in again.

4. **Cut two back *envelope* pieces of the width that you calculate in Step 3 and the length that you calculate in Step 1 (See Figure 15-6).**

Figure 15-6:
Cut two back envelope pieces to make the back of the sham.

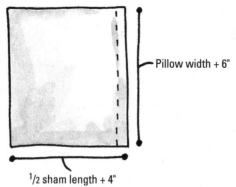

Pillow width + 6"

¹/₂ sham length + 4"

5. **Finish one short edge of each back envelope piece.**

   See Chapter 6 to read more about finishing raw edges.

6. **Fold, press, and topstitch a 2-inch hem on the finished edge of each back envelope piece.**

   See Chapter 5 for more information on topstitched hems.

7. **Overlap the back envelope pieces 2 inches at the hemmed edges, pinning the back envelope pieces together at the top and bottom of the hemmed opening.**

8. **Place and pin the top sham and envelope back, right sides together, so that the raw edges of the front and back sham pieces are even around the perimeter.**

9. **Using a ¹/₂-inch seam allowance and a straight stitch, sew the top and back sham pieces together, backstitching at the ends of the seam.**

   I want to tell you what settings to use on your machine, but you could be using any one of hundreds of fabrics. I suggest starting with a 2.5 mm/10 to 12 spi stitch length, sewing a test strip of stitches on your fabric, and then adjusting your stitch length, if you need to.

10. **Trim away the excess fabric at the corners (see Chapter 6 and read up on trimming seam allowances at the corners) and press the seams flat and together, as shown in Figure 15-7.**

11. **Put the sham on the ironing board and press as much of the seam open as possible, pressing around all four sides of the sham.**

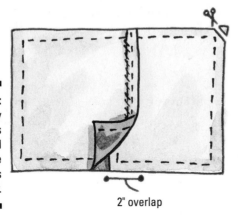

Figure 15-7:
Cut away the excess fabric and press the seams together.

2" overlap

12. **Turn the sham right side out through the envelope opening and press the seam flat and together along the seam line.**

13. **Using your fabric marker or dressmaker's chalk, mark a border around the sham 3 inches in from the seamed edge.**

    This border marks the stitching line of the flange.

14. **Stitch around the sham, as shown in Figure 15-8, sewing on the markings made in Step 13, 3 inches in from the finished edge.**

    Instead of machine-stitching the flange, thread a large tapestry needle with yarn and sew several rows of running stitches around the flange, starting 3 inches from the finished edge (see Chapter 5 for the how-to's on working the hand running stitch).

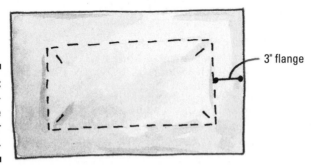

3" flange

Figure 15-8:
Stitch the 3-inch flange around your sham.

The 15-minute flanged pillow cover

I made the bright orange and yellow pillows shown in the color section in 30 minutes by covering two pillow forms with napkins. When the covers are dirty, simply loosen a few stitches, remove the pillow forms, wash the covers (you can wash napkins, after all), press, pop in the forms, and then restitch. Easy, easy, easy.

Follow these simple steps to become a pillow cover pro:

1. **Buy two 20-inch napkins to cover one 16-inch pillow form.**

   This way the flange ends up measuring 2 inches all the way around the pillow cover.

2. **Preshrink the napkins and press them.**

3. **Place the napkins wrong sides together.**

4. **Set your sewing machine like this:**

   • **Stitch:** Straight

   • **Length:** 2.5 to 3 mm/10 to 12 spi

   • **Width:** 0 mm

   • **Foot:** All-purpose

5. **Stitch around about three and a half sides of the napkins, guiding 2-inches from the edge, and leaving a 6-7-inch opening.**

6. **Pop the pillow form through the opening in the stitched napkin cover.**

7. **Machine stitch the opening closed, backstitching at the ends.**

   Tada! I told you it was easy.

Sewing a One-Piece Fringed Envelope Pillow

Make this really easy pillow using a fabric that complements your decor and a sensational decorator trim called bullion fringe (I discuss bullion fringe in Chapter 13). After making this easy pillow, you may amaze even yourself with your newfound creativity and sewing skills.

To make this project, you need the following materials in addition to your Sewing Survival Kit (See Chapter 1 for a kit rundown):

✔ One 18-inch pillow form

✔ ½ yard of 48-or-54-inch-wide home decor fabric

✔ Thread that matches the fabric

✔ One-yard bullion fringe to coordinate with the fabric

Follow these steps to create the pillow:

1. **Cut the fabric 18 x 46 inches, as shown in Figure 15-9.**

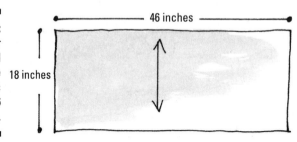

Figure 15-9:
Cut your fringed envelope pillow fabric 18 x 46 inches.

2. **Finish the short ends of the pillow cover.**

   See Chapter 6 for more information on edge finishing.

3. **Press and stitch a ½-inch hem on both short ends of the fabric.**

4. **Cut the bullion fringe in half and place the two 18-inch lengths on the pillow cover, as shown in Figure 15-10.**

   See information in Chapter 13 on how to safely cut the fringe so that it doesn't unravel unexpectedly.

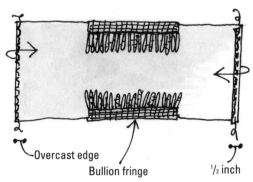

Figure 15-10:
Hem both short ends, and then center the two lengths of fringe on the pillow cover fabric.

5. **Place the trim on the right side of the fabric, centering it on the sides of the fabric strip so that the lip edge of the fringe is even with the raw edges.**

6. **Fold the short ends toward the center, right sides together, so that the pillow cover measures 18 inches square, as shown in Figure 15-11.**

   The short ends overlap each other about 4½ inches and sandwich the bullion fringe in the seam line.

7. **Set your machine like this:**

- **Stitch:** Straight
- **Length:** 3 to 4 mm/6 to 9 spi
- **Width:** 0
- **Foot:** All-purpose

8. **Sew a ½-inch seam on both sides of the pillow cover, backstitching at both ends of each seam.**

9. **Press the seams flat and together.**

10. **Turn the pillow cover right side out and pop the pillow form into the cover through the opening in the back.**

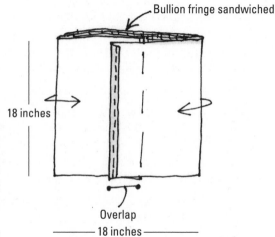

Bullion fringe sandwiched

18 inches

Overlap

18 inches

Figure 15-11:
Fold and overlap the short ends toward the center.

Making a Trim and Border Pillow

You can get some experience sewing in piping and cord-edge trim by making this fun trim and border pillow. To make a trim and border pillow, you need the following supplies (in addition to the Sewing Survival Kit that I tell you about in Chapter 1):

- ✔ One 14-inch pillow form
- ✔ ½ yard of 48-inch-wide to 54-inch-wide upholstery velvet
- ✔ One 10-inch square of home decor fabric that coordinates with the velvet
- ✔ Thread that matches the fabric
- ✔ 1½ yards of cord-edge trim that coordinates with the fabric
- ✔ (Optional) Four decorator tassels to coordinate with the fabric (see Chapter 13 for more information on tassels)

Follow these steps to create the pillow:

1. **Cut a 14-inch square from the upholstery velvet and set it aside.**

2. **From the remaining velvet, cut two 2¾-x-14-inch strips and two 2¾-x 10-inch strips.**

3. **Set your sewing machine like this:**

   • **Stitch:** Straight

   • **Length:** 3 mm/9 spi

   • **Width:** 0 mm

   • **Foot:** Zipper or piping

   Take your needle position off of center so that it sews next to the piping on the lip edge of the trim (turn to Chapter 1 for information on needle position).

4. **Sew the cord-edge trim to two opposite sides of the 10-inch fabric square, using a seam allowance the width of the lip of the cord.**

   See Chapter 13 if you need more information on attaching the trim.

5. **Sew the short fabric strips onto the same two opposite ends of the 10-inch pillow square where the cord is sewn, sandwiching the cord-edge trim between the velvet strip and coordinating fabric.**

6. **Repeat Steps 3 through 5 for the other, longer sides of the pillow square using the remaining cord edge trim and longer velvet strips.**

7. **Press the cord-edge-trimmed pillow square from the wrong side, pressing the seam allowances to one side.**

8. **Using your dressmaker's chalk and trimming scissors, mark and trim each corner on both pillow squares into a gentle curve.**

   Doing so makes it easier to sew the tassels and prevents the bunny ear effect in each corner of your pillow when you finish it, as I discuss in the section "Preparing the corners" earlier in this chapter.

9. **If you're using tassels, pin one in each corner of the decorated square as shown in Figure 15-12, pinning them so that the loops catch in the seam allowance.**

   Check out Chapter 13 to get the lowdown on tassels.

10. **With the right sides joined, pin and stitch the pillow together, using a ½-inch seam allowance and leaving a 5-inch opening on one side to turn the pillow through, as shown in Figure 15-13.**

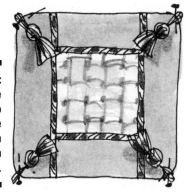

Figure 15-12:
Pin the
tassels so
that the
loops catch
in the seam
allowance.

5-inch opening

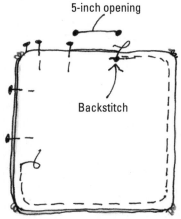

Backstitch

Figure 15-13:
Pin and
stitch the
pillow cover
together,
leaving
a 5-inch
opening on
one side.

11. **Press the seams flat and together.**

    See Chapter 5 for more information on pressing seams.

12. **On either side of the opening, clip into the seam allowance just shy of the seamline. Press the seam allowance toward the center of the pillow cover, as shown in Figure 15-14.**

13. **Trim the seam allowance to about ¼ inch, taking out the fabric bulk at the corners. (See Figure 15-14 for a visual.) Turn the pillow cover right side out.**

14. **Stuff the pillow form into the pillow cover and hand slipstitch the opening to close it.**

    See Chapter 5 for more information on hand slipstitching.

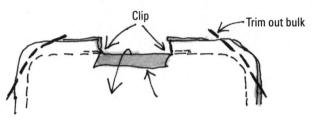

Figure 15-14:
Clip into
the seam
allowance
and trim
away bulk at
the corners.

Making a Box-Edged Pillow

Box-edged pillows, popular in the 1950s, have popped back onto the decorating scene. They look like small sofa cushions — two rows of piping with a strip of fabric in between called a *boxing strip* — and they often have a fabric-covered button stitched in the center (check out the pillow in the color section).

To make a box-edged pillow, you need the following supplies in addition to the Sewing Survival Kit (see Chapter 1 for details):

- One 14-inch pillow form (If you can find a boxed edge pillow form the size that you need, buy it; otherwise, use a regular pillow form.)
- ½ yard of 48-inch-wide to 54-inch-wide home decor fabric
- One 60-inch-x-2-inch contrasting home decor fabric for the boxing strip
- Thread that matches the fabric
- Four yards of piping that contrasts with the pillow and boxing strip fabric (See Chapter 13 for piping instructions.)
- Two ½- to 2-inch covered button sets (they come in a kit with several buttons per kit)
- Long hand-sewing needle used in doll making

Just follow these steps to create the pillow:

1. **Cut two 14-inch squares of home decor fabric; set one aside.**

   The boxing strip adds room that you need for creating the flat sides to the finished pillow. Because of the softness of the pillow forms, if you add seam allowances, the pillow covers come out too big.

2. **Using a ½-inch seam allowance, pin and stitch the piping to the right side and all the way around the first pillow square, pulling out the pins as you get to them (see Chapter 13 for a more detailed explanation of attaching piping).**

3. **Repeat Step 2 for the other pillow square.**

4. **Pin the boxing strip to the first pillow square as shown in Figure 15-15.**

   Starting anywhere but at a corner, pin the boxing strip to the right side of the pillow square so that the raw edges of the piping and the fabric are even.

   The boxing strip is intentionally cut longer than needed to go around the pillow square. This way, you don't run short of boxing strip fabric, and you can cut it to fit.

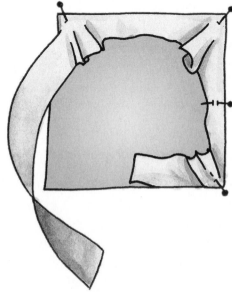

Figure 15-15:
Starting anywhere but a corner, pin on the boxing strip.

5. **Set your sewing machine like this:**

   - **Stitch:** Straight
   - **Length:** 3 mm/9 spi
   - **Width:** 0 mm
   - **Foot:** Zipper or piping

6. **Sew on the boxing strip at the ½-inch seamline, pulling out the pins as you get to them. Stop sewing about 2 inches before the end of the boxing strip.**

   When pinning and sewing around a corner, clip the seam allowance of the boxing strip up to, but not through, the seamline. With the needle in the fabric, raise the foot and pivot slightly. Lower the presser foot and continue sewing a gentle curve rather than a sharp corner to accommodate the bulk of the piping and boxing strip fabrics.

7. Pin and seam the short ends of the boxing strip together and then press the seam open.

8. Stitch the rest of the boxing strip to the edge of the first pillow square.

9. Repeat Steps 2 through 7, attaching the second piped pillow square to the other side of the boxing strip but leaving a 5- to 6-inch opening for the pillow form to fit through.

10. Turn the pillow right side out and push the pillow form through the opening of the pillow cover and slipstitch it closed.

    See Chapter 5 for more on slipstitching.

11. Make two covered buttons with the same fabric as the piping or boxing strip, following the manufacturer's instructions.

12. Sew both buttons to the center of the pillow.

    • Thread the long needle with a doubled thread and knot the end. Poke the end of a long thread through the eye of the needle, pulling it so both thread ends are even; treating them as one, tie a knot (see Chapter 5 for more on tying the perfect knot).

    • Push the needle through the center of one side of the pillow and bring it through the other side.

    • Push one button onto the threaded needle, snugging the button down to the surface of the pillow.

    • Push the needle through to the other side of the pillow and repeat for the second button. Now both buttons are secured to the pillow and each other.

    • Repeat this stitching process several times so that you secure both buttons together through the pillow, as shown in Figure 15-16; afterward, secure the stitch by sewing a knot (see Chapter 5 for more on securing hand stitches).

Piping

Figure 15-16:
Sew both buttons to the center of the pillow.

Chapter 16

Wowing Up Your Windows

· ·

· ·

"**S**ave money. Make your own window treatments." This message may make a great mantra for people transitioning to a new apartment or home or updating their current abode. This chapter tells you how to work with windows, and it tells you how to make window treatments (and even a simple shower curtain to spice up your bathroom) that you find easy on the eyes — and the pocketbook!

Wandering through the Wide World of Window Treatments

When starting your journey through this vast world of window treatments, you first need to consider some basic design elements. No matter what room you work in, remember that every room has three common elements:

✔ Eye-level decor

✔ Mid-level decor

✔ Floor-level decor

Most people do a great job on the floor-level decor. They have to walk on something, which includes flooring, carpet, area rugs, and floor pillows. Many people also do a good job with the mid-level decor. People have to sit and eat on something, which includes sofas, chairs, tables, and lamps.

The most neglected design element in a room (and the one that makes the most impact) is the eye-level decor — or the window treatments. If you have checked out custom window treatments and their prices, you're probably not surprised at the number of naked windows in so many homes and apartments. But before you take out a second mortgage for your window treatments, I want you to know that affordable alternatives are available, many of which I cover in this chapter, which can save you up to 75 percent of custom treatments. So no more excuses — now's the time to dress those naked windows.

Use *curtains,* or short treatments that stop at or just below the windowsill for shorter, narrower windows:

- ✔ **Double cafe curtains:** Hang on rings that you string onto a rod
- ✔ **Sheer panel curtains:** Have a stitched casing at the top and are slipped over a flat curtain rod

Use *draperies*, long treatments that stop at the floor or *puddle* onto the floor, for longer, wider windows.

- ✔ **Full-length triple pinch pleat draw draperies:** Hang on a two-way traverse rod. See the section "The anatomy of windows, rods, and treatments" later on in this chapter to learn more about a traverse rod.
- ✔ **Pinch-pleated draw draperies:** Hang on a traverse rod, which has slides that hold the drapery hooks. See the section "The anatomy of windows, rods, and treatments" later on in this chapter to learn more about a traverse rod.
- ✔ **Sheer panel draperies:** Have a stitched casing at the top that you slip over a flat or continental curtain rod
- ✔ **Shirred draperies:** *Shirred* (gathered) onto a continental rod you thread through a stitched casing or pocket at the top of the drapery panel and tie back to the window frame

Use the following ideas alone or together with curtains or draperies for just about any window:

- ✔ **Bishop sleeves:** You create these sleeves by tying back drapes and then pulling up slack so that the drapery blouses over the tieback and looks like a puffed sleeve when gathered in at the cuff.
- ✔ **Cornice:** A rigid box covered with fabric and padded with a soft batting or contoured foam. Use a cornice alone over the top of a window, over draperies, or over vertical blinds mounted on a traverse rod (see the next section for information on the different rod types).
- ✔ **Poufs and rosettes:** Short lengths of fabric pulled into a loop along the length of a drapery scarf that fan out, creating soft, roselike poufs that look sort of like puffed sleeves at the corners of the window. Check 'em out in Figure 16-1.

✔ **Puddles:** A puddle uses drapery fabric that measures 12 to 20 inches longer than a standard drapery from the top of the rod to the floor. The hem edge is shirred in with a rubber band or cord and then spreads out or "puddles" onto the floor.

✔ **Scarf or swag:** A soft, usually sheer fabric that drapes over the top of swag holders at each corner of the window. (You can find several types of swag holders where drapery hardware is sold.)

✔ **Tiebacks:** Made of fabric or drapery cord and tassels, tiebacks (see Figure 16-1) hold a drapery open at the side of a window.

✔ **Window topper:** Any treatment mounted at the top of the window — from a cornice to a short skirt shirred onto a rod.

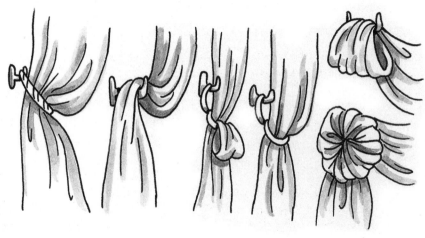

Figure 16-1:
Add poufs, rosettes, or tiebacks to create drama and add dimension to your draperies.

If you're itching to know more about other aspects of design, check out *Home Decorating For Dummies,* 2nd Edition, by Katharine Kaye McMillan and Patricia Hart McMillan (Wiley).

The anatomy of windows, rods, and treatments

The mullion's connected to the . . . window sash; the sash slides into the . . . window frame; the window frame is surrounded by the . . . trim mold. If you know the song but this still makes no sense to you, now's the time to discover the language of windows (as shown in Figure 16-2) and window treatments (see Figure 16-3) in this section.

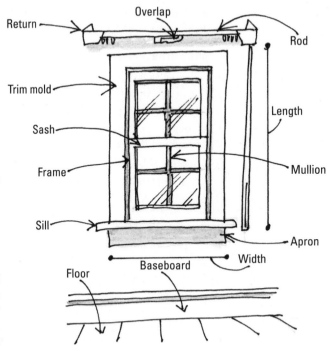

Figure 16-2:
The anatomy
of a window.

Check out these standard window parts:

- **Apron:** A piece of wood that attaches under the *windowsill*. On windows that don't have sills, the apron looks like a continuation of the *trim mold*.

- **Overlap:** The piece of hardware attached in the center where one drapery crosses over the other on a two-way draw traverse rod.

- **Return:** Where the rod or cornice turns the corner and returns to the wall. Depending on the depth of the return, you may have enough room for another rod to fit behind it, allowing you to layer your draperies.

- **Rod:** Holds the drapery or curtain in place over the window.

- **Trim mold:** The wood that has been nailed around the window to trim or finish the opening.

- **Window length:** The distance measured from the top to the bottom of the window. Outside window length is measured from the outside edge of the *trim mold* to the bottom of the *apron*. Inside length is the distance from the top of the window frame to the *sill*.

- **Windowsill:** This piece of trim extends from the window and runs parallel to the floor, usually at the bottom of the window. This is the part you set your coffee cup on.

 ✔ **Window width:** The distance measured across the window. Outside window width measures from one outside edge of the *trim mold* to the other outside edge of the trim mold. Inside window width measures from one side of the window to the other, inside the window frame.

Rods come in a variety of shapes and sizes (see Figure 16-3). The type of rod you use depends on what sort of window treatment you want to make:

 ✔ **Cafe rods:** Mounted either inside or outside the window frame. Cafe rods work well for straight, shirred, or pleated curtains.

 ✔ **Continental rods:** Available in wider 2-inch to 4-inch *drops* (the height of the rod from its top to bottom edges). You use continental rods for shirred panels like those described in "Creating Simple Reversible Curtains and Draperies to Fit Any Window" later in this chapter.

 ✔ **Flat rods:** Hold shirred drapery panels by threading the rod through the casing at the top of the panels. This very basic window treatment does not finish the window treatment until you add a cornice, valance, or other window topper that goes over a curtain at the top of the window frame.

 ✔ **Tension rods:** Best for lightweight curtains. Tension rods are held between walls or inside a window frame by a spring-type mechanism inside the rod rather than by a bracket that you screw into the wall.

 ✔ **Traverse rods:** Include a drapery cord that you pull to open or close the draperies. Some traverse rods let you pull the draperies across to one side and others move the drapery panels from the center so that one ends up on each side.

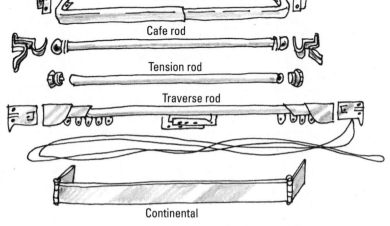

Figure 16-3: Choose a rod according to which type of curtain you want.

Measuring the finished width and length

After you select the curtain or drapery style you want to use for your window and determine the sort of rod you need, measure your windows to determine the finished width and length of the treatment.

Use the following information to determine the finished length of your specific treatment:

- ✔ **Curtains and draperies:** Measure from the top of the rod to the desired length — to the sill, apron, or floor.
- ✔ **Shower curtains:** Measure from the top of the rod to the floor.

And now for the finished width:

- ✔ **Curtains and draperies:** Measure the rod from end to end plus returns.
- ✔ **Shower curtains:** After you install it over the tub, measure the rod width from end to end.

Keep these guidelines in mind for accurate measurements:

- ✔ **Install the curtain rod first.** When you take your measurements, you're able to measure accurately the finished width and length when you have already installed the rod. Rods can attach to the window frame inside the window frame (called an *inside mount*), outside the window frame or trim mold (called an *outside mount*), or at the ceiling (called a ceiling mount).
- ✔ **Use a metal measuring tape.** Cloth measuring tapes may stretch or sag, causing inaccurate measurements.
- ✔ **If you're making window treatments for several windows, take measurements for each window.** Even in the same house where the windows look the same size, window measurements may vary. You want to make sure each treatment fits each window.
- ✔ **Curtains for a window without an apron should have a finished length that's at least 4 inches below the windowsill or below the bottom of the frame.** This way, your curtain is in proportion to the window. (See "The anatomy of windows, rods, and treatments" earlier in this chapter.)

Calculating Cut Fabric Length and Width

After you know the finished measurements for your window treatment (see the previous section), you need to calculate the cut length of the fabric.

Pattern instructions for curtains, draperies, slipcovers, dust ruffles, and other home-decor projects that require a lot of fabric tell you to cut so many *panels* for a particular project. Panels are nothing more than a length of fabric used at the widest width of the fabric.

Looking for length

You determine the cut length of the curtain or drapery by taking the finished length (the length of the curtain or drapery when you finish it and hang it over the window) and adding additional fabric to allow for the following parts, as shown in Figure 16-4:

- ✔ **Casing:** A fabric tunnel at the top of a curtain or drapery panel that you thread onto a rod

- ✔ **The heading:** Decorative extra fabric above the casing that looks like a little ruffle after you thread the casing onto the rod

- ✔ **Doubled lower-hem:** Twice-folded hems to give the curtain weight

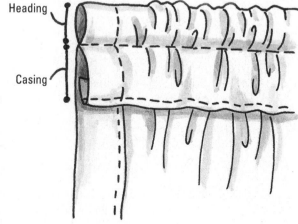

Heading

Casing

Figure 16-4:
Take into account the extra fabric you need for a heading and casing.

When you begin making window treatments, choose fabric that is a solid color or has a very small design. Treatments become much more difficult to work with when you have to try to match a large-pattern design.

Follow these easy steps to determine how much extra fabric to add to the finished length of your curtain or drapery to account for the casing and heading:

1. **Using your tape measure, measure the curtain rod's diameter.**

2. **Add an inch to the measurement you determined in Step 1.**

   This extra inch accounts for a ½-inch seam allowance, and you also have plenty of extra room for the rod to slide smoothly through the casing.

3. **Decide how high you want the heading to extend above the rod and double that length.**

   For example, if you want a 2-inch heading, add another 4 inches to the length of the fabric you need to cut.

4. **Determine how much extra length to add for the doubled hem, according to the following guidelines:**

   - **Sheer and lightweight fabrics:** Use a 6-inch double-fold hem by adding 12 inches to the cut length

   - **Medium-weight fabric:** Use a 4-inch double-fold hem by adding 8 inches to the cut length

   - **Heavyweight fabric:** Use a 3 -inch double-fold hem by adding 6 inches to the cut length

5. **Add the measurements from Steps 2, 3, and 4 to the finished length of your curtain and you have the cut length needed for one drapery panel.**

Determining width

To determine the cut curtain or drapery width, you need to take the following into account:

- ✔ **Fabric weight:** The lighter the fabric weight, the more fullness you want in the treatment. Lightweight fabric is more likely to look skimpy. Follow these general guidelines to figure out the ideal drapery width for your situation:

  - When using sheer and lightweight fabrics, use 2½ to 3 times the rod width (including the returns) for the finished width of the fabric panel.

  - When using mid-weight fabrics, use 2 to 2½ times the rod width (including the returns) for the finished width of the fabric panel.

  - When using heavyweight fabrics, use twice the rod width (including the returns) for the finished width of the fabric panel.

- ✔ **Fabric width:** Most treatments use more than one fabric width, or panel, so that you have enough fabric spanning across the window for pulling up the gathers, pleats, and shirring. For example, in a set of sheer panel draperies, you may see three separate panels shirred onto a rod and each finished panel may be made from two cut panels.

If, for example, a fabric is 54 inches wide, and you need two and a half widths to make a drapery, that means that you need two 54-inch panels and one 27-inch panel.

Home-decor fabrics, which run from about 48 to 72 inches wide, are typically wider than fabrics used to make clothing. As a result, they work better than the 36- to 45-inch fashion fabrics to cover large areas.

✔ **Seam allowances:** Seam allowances for home-decor projects are usually ½ inch. For easy pattern matching, home-decor fabrics have match points or color bars printed in the selvages (the finished edges that run the length of the fabric), and if the fabric is printed, the print usually starts ½ inch in from the selvage (see Figure 16-5 to see the selvage match points). So, when you decide how wide to make each fabric panel, remember to add 1 inch *per panel* for the seam allowances (½ inch + ½ inch = 1 inch).

✔ **Doubled side hems:** You sew side hems on both sides of a curtain or drapery panel. Like lower hems, side hems are doubled so that the fabric hangs straight and even on the edges.

Use the following formulas to determine how much to add to your width measurement:

- For treatments using only one panel (like a shower curtain), add 4 inches for a 1-inch double hem on each side (1 inch x 2 [doubled side hems] x 2 sides = 4 inches).

- For treatments using two or more panels, add 4 inches to the finished width of the treatment for 1-inch doubled side hems.

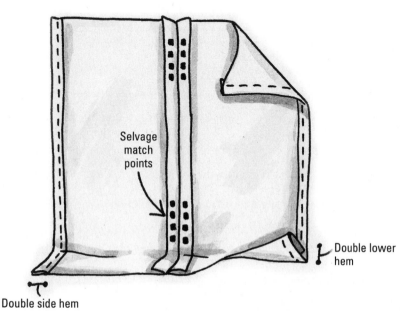

Figure 16-5: Use the selvage match points to align the fabric pattern from panel to panel.

Selvage match points

Double lower hem

Double side hem

Figuring fabric for fancy flourishes

Add dimension to your draperies with a pouf or rosette. Add drama (and hardly any sewing) with a bishop sleeve or puddled hems (refer to Figure 16-1). All you need is a little more fabric.

✔ For each pouf, rosette, or puddle, remember to add an additional 20 inches to the cut length so that the fabric drapes properly.

For example, if a drapery has two poufs and two puddles, add an additional 80 inches to the cut length (20 inches x 4 = 80 inches).

✔ When making bishop sleeves, add an extra 18 inches of fabric to the length of the finished draperies.

Constructing a Window Cornice

Want to make quick and easy changes to your window treatments? The cleverest home-decor product I've found, called the Quick-Change Window Cornice (by Naked Room Solutions . . . At Your Door Home Décor) gives you the tools to do just that. The best part is that the Quick-Change Cornices look like expensive custom treatments for a fraction of the custom price. See Figure 16-6 to become familiar with cornice terminology before starting the project and check out the color section to find your favorite. Become a quick-change artist and give any room a new, custom look in an evening or less.

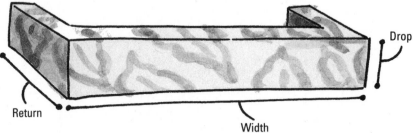

Figure 16-6: Anatomy of a cornice.

Parts of the cornice include the following:

✔ **Width:** The distance the cornice spans across the window's width

✔ **Drop:** The length the cornice *drops* down from the window

✔ **Return:** The part that bends back or *returns* to the wall

To make this window cornice, you need the following materials in addition to your Sewing Survival Kit (which I tell you about in Chapter 1):

✔ One Quick-Change Cornice Window Kit (see the appendix)

✔ 3½ yards of home-decor fabric to cover two average-sized cornices that fit 48-inch windows

Covering your cornice

The cornice's body is actually polyurethane foam, which you cut to fit your window according to the manufacturer's instructions.

I like to change my decor for the season or for a change of scene. If you're like me, cover your basic cornice with a solid or small-scale print, and then when you want to change the look of the room, just change the accent fabric. Check out the sections "Adding a long bow to a cornice" and "Creating a French country cornice" later on in the chapter.

After preparing the body of the cornice, follow these steps to cover it with your fabric:

1. **Cut a piece of your fabric in the following dimensions:**

   • **Length:** 38 inches

   • **Width:** The width of the cornice (from the end of the left return to the end of the right return) plus 13 inches

2. **Lay the fabric wrong side up on a table or the floor and place the cornice on the fabric, contoured side down.**

   Position the cornice so that you have a 6½-inch border at the top and both sides and the groove on the back is closest to the top.

3. **Using a credit card, tuck the fabric into the groove on the back of the foam from the center out.**

4. **Roll the cornice toward you, turning it so the contoured side is face up. Begin tucking the fabric into the top horizontal groove, smoothing the fabric from the center out.**

5. **Tuck the second, third, and/or fourth tuck grooves, keeping the fabric loose and straight ahead of the groove that you're tucking.**

   This way, the fabric tucks easily in the grooves as you work toward the bottom edge.

   You can tuck the fabric into one groove, all the grooves, some of the grooves, or none of them. This cornice offers options for almost any decorating taste.

6. **Roll the cornice toward you again so that you see the back. Tuck the fabric into the tuck groove on the back, pinning it into place with T-pins that come in your kit.**

   If you didn't tuck fabric into all the grooves on the face of the cornice, you may need to trim off the excess fabric so there isn't a lot of fabric bunching up inside the groove on the back.

   If you want to embellish your cornice like the ones you see in this book's color insert, do it now. Skip ahead to the next sections on "Adding a long bow to a cornice" or "Creating a French country cornice," add your embellishment, and then finish the returns as described from Step 6 on.

7. **Insert the curtain rod that comes with the kit.**

8. **Fold the fabric at the return ends, as you would wrap a gift.**

9. **Finish the returns of the cornice, following the manufacturer's directions.**

   Note that the curtain rod buried into the back of the cornice becomes the backbone and prevents the cornice from sagging after you install it above the window.

10. **To finish, hang the cornice over the window by following the manufacturer's instructions.**

Adding a long bow to a cornice

After you cover your Quick-Change Cornice with your basic fabric, you can add a long strip of contrasting fabric cinched in with a napkin ring. When you get tired of it, just quick-change it.

Because you're adding another fabric onto your basic fabric-covered cornice, buy a little extra, and then make a couple of throw pillows or a table topper to match (see Chapters 14 and 15 for yardage requirements for table toppers and pillows).

To make this cornice, you need the following materials in addition to your Sewing Survival Kit (see Chapter 1):

- Napkin ring (one per cornice)
- Strip of fabric 16 inches long and 12 inches wider than the width of the window
- T-pins (they look like a letter "T" and are available in the home-decor department of fabric or craft stores)

Follow these steps to make a great-looking window topper:

1. **Press a 2-inch hem on both long edges of the fabric strip. (See Figure 16-7.)**

2. **Thread the hemmed fabric strip through the napkin ring, centering the ring in the center of the strip — see why I call it the *long bow*?**

3. **Place the long bow across the face of the covered cornice.**

4. **Turn the cornice so that the backside faces you.**

5. **Insert the curtain rod into the groove on the back of the cornice.**

6. **Pin the fabric ends (including the long bow), creating the cornice returns as shown in the manufacturer's instructions.**

7. **Turn the cornice over and adjust the napkin ring, putting it in the center of the bow as shown in Figure 16-7.**

8. **Install your cornice following the manufacturer's instructions.**

Figure 16-7:
Simply add a strip of fabric cinched in the middle with a napkin ring for the long bow cornice embellishment.

Press two hems

Creating a French country cornice

When I started working with this Quick-Change Cornice product, my imagination took over. The tuck grooves are deep enough to hold an extra piece of fabric and two lengths of cord-edge trim — and without sewing! Cover the basic cornice as described in the previous section and before finishing the return ends, just follow these easy steps for the added embellishment used on the great-looking cornice you see in the color section.

To make this cornice, you need the following materials in addition to your Sewing Survival Kit (see Chapter 1):

- ✔ A ½ yard of home-decor fabric to coordinate with the base cornice fabric

- ✔ Two lengths of cord-edge trim the width of the cornice plus 13 inches in a color that coordinates with the fabric

- ✔ T-pins (they look like a letter "T" and are available in the home-decor department of fabric or craft stores)

Follow these steps to create the embellished cornice:

1. **Cut the coordinate fabric in half, creating two strips measuring the width of the fabric and 9 inches long.**

   When laid end to end, these two fabric strips are longer than the cornice is wide, and you can scrunch and gather them to fit across the face of cornice, giving a textural look to your window treatment. Keep reading!

2. **Lay the covered cornice flat and face-up on the table or floor.**

3. **Starting in the center of the cornice, take the first strip of coordinate fabric and poke the top edge into the top tuck groove and the bottom edge into the bottom tuck groove, centering the strip on the face of the cornice.**

   This step anchors the strip.

4. **Using both hands, begin scrunching and gathering the long cut edges of the fabric strip, tucking the long edges into the tuck grooves from the center of the cornice out to one end and over the returns.**

   The fabric has a three-dimensional shirred look to it.

5. **Take the second strip of coordinate fabric and repeat Steps 3 and 4, scrunching and gathering from the center out to the other end of the cornice. Your cornice will look something like Figure 16-8.**

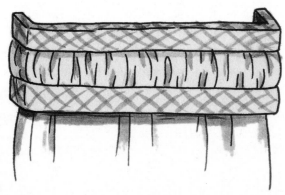

Figure 16-8:
Scrunch
the fabric
around the
cornice.

6. **Take one length of cord-edge trim and tuck it in the top tuck groove. Tuck the second length of cord-edge trim in the bottom tuck groove, securing both lengths of trim with T-pins.**

Figure 16-9 shows you how to attach the trim. ***Note:*** The variation shown in this illustration is made simply by attaching the fabric flat rather than scrunched.

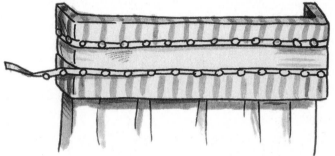

Figure 16-9:
Add cord-edge trim to complete your cornice.

Sewing the Easiest Shower Curtain Ever

I know what you're thinking . . . "A shower curtain doesn't go on a window — at least not on any window in my house." In my mind, though, the word *curtain* makes this a perfect warm-up project for making other types of curtains and draperies you find in this chapter. You take the same width and length measurements as you do when making a curtain for a window, and you use the same types of fabrics.

Handmade shower curtains look better and cost less than ready-mades, and you can easily create color flow from a bedroom to a nearby bathroom simply by matching or coordinating your fabric choices. Because you hang a plastic liner behind the shower curtain, you have no need to line this curtain, so this project is a snap to make.

This shower curtain also uses a wonderful product called Qwik-Tach tape (available at your local fabric store). You sew the tape as a header at the top of the curtain — no buttonholes or eyelets to make, and the tape comes in many great colors that coordinate with a variety of curtain fabrics. To attach the curtain to the rod, large, fashionable grommets snap into place on the header and the curtain just pops onto the rod.

Shower curtains range in finished sizes from 60 to 80 inches wide x about 70 to 80 inches long. The shower curtain you make in this section is likely to fit most shower and bathtub stalls. You may need to adjust the hem length slightly to fit your stall.

To make this shower curtain, you need your Sewing Survival Kit (which I tell you about in Chapter 1), plus the following items:

- ✓ One square or rectangle of fabric. One of the simplest fabrics to use is a full-sized unfitted bed sheet — it comes with a ready-made hem! You can also use 2¼ yards of any 60- to 72-inch home-decor fabric.
- ✓ Thread that matches the fabric
- ✓ One package of Qwik-Tach tape with header fabric that coordinates with curtain fabric
- ✓ Qwik-Tach grommet set
- ✓ One tension-type shower curtain rod with a diameter of 1-inch or less

Follow these steps to create your custom shower curtain:

1. **Cut your fabric.**

   If you're using a sheet with a ready-made hem, cut the sheet 76 inches wide. Measuring from the wide decorative hem-end of the sheet, cut the sheet 71½ inches long. Place this hem at the bottom of the shower curtain. Now you can skip ahead to Step 5.

   If you're using 60- to 72-inch-wide home-decor fabric, cut it the width of the fabric x 77½ inches long.

2. **Make the doubled lower hem.**

   Fold up, pin, and press a 3-inch hem toward the wrong side of the fabric on the lower edge of the shower curtain. Fold up, pin, and press the hem up another 3 inches so that the hem is doubled.

3. **Set your machine like this:**

   - **Stitch:** Straight
   - **Length:** 3 mm/9 spi
   - **Width:** 0 mm
   - **Foot:** All-purpose

4. **Sewing with the wrong side up, topstitch along the top edge of the hem, backstitching at each end. (See Chapter 5 for more information on topstitching and backstitching.)**

5. **Make the doubled side hems.**

   Fold, pin, and press a 1-inch hem toward the wrong side of the fabric on one side of the shower curtain. Fold, pin, and press the side hem another inch so that the hem is doubled. Repeat for the other side hem of the shower curtain.

6. **Sewing with the wrong side up, topstitch along the hem edge, back-stitching at each end. Repeat for the other side hem.**

7. **Make the heading (the part that slides over the shower curtain rod) using the Qwik-Tach tape.**

   Lay the finished curtain face up on the floor or on a table. Place the finished end of the Qwik-Tach tape even with the finished width of the curtain, cutting off just enough tape to fit the curtain.

8. **Following the manufacturer's instructions, cut and hem one end of the tape (the other end is already finished, ready for application).**

9. **Sandwich the top of your shower curtain between the finished edges of the Qwik-Tach tape, following the manufacturer's instructions, as shown in Figure 16-10.**

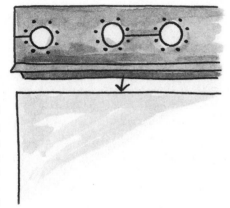

Figure 16-10:
Attach the Qwik-Tach tape to the curtain.

10. **Set your machine like this:**

    - **Stitch:** Straight
    - **Length:** 3 mm/9 spi
    - **Width:** 0 mm
    - **Foot:** All-purpose

11. **Topstitch the tape into place.**

12. **Snap the grommets together over the eyelets in the tape, lining up the slits in the grommets with the slits in the Qwik-Tach tape as shown in Figure 16-11.**

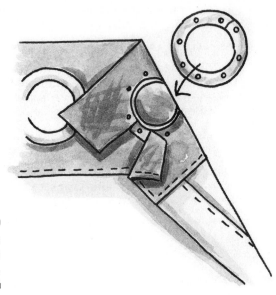

Figure 16-11:
Attach the
grommets.

13. **Press the shower curtain and hang it up, flexing the slits in the grommets open, and then snapping them over the rod as shown in Figure 16-12.**

To keep your new shower curtain dry, install a plastic liner on another rod behind your new shower curtain.

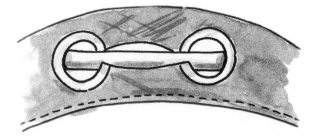

Figure 16-12:
Snap the
grommets
over the rod.

Creating Simple Reversible Curtains and Draperies to Fit Any Window

You make curtain or drapery panels in almost the same way you make a shower curtain. (Check out the previous section to try your hand at making a shower curtain.) This project uses two home-decor fabrics, so it looks reversible; when the treatment is open, both sides show, bringing two coordinating fabrics into the room.

To make this curtain, you need your Sewing Survival Kit (which I tell you about in Chapter 1), plus the following items:

✔ Yardage of two coordinating 60- to 72-inch home-decor fabrics (See "Determining how much fabric you need" in the next section to calculate the specific yardage.)

✔ A decorator drapery rod and hardware (See the section earlier in this chapter called "The anatomy of windows, rods, and treatments" that describes the different types of rods.)

✔ Enough drapery rings with *mitten clips* to fit across the panel(s)

✔ Thread that matches the fabrics

Determining how much fabric you need

Follow these steps to determine how much fabric you need to buy for your curtain:

1. **Measure the width of your window in inches.**

2. **Multiply the window width by 1½.**

   For example, if your window is 58 inches wide, then 58 inches × 1½ = 87 inches.

3. **Divide the number you get in Step 2 by the width of your fabric.**

   This is the number of panels of fabric you need. In the same example, 87 inches divided by 60-inch wide fabric = 1.45, rounded up to 1.5 panels.

4. **Measure the length of the window from the top of the rod to the floor or just below the windowsill or apron.**

   See "The anatomy of windows, rods, and treatments" section earlier in this chapter for definitions of windowsill, apron, and other applicable terms.

5. **Add 6 inches for the double hems.**

6. **Multiply the number you get in Step 5 by the number of panels you need (see Step 3). This is the length of fabric you need in inches.**

7. **Divide the number you get in Step 6 by 36. This is the length of fabric you need in yards for one side or *face* of the curtain.**

   You need the same amount for a second, coordinating fabric for the lining.

Putting the curtain together

Follow these steps to create a great-looking drapery:

1. **If you're using more than one panel, seam the fabric panels together at the selvages. (See Chapter 6 for more information on seaming.)**

2. **Using a half-inch seam allowance, place, pin, and sew the face and coordinating fabrics, right sides together at one short end, as shown in Figure 16-13a.**

   The seam needs to be straight and smooth. After you sew the seam (see Chapter 6), press it flat and together, and then press it open.

3. **Gently rip out a few stitches from both ends of the seam you stitched in Step 2, and then trim away 1 inch from each long side of the coordinating fabric.**

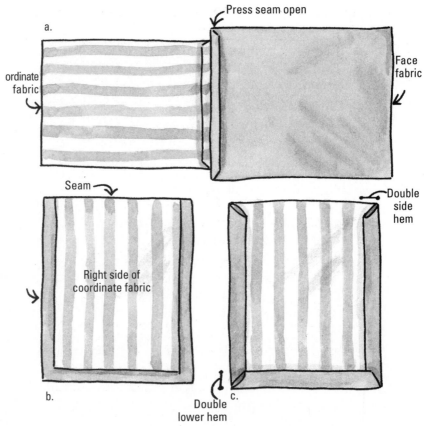

Figure 16-13:
Sew short ends of fabrics together. Fold the panel so the seam is at the top and the wrong sides are together. Make double lower and side hems.

When making your double side hems, you incorporate two layers of fabric twice, making four layers of fabric. By trimming away an inch from each side of the coordinate fabric, you eliminate bulk so that working with the project is a lot easier.

4. **Fold the coordinate fabric and the face fabric, so the seam is at the top and the wrong sides are together, as shown in Figure 16-13b.**

5. **Make the doubled lower and side hems (shown in Figure 16-13c) by following Steps 2 through 6 of the instructions given in the "Sewing the Easiest Shower Curtain Ever" section earlier in this chapter.**

   Press the curtain, smoothing out any wrinkles.

   When you have very long draperies, machine blind hemming the doubled hems (and all that yardage) is easier than topstitching them. See Chapter 7 for more on machine blind hemming.

6. **Clip the mitten clips that are attached to the drapery rings to the top of the curtain, spacing them equidistantly across the width of the drape as shown in Figure 16-14.**

7. **Thread the rod through the rings and hang up your creation.**

   If your rod has a knob or *finial* (a decorative doo-dad) on the end, remove it by gently pulling it off. Thread your drapery rings onto the rod, and then put the knob back onto the rod and hang up your treatment. Follow these same simple steps to remove your drapery for cleaning.

   Open the draperies, allow the sunshine in, and admire your work.

Figure 16-14:
Space drapery rings evenly across the top of the curtain.

Whipping Up a Shirred and Flipped Panel Window Treatment

A shirred and flipped window treatment (see this book's color section) works well on windows of just about every size because both the rod and the treatment adjust to fit each window. Each panel of a shirred and flipped treatment has a casing and heading. You thread both ends onto a continental rod and gather them across the window. (You can easily create a coordinated look in a bedroom by choosing fabric for this window treatment that matches the duvet cover; see Chapter 17 for more information on creating a duvet cover.)

 One yard each of two companion or coordinating fabrics makes two reversible panels that shirr to about a 24-inch width. For each 24-inch increment in window width, buy another yard each of your companion fabrics.

You need the tools in your Sewing Survival Kit (see Chapter 1), plus the following, to make this window treatment:

- ✔ A continental rod with a 3-inch drop
- ✔ Thread that matches the fabric
- ✔ A yard each of coordinating fabric to make two panels

Follow these steps to shirr and flip to your heart's content:

1. **Cut each yard into two panels measuring half the width of the fabric and 36 inches long.**

   For example, if you start with a yard of 54-inch-wide fabric, the resulting panel is 27 inches wide and 36 inches long.

2. **Pin two cut companion fabric panels, right sides together.**

   This way, the finished panel is reversible, and both fabrics show when the panel is threaded onto the rod.

3. **Set your machine like this:**
   - **Stitch:** Straight
   - **Length:** 3 mm/9 spi
   - **Width:** 0 mm
   - **Foot:** All-purpose

4. **Starting in the center of one long side, sew around the four sides of the panel, using a ½-inch seam allowance.**

Leave a 6-inch opening on one side of the panel so that you can turn it right side out. To prevent the stitches from ripping out, backstitch at both ends of this opening.

5. **Turn the reversible panel right side out by reaching through the opening, grabbing the fabric, and pulling it through the opening.**

6. **Using the blunt end of your scissors, push the corners out to make them crisp and sharp, and then press the seams flat and together around all four edges.**

This step takes a little bit of time, but the results are well worth it.

7. **Edgestitch the opening closed, backstitching at the beginning and the end. (See Chapter 6 for more information on edgestitching.)**

8. **On one of the short ends, run a row of stitching parallel to and 2 to 3 inches from the edge, backstitching at the beginning and end. Repeat for the other short end of the panel.**

9. **Sew another row of stitching 3½ inches below and parallel to the line of stitches you sewed in Step 8, backstitching at both ends. (See Figure 16-15.) Repeat for the other short end of the reversible panel.**

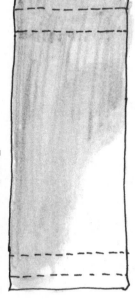

Figure 16-15:
Two rows of stitching create a pocket for the rod to slide through.

10. **Using your seam ripper, carefully remove the stitches at the edge of the panel between the rows of heading and casing stitches that are 3½ inches apart.**

   This is the casing pocket that the rod fits through. Repeat for the other end of the pocket casing.

11. **Put the panel on the rod through both pocket casings, as shown in Figure 16-16.**

   Thread the top of the panel casing onto the rod, and then flip the bottom of the panel up and thread the bottom casing onto the rod. Shirr the first panel to one end of the rod, pushing the end of the casing around the return so it covers the rod.

   Repeat for as many panels as you make to fit across your window.

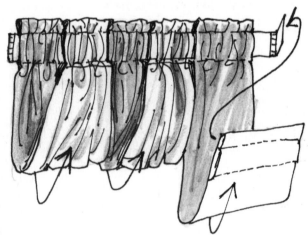

Figure 16-16: Put the panel on the rod through both pocket casings.

Chapter 17

Making Ho-hum Linens Luxurious

*W*ant to make changing your bedroom decor as easy as changing your clothes? If so, you're reading the right chapter. First, discover the easiest-to-work-with fabric by making a fleece throw, perfect for cuddling up in any bedroom. Next, refresh the look of your sleeping chambers by making the easy dust ruffle and duvet cover that I describe in this chapter. Create matching pillow shams from Chapter 15 and terrific window treatments from Chapter 16. Finally, leftovers have never looked so good — your fabric leftovers, that is. Create the focal point of any room by making a knotted neck roll pillow that accents your bedding with fabric leftovers. It's easier than you think.

The biggest challenge with most home decor projects is handling the length, bulk, and weight of the larger pieces of fabric. Clear away some space on the floor, move the stuff off the dining room table, and get sewing!

Creating a Fleece Throw

Polyester fleece is a warm, versatile, easy-to-work-with fabric. Trade names for it include Polartec, Polarfleece, Citifleece, Kinderfleece, and many others. So when you go to a fabric store looking for fleece for this project, ask for a high-quality, double-sided (thicker), napped polyester fleece. This type holds up to a lot of cuddling, is a little more expensive than the thinner fleeces, and is unlikely to get those annoying little fuzz balls.

The no-sew fleece throw you create in this chapter gives you a great introduction to this magical fabric and adds color and warmth to any room.

Working with fleece: The do's and don'ts

Treat it right, and fleece provides you with durable projects that look as good as they feel. But, as great as fleece is for home decor projects and clothing, it does require some special treatment.

Here are a few general do's and don'ts to help you work well with fleece:

- ✔ **Do know the right from wrong side of the fleece:** As fleece wears, the color ages differently on the right and the wrong sides of the fabric. This is no big deal unless you use two different sides for one project. Here's an easy way to figure out which side is which: When stretched on the selvage (the long finished edge of the fabric when it comes off the loom — see Chapter 4), fleece curls to the right side; when stretched across the grain, it curls to the wrong side.

- ✔ **Do mark the wrong side of the fabric by using a dressmaker's pencil or chalk after cutting out your pattern:** Mark the center front with a single hash mark and the center back with a double hash mark. If the front and back pattern pieces look similar to one another, you can tell them apart by the markings. Dressmaker's chalk or pencil marks fleece easily and doesn't smudge.

- ✔ **Do mark notches with a chalk pencil instead of clipping into the seam allowance:** Most fleece projects use ½-inch seam allowances, and if you clip too far into the seam allowance, the snip is hard to fix.

- ✔ **Do wash your finished project by turning it inside out:** Use lukewarm water, the gentle wash cycle, and powdered detergent. Liquid detergents can damage the chemical finish on the lighter-weight fleeces, impairing their moisture-wicking capabilities.

- ✔ **Don't prewash fleece:** Prewashing is not necessary. Fleece is usually made of polyester or a polyester blend that doesn't shrink. You won't damage the fabric if you do preshrink it, you just don't need to.

- ✔ **Don't press the fleece after you sew seams:** Placing a hot iron directly on the fabric crushes the nap and can melt the fibers. You won't be seaming anything in this project, but if somewhere down the road you find yourself with a pesky seam that needs shaping, set the iron for *steam* and hold it 3 to 4 inches above the seamline, letting the steam penetrate the fibers. Finger-press the seam in shape by holding and patting your hand over it until the fabric cools.

The fleece throw

This throw is sure to be a hit for you or someone on your gift list. The version you see in the color section of this book takes color inspiration from the cowboy shirt pillows I show you how to make in Chapter 15. Try this color-scheming trick the next time you're stuck for color ideas: Take an inspiration piece to the fabric store (in this case, the cowboy shirt), and match five colors of fleece to colors in your inspiration piece.

To make this project, you need the following materials in addition to your Sewing Survival Kit (see Chapter 1):

- ✔ 1⅔ yard fleece (54 to 60 inches wide), which makes one square throw or two rectangular throws
- ✔ Four to five contrasting colors of fleece, each ¼ yard, to create the fringe (This makes fringe for one square throw or two rectangular throws.)
- ✔ A new leather hole punch that you tap with a hammer (available in your local craft store)
- ✔ A hammer
- ✔ A flattened corrugated box to help in punching the holes
- ✔ A clean concrete floor, sidewalk, or equally hard surface

Follow these steps to make the fleece throw:

1. **Carefully trim off the selvages from both sides of the fleece square, making sure the edges are straight and have a clean cut (see Chapter 4 for more on cutting fabric).**

   These clean-cut edges are what I refer to from here on out as the *side edges* of the throw.

2. **Carefully cut the top and bottom edges of the throw, making them clean cut and perpendicular to the side edges.**

   My rotary cutter, rotary cutting board, and O'Lipfa ruler really come in handy for cutting fleece edges straight and true (see Chapter 1 for more on these great tools).

3. **Fold the fleece in half so that the fold is parallel with the side edges — the short edges, if you're making a rectangular throw, and whichever sides you choose for a square throw.**

   If you're making two rectangular throws, cut the fleece in half the long way on the fold, being careful that the cut is straight, smooth, and perpendicular to the bottom and top edges.

4. **Unfold the fleece square or rectangle and mark the fringe placement holes, as shown in Figure 17-1.**

   Using your dressmaker's chalk, mark the holes 1 inch from the top and 1 inch from the bottom edges, marking off the fringe placement with dots every inch.

Figure 17-1:
Mark the
holes at
1-inch
intervals.

5. **Using your sharp, new leather hole punch, cut out the fringe holes every inch over the marks made in Step 4.**

   The leather punch I use has several interchangeable tips; I use the tip that makes the biggest hole (about ¼- to ⅜-inch in diameter). To get started with the punches

   • Place the flattened cardboard box on a concrete floor (like the basement floor or an equally hard surface), and lay the fleece on top of the cardboard.

   • Place the punch over the mark you made in Step 4 and, with your hammer, tap the top of the punch firmly until it cuts a clean hole through the fleece (you cut through the corrugated box at the same time).

   • After you punch a few holes, clean out the excess fleece and cardboard from the tip of the punch and continue punching.

6. **Cut 30 strips of fringe ⅜ inch wide and 20 inches long from each of the other four fleece colors, as shown in Figure 17-2.**

7. **Alternating fringe colors, thread a fringe strip through each punched hole and knot the ends as shown in Figure 17-3.**

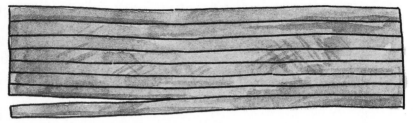

Figure 17-2:
Cut 30
⅜-inch x
20-inch
strips of
fringe.

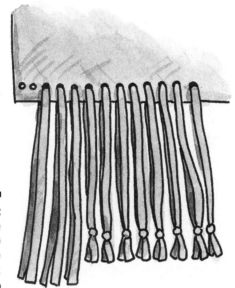

Figure 17-3:
Knot the
fringe to
finish the
throw.

Now curl up with a good book and your colorful new throw.

Trimming Sheets and Towels

Want to get the most bang for your sewing buck? Buy towels and sheets on sale and add your own trim. See the color section for a look at the lace-trimmed sheets I show you how to make in this section. It takes just minutes and about 4 yards of lace to turn the ordinary into *Wow!* You can use a similar technique to coordinate your towels and shower curtain. You can even personalize towels for your family members by using a different trim for each person. It just takes a little know-how.

Decorating sheets

I love to get decorating ideas from mail order catalogs. One of my favorites had a lace-trimmed sheet and pillowcase set that retailed for about $400! I knocked off these linens for a fraction of that price by adding a little lace trim to the hems of sheets I bought at a clearance sale. In this section, I show you how to add lace to your linens.

To make this project, you need the following materials in addition to your Sewing Survival Kit (see Chapter 1):

- ✔ One flat sheet
- ✔ Two pillowcases
- ✔ Four yards of lace for a full or queen sheet and pillowcases; five yards of lace for a king sheet and pillowcases
- ✔ Thread to match the lace

Follow these steps to add new life to your sheets:

1. **Preshrink the sheets and lace the way you plan to care for the sheets (see Chapter 2 for more on preshrinking).**

   I used polyester lace on the cotton/poly blend sheets you see in the color section. Polyester doesn't shrink, but cotton does, so what to do? Preshrink only the sheets.

2. **Cut a length of lace long enough to go around the hem of one pillowcase plus 1 inch for seam allowances. Repeat for the second pillowcase.**

3. **Set your machine like this:**

   - **Stitch:** Straight
   - **Length:** 3 mm/9 spi
   - **Width:** 0 mm
   - **Foot:** All-purpose

4. **Using a ½-inch seam allowance, sew the short ends of the pillowcase lace together. Seam one lace circle for each pillowcase.**

5. **Press the seams open and then turn the lace circles right side out.**

6. **Pin the lace onto each pillowcase, on the right side, so that the straight edge of the trim is just below the ready-made stitching on the pillowcase hem edge, as shown in Figure 17-4.**

7. **Stitch the lace to the pillowcase, sewing it on just below the ready-made stitching at the hem.**

8. **Cut the lace the length needed to span across the hem of the flat sheet plus 1 inch for seam allowance.**

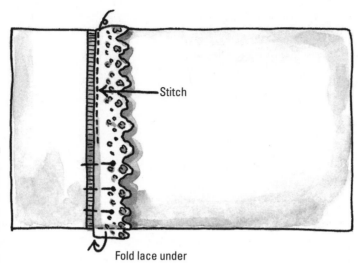

Stitch

Fold lace under

Figure 17-4:
Pin and
stitch the
lace to the
pillowcase
hem edge.

9. **Turn back the two short ends of the lace ½ inch and press.**

10. **On the right side of the sheet, pin the lace so that the straight edge is just below the ready-made stitching on the hem edge and the short ends of the lace are turned under and pinned to the sheet.**

11. **Stitch the lace to the sheet.**

    Stitch up one short edge of the lace (where you turned in and pinned the edge), across the long straight edge and down the other short edge on the other side, backstitching at each end of the lace (see Chapter 6 for more on backstitching).

12. **Press your creation.**

    Show off your new, fancified sheets by making the bed so that the decorated side of the sheet shows as a cuff over the blanket or duvet cover.

Trimming towels

Want to add a custom look to your bathroom? Trim your towels to match your shower curtain. This project is easy, looks great, and costs a fraction of the price you pay for a similar designer towel.

Because only one side of a towel shows when you hang it from a towel rack, you may as well save yourself some trouble and decorate just one side. The instructions in this section show you how to decorate one side of two towels, but you can also decorate both sides of one towel or double the materials and repeat the steps to have two super-fancy, fully decorated towels.

To make this project, you need the following materials in addition to your Sewing Survival Kit:

- ✔ Two bath towels

- ✔ ¼ yard of fabric that's a little more than twice as long as your towel is wide (If you made a shower curtain, use the leftover fabric to trim towels to match.)

- ✔ 2½ yards of ⅝-inch-wide grosgrain ribbon (The kind with ribs — see Chapter 2.)

- ✔ All-purpose thread to match the ribbon

Follow these steps to trim a towel at both ends:

1. **Preshrink the towels, ribbon, and fabric (used for banding the towel) the way you plan to care for the towels (see Chapter 2 for more on preshrinking).**

   Preshrinking makes your towels last longer and wear better, and the decorative bands don't shrink as much when you dry them on the permanent-press setting of your dryer.

2. **Cut a fabric band 3 inches wide and twice as long as your towel is wide, plus 2 inches for seam allowances.**

   For example, if your towel is 24 inches wide, your fabric band should be 50 inches long.

3. **Cut two lengths of the grosgrain ribbon the same length as the fabric band.**

4. **Pin one length of ribbon along the top edge, and one length of ribbon along the bottom edge of the fabric band, overlapping the fabric with the ribbon by ½ inch, as shown in Figure 17-5.**

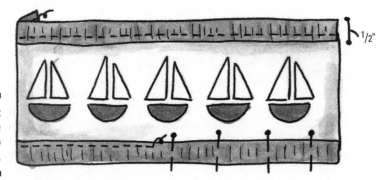

Figure 17-5:
Pin the ribbon to the fabric.

5. **Set your machine like this:**
   - **Stitch:** Straight
   - **Length:** 3 mm/9 spi
   - **Width:** 0 mm
   - **Foot:** All-purpose

6. **Stitch both lengths of ribbon to the fabric band, sewing just inside and right next to the straight edge of the ribbon, as shown in Figure 17-5.**

7. **Press the band smooth and flat.**

8. **Cut the long band in half so that you have two shorter strips the same length.**

9. **Center one fabric band over the woven decorative part of the towel and pin it in place.**

10. **Turn under the short ends of the fabric band ½-inch, making them even with the edges of the towel, and then press and pin them.**

11. **Topstitch the fabric band in place, sewing around all four edges of the band (see Chapter 5 for more on topstitching).**

12. **Repeat Steps 9 through 11 with the other fabric band, placing it on another towel or on the opposite end of the towel you've already decorated.**

Now hang up your newly decorated towels, stand back, and admire your work. Pretty easy, huh?

Making a Dust Ruffle

A bed skirt, often called a dust ruffle, fits between the mattress and box springs and drops to the floor, covering up the unsightly bed frame or side rails.

I like making my own bed skirts, even if I buy a ready-made comforter, because I use better fabric and sew in more gathers to add a really rich look to the bedroom. Like other home decorating projects, the most challenging part is handling the volume of fabric.

When working with a great volume of fabric, hold the fabric taut in front of and behind the presser foot as you sew. Sew a few inches and then reposition your hands, keeping even tautness in front of and behind the foot as you proceed along the length of the seam. Doing so keeps the machine from getting clogged by a backup of fabric.

If you are in quandary about how to coordinate your dust ruffle fabric with the other fabric in your room, see Chapter 13. Also check out "Ten Tips for Mixing Prints" in Chapter 21.

The dust ruffle that I present in this section is three-sided — the headboard side doesn't have a ruffle on it. The ruffle is also designed for a bed without posts or a footboard. You can buy a bed skirt pattern specifically suited for these beds.

Measuring the box springs

In order to make the ruffle the right size to cover the box springs entirely, you need to measure your box springs. Take the mattress off your bed and follow these steps:

1. **Measure the top width, the top length, and the drop.**

   Remember, the _drop_ is the measurement from the top of your box springs to the floor.

2. **Add the following to the measurements you took in Step 1 to account for the seam allowances and hems:**

   - **Top width:** Add 1½ inches
   - **Top length:** Add ½ inch

These measurements help you determine you how much fabric to cut out for the base of the dust ruffle. For more information, see the section "Cutting the fabric and sheet."

Buying your fabric

To make this dust ruffle, you need not only your Sewing Survival Kit (see Chapter 1), but also enough base fabric to cover your box springs and enough ruffle fabric to fall, or _drop,_ the distance from the top of the springs to the floor. One flat sheet does the trick for the base fabric that goes between the mattress and the box springs; select a size as close to the dimensions of your box springs as possible (this sheet doesn't show, so it doesn't matter what color it is).

On the dust ruffle pictured in the color section, I made a base dust ruffle as described in this section, and then I made another dust ruffle that's 2 inches shorter and lays on top of the first for a two-tiered effect. If making two dust ruffles is biting off more than you care to chew, get the same effect by buying an inexpensive dust ruffle and making a second, shorter ruffle out of your duvet fabric or a coordinating fabric.

You make the ruffle itself by sewing strips of fabric together. The number of strips you need (and consequently, the amount of fabric) depends on the size of your bed and the width of your fabric. A normal drop (the distance the dust ruffle measures from the top of the box springs to the floor) is 16 inches, so 20-inch strips are long enough for nice 2-inch double hems. Consult Table 17-1 to determine the correct yardage.

You can use the instructions I give you for any size ruffle. Just adjust like this:

- ✔ For a shorter dust ruffle that layers over a longer ruffle, cut 18-inch ruffle strips rather than 20-inch ruffle strips.

- ✔ For a longer dust ruffle on taller beds, cut longer ruffle strips. If you have a very high bed, where the drop is longer than 16 inches, subtract 16 inches from your drop measurement and then multiply that number by the number of strips you need (see Table 17-1) and divide by 36 to determine how much extra fabric to buy.

  So if your drop is 24 inches, it measures 8 inches longer than the normal drop. Multiply eight by seven (the number of 6-inch strips needed for a queen-sized ruffle), and you get 56. Divide 56 by 36, and you get 1.5. You need 1.5 extra yards fabric for your ruffle.

I recommend that you stick to polyester-cotton blends (for easy care) in solid colors (tasks get more complicated when you have to match patterns). Also pick up thread that matches the fabric, masking tape, and pearl cotton.

Table 17-1	Yardage for Bed Skirt		
Bed Size	**Fabric Width**	**Yardage**	**Number of 20-Inch Strips to Cut**
Twin	45-inch	4½	8
	54-inch	4	6
	60-inch	4	7
Double	45-inch	5⅛	9
	54-inch	4½	8
	60-inch	4½	8
Queen	45-inch	5⅛	9
	54-inch	4½	8
	60-inch	4	7
King	45-inch	5⅝	10
	54-inch	4½	8
	60-inch	4½	8

Cutting the fabric

Have the measurements you took in the previous section handy as you follow these steps:

1. **With the hem edge of the sheet at the top (the head end of your mattress), cut the flat sheet the width and length that you calculated in Step 2 of the previous section.**

   This piece is your *base fabric* — the part of the dust ruffle that fits between the box spring and the mattress.

2. **Cut the appropriate number of fabric strips for your bed's size (see Table 17-1).**

   The strips should be 20 inches long by the width of the fabric; cut the strips across the width of the fabric, perpendicular to the selvage, as shown in Figure 17-6.

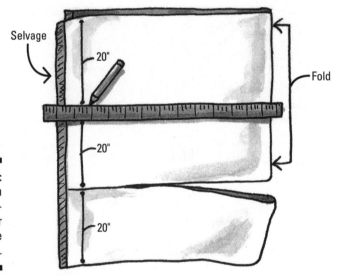

Selvage

20"

Fold

20"

20"

Figure 17-6: Cut 20-inch strips perpendicular to the selvage.

Sewing the ruffle strips together

As you follow these steps, you create a very long strip of fabric. As the long strip takes shape, fold it up and let it rest in your lap for easy handling:

1. **Finish and hem one short side of one of the fabric strips with a ¾-inch hem (see Chapter 6 for more information on finishing seams and Chapter 7 for details on hems). Repeat for a second fabric strip.**

The hemmed edges of these two strips are the head ends of the bed skirt.

2. **Set your machine like this:**

   - **Stitch:** Straight

   - **Length:** 3 mm/9 spi

   - **Width:** 0 mm

   - **Foot:** All-purpose

3. **Place the short raw edge of the hemmed strip to the short raw edge of one of the unhemmed strips, with the right sides joined, and pin the edges together.**

4. **Sew a ½-inch seam, backstitching at both ends, and then press your seam open.**

   See Chapters 5 and 6 for more on backstitching.

5. **Place, pin, and stitch another unhemmed strip to the longer strip, sewing the short raw edges, right sides together, as shown in Figure 17-7.**

   Continue adding shorter strips to the longer one so that the last strip added is the other hemmed strip.

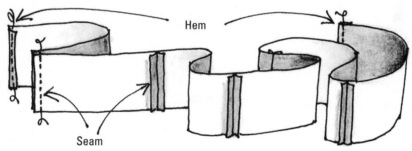

Figure 17-7: Seam the strips together to make the ruffle.

Hem

Seam

Double hemming the ruffle strip

Home decorating projects are made with double hems. This gives the fabric extra weight at the hem edges and a professional, finished look.

Before you double hem your dust ruffle, try it on the bed for size. Pin up the raw edge 4 inches to simulate a 2-inch double hem. Hold the test double hem even with the top edge of the box springs, letting the ruffle drop down to the floor. If the length isn't right, lengthen or shorten your hem allowance as needed so that the ruffle raw edge touches the floor, and then hem the ruffle according to the following steps.

Because the hem is turned up twice, you don't need to finish the edge before hemming. Just follow these steps:

1. **Place the fabric on the ironing board, wrong side up, so that the hem edge is on the board the long way.**

2. **Press up half the width of the finished hem width determined earlier the length of the long strip.**

3. **Turn up, press, and pin up the hem again so that the hem is doubled.**

   Your finished hem width should be approximately 2 inches (for more on double hemming, see Chapter 16).

4. **Set your machine like this:**

   - **Stitch:** Straight
   - **Length:** 3 mm/9 spi
   - **Width:** 0 mm
   - **Foot:** All-purpose

5. **Sewing with the right side of the ruffle strip up, topstitch your hem, guiding an even distance from the hem edge.**

   For a 2-inch hem, guide approximately 1¾-inch from the folded hem edge. For more on hemming, see Chapter 7.

   Stick a strip of masking tape across the bed of the machine so that the left edge of the tape is the finished hem width to the right of the needle and parallel to the lines marked in the needle plate. Use the edge of the tape as your stitching guide.

6. **Iron over the hem to smooth out the stitching.**

Speed gathering the ruffle strip

As you follow these steps, you see the dust ruffle coming together in front of your eyes:

1. **Find a ball or skein of pearl cotton (a twisted embroidery floss available through your local fabric or craft store) or any fine string.**

   You use the pearl cotton or fine string as a cord to help you evenly gather the fabric. This cord must be long enough to fit the length of the ruffle strip. To prevent it from tangling, leave the cord in the ball, skein, or package until you're ready to use it.

2. **Set your machine like this:**

- **Stitch:** Zigzag
- **Length:** 2.5 to 3 mm/9 to 13 spi
- **Width:** 3 to 4 mm
- **Foot:** Embroidery

3. **Place the dust ruffle fabric under the needle, ½ inch from the raw edge and with the *wrong side of the fabric up.* Leaving the foot up, pierce the fabric with the needle.**

   The long strip is in your lap and on the floor.

4. **Center the end of the cord under the foot and on top of the fabric.**

   Anchor the beginning end of the cord by putting a pin 2½-inch from, and perpendicular to, the long raw edge. Wrap the cord around the pin in figure-eight style.

   This way, the cord doesn't slide out of the stitching as you sew. It doesn't matter which side of the needle the cord is on.

5. **Zigzag over the cord the length of the ruffle strip, guiding the stitching and cord ½-inch from the raw edge.**

   Leave a 3- to 4-inch cord tail at both ends of the ruffle strip.

   The stitches create a channel for the cord to slide through — gathers are easily adjusted, and the cord doesn't break as you work with the fabric.

6. **Mark the edge of the ruffle and the edge of the base fabric into eight equal sections.**

   - Fold the ruffle strip in half so that the short edges line up, and then in half again, and in half again until you have folded the ruffle strip into eighths. At the edge where the gathering stitches are, press a short crease at the folds, pressing from the gathering stitches to the raw edge. These are your eight match points.

   - Using your tape measure and fabric marker, measure around the three sides of the base fabric and divide that measurement into eighths. Using a fabric marker or pencil, mark the base fabric into eighths along the three raw edges, as shown in Figure 17-8.

7. **Pin the ruffle to the base fabric, right sides together, matching the marks around the three sides of the base fabric.**

8. **Pull up and adjust the gathers.**

   Starting at the head end of the bed skirt, pull on the gathering cord, adjusting the ruffled fullness to fit from the end to the first pin. Continue this way, spacing the gathers evenly from pin to pin, until you gather the ruffle to fit the base fabric.

   When you finish pulling up the gathers, the gathered strip fits the flat base fabric, and the gathers are even.

9. **Before sewing, pin the ruffle to the base fabric, pinning every 4 to 5 inches.**

This way, your ruffle is pinned securely and is easier to work with.

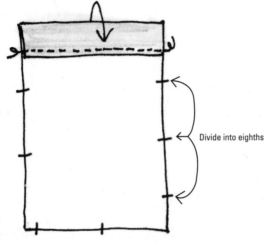

Figure 17-8:
Divide the base fabric into eighths for easy ruffle placement.

Divide into eighths

Attaching the ruffle to the base fabric

Follow these steps to complete the dust ruffle:

1. **Set your machine like this:**

   - **Stitch:** Straight
   - **Length:** 3.5 to 4 mm/6 to 8 spi
   - **Width:** 0 mm
   - **Foot:** All-purpose

2. **With the ruffle side up, sew the ruffle to the base fabric using a ⅝-inch seam allowance, and backstitch at the beginning and ends of the seam as shown in Figure 17-9.**

   Clip off and discard the excess cord ends.

   Your gathering stitches are ½ inch from the raw edge. When sewing the seam, you find that the ⅝-inch seamline is just to the left of the gathering stitches. For more on gathering, check out Chapter 8.

TIP

Hold the fabric taut in front of and behind the presser foot as you sew. Sew a few inches, removing pins before sewing over them. Reposition your hands, keeping even tautness in front of and behind the foot and along the length of the seam — doing so keeps the seam smooth and pucker-free.

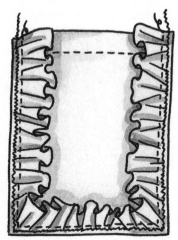

Figure 17-9:
Sew the ruffle to the base fabric.

Creating a Custom Duvet Cover

A duvet is a fluffy comforter that you slip into a duvet cover. You make the duvet cover in this section out of bed sheets, so your duvet is as easy to care for as the sheets on your bed.

Because duvet covers are much cheaper than the duvet itself, you can afford to have several color-coordinated covers — a wardrobe of room accessories to match your moods or the changing seasons.

Before you start, measure the length and width of the duvet or comforter you intend to cover. You need this measurement to buy sheets in the right size.

To make a duvet cover, you need the following materials, in addition to your Sewing Survival Kit:

- ✔ Flat sheets slightly larger than the length and width of your duvet

    Duvets and flat sheets vary in size by manufacturer, so double-check that the sheets you buy are large enough to cover your duvet.

- ✔ Thread that matches the sheets
- ✔ One standard-weight zipper in a length that measures half the width of the finished duvet cover

Follow these steps to make your duvet cover:

1. **Lay one sheet on the table or floor, wrong side up. Center your duvet on the sheet so that the edges of the duvet are inside the hemmed edges of the sheet, as shown in Figure 17-10.**

Figure 17-10:
Center your duvet on the wrong side of the sheet and prepare to cut.

Duvet   Wrong side
                         of sheet

If you need a little more length, rip out the hems at the top and bottom of each sheet and then press the hems flat.

2. **Cut out the sheet, making it ½-inch bigger than the duvet on each side.**

   Cut off the excess fabric from the bottom, sides, and top. This piece is the duvet top.

3. **Using the first cut sheet as a pattern, cut the second sheet the same size as the first sheet.**

   This piece is the duvet back.

4. **Insert the zipper on one short end of the duvet cover, using a centered zipper application (read more about zipper application in Chapter 9).**

   After you stitch in the zipper, remove the basting stitches (check out Chapter 5 for more on basting) and unzip it. (You need the zipper unzipped to turn the duvet cover right side out.)

5. **With the right sides of the fabric together, pin the top, bottom, and sides together, starting at one end of the zipper and ending at the other.**

6. **Set your machine like this:**

   - **Stitch:** Straight

   - **Length:** 3 to 3.5 mm/8 to 9 spi

   - **Width:** 0 mm

   - **Foot:** All-purpose

7. **Sew the duvet cover together, using a ½-inch allowance and back-stitching at each end of the zipper as shown in Figure 17-11.**

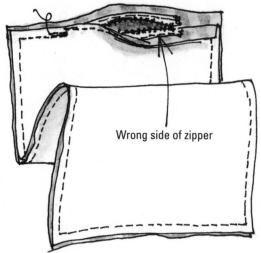

Figure 17-11:
Sew the top, bottom and sides together, starting at one end of the zipper and ending at the other.

Wrong side of zipper

8. **Turn the duvet cover right side out through the zipper opening and then slide in your duvet.**

If you struggle to get the duvet into the cover, try this: Place the duvet cover wrong-side-out on the floor, and then place the duvet on top. Wrap rubber bands around the cover and the comforter at each corner (like you would wrap a ponytail — see Figure 17-12). Wrap the corners very tightly. Now, turn the duvet cover right side out through the zipper opening. The rubber bands keep the corners of the comforter and the corners of the cover together, and prevent the duvet from moving around and bunching up inside the cover.

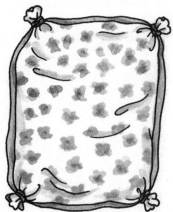

Figure 17-12:
Rubber band the corners of your duvet to the cover before turning the cover right side out.

Now that you have made your duvet cover, put it on your bed, stand back, and admire your work for a moment, and then hop in for a nap.

Making a Bow-Tie Neck Roll

After you revamp your bedroom, you may have some fabric left over. Make use of every last bit by making a clever knotted neck roll. My sewing friends Naomi Baker and Tammy Young dreamed up this project. Bow-tie neck rolls are super easy to make and a real focal point on any bed. I use a striped fabric on one side because the stripes visually accentuate the knot in the pillow. You can check it out in the color section.

To make this project, you need the following materials in addition to your Sewing Survival Kit:

- ✔ Two pieces of fabric measuring 14 inches x 46 inches
- ✔ One small bag of polyester fiberfill (available at your local fabric store)
- ✔ Thread to match the fabric

Follow these steps to create your neck roll:

1. **Place and pin your two fabrics right sides together.**

2. **Using a ½-inch seam allowance, sew around all four sides, leaving an 8-inch opening on one long side to turn the pillow through (for more on making pillows, see Chapter 15).**

3. **Press seams flat and together and then press them open over a seam roll.**

4. **Turn the pillow cover right side out and loosely stuff it with fiberfill.**

5. **Hand slipstitch or machine edgestitch the opening closed so that the stuffing stays put (see Chapter 5 for more on slipstitching and Chapter 6 for info on edgestitching).**

6. **Shake the fiber fill around and tie a loose knot in the center of the pillow.**

   Put your new pillow in a place of honor.

Chapter 18

Give Your Furnishings a Face-lift with Slipcovers

Slipcovers aren't just for hiding that ratty hand-me-down sofa anymore. In fact, slipcovers are the latest decorating craze — even for covering new furniture. They refresh a tired room, protect upholstered furniture, and you can wash and easily change them for the season. You can slipcover chairs, sofas, and folding chairs or decorate your kitchen or dining room chair backs for special occasions. Look in the color section to see what slipcovers do to spruce up any room and then try it yourself. The step-by-step instructions in this chapter keep you on track.

Creating a Double-duty Hamper Liner

Okay, okay — *technically* a hamper liner isn't a slipcover. Still, I call it a *reverse* slipcover because it goes inside rather than over the top of something. This liner is also removable, and you can use it as a laundry bag.

To make this hamper liner, you need the following materials in addition to your Sewing Survival Kit (which I tell you about in Chapter 1):

✔ A laundry hamper

✔ Washable cotton fabric that measures the perimeter plus 1-inch-x-1½-times the height of the hamper

  ✔ 2½ yards of ⅝-inch ribbon that coordinates with hamper fabric

  ✔ Thread to match the fabric

  ✔ A large safety pin

Follow these instructions to make your hamper liner:

1. **Fold the fabric in half with the right sides together so the fold is on the lengthwise dimension of the hamper and on the lengthwise grain of the fabric.**

   See Chapter 4 and Figure 18-1 for more on grainlines.

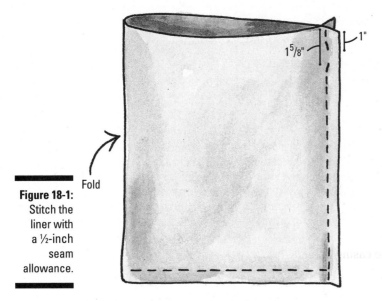

1⁵⁄₈" 1"

Figure 18-1:
Stitch the
liner with
a ½-inch
seam
allowance.

Fold

2. **On the seamline, measure and mark 1 inch from the top of the opening; measure and mark 1⅝ inch from the top of the opening on the seamline.**

   These marks indicate the opening where you thread the ribbon drawstring at the top of the liner.

3. **Set your machine like this:**

   • **Stitch:** Straight

   • **Length:** 3 mm/9 spi

   • **Width:** 0 mm

   • **Foot:** All-purpose

4. **Using a ½-inch seam allowance, sew the hamper liner.**

Stitch across the bottom and up the side, backstitching at the beginning and ends of the seam and below and above the marks made in Step 2 (see Figure 18-1).

5. **Press the seams flat and together and then press them open.**

6. **Make a double-hem casing (see Chapter 16 for more on doubled hems).**

   At the opening of the liner, press a ½-inch hem; turn the hem over another ½ inch and press.

7. **Stitch around the casing, sewing close to the folded edge as shown in Figure 18-2.**

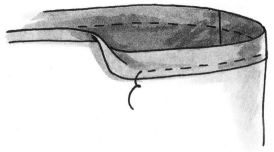

Figure 18-2:
Sew the casing close to the folded edge.

8. **Thread the ribbon through the casing as shown in Figure 18-3.**

   Attach a safety pin to one end of the ribbon. Use the safety pin to thread the ribbon through the opening of the casing at the upper edge of the liner. Pull the lead end through and extend both ends of the ribbon evenly from the casing opening.

9. **Cut each end of the ribbon diagonally and make a knot on each end as shown in Figure 18-3.**

Figure 18-3:
Use a safety pin to guide the ribbon through the casing.

10. **Turn the liner inside out and put it in the hamper so that the top cuffs over the top of the basket.**

I use a red-and-white check fabric that coordinates with the shower curtain so that the cuff peaking over the top of the hamper adds another touch of color to the bathroom.

Covering a Chair Back with a Bow-Back Cover

Almost as many types of chairs inhabit the world as do people. So for this project you use an old sheet to make a basic pattern that fits the chair population in your home. Now you have a custom pattern when you're ready to make covers from other fabrics.

Check out the color section in this book to see how this bow-back cover (I call it that because a bow strip and knot are stitched to the cover for interesting chair back detail.) livens up a simple cane-back chair. These covers are so fast and easy to make, you can have a set for every day, another for seasonal meals, and even another for special occasions.

Making your pattern

To make this pattern, you need the following materials in addition to your Sewing Survival Kit:

- A chair you want to cover
- An old sheet you don't mind cutting up
- Thread to match the fabric
- Pencil

Follow these steps to make a pattern that's just right for your chairs:

1. **Cut two rectangles, each 24 inches wide x 20 inches long.**

2. **Pin the rectangles together at the top and sides, about ½ inch from the cut edge.**

3. **With the pins on the outside, place this cover over the back of the chair to check the fit.**

   This is called *pin-fitting*.

4. **Adjust the pins so that the cover fits smoothly over the back of the chair.**

5. **Remove the cover and, if necessary, trim away the excess fabric so that you end up with a ½-inch seam allowance at the pinned edges and a 1-inch hem allowance at the open end.**

If you want to check the fit of your sheet pattern before cutting into your decorator fabric, baste the chair back pattern pieces together. Press the seams open, turn the cover right side out, and try it on your chair back. If an adjustment needs to be made, remove the cover from the chair, turn it wrong side out, put it over the chair back again, and mark the adjustments with pins or your pencil. Rebaste and then try it on the chair until it fits the way you want it to.

After you adjust the fit, use your pencil and write "Chair Back Cover – Cut 2" on your custom pattern. This means that you cut two chair back pieces to make one chair back cover. Also write "½-inch seam allowance" and "1-inch hem allowance." This reminds you to use a ½-inch seam allowances around the three sides of the cover and a 1-inch hem allowance at the opening when you make another set of chair covers.

6. **To make the bow band pattern piece, cut a strip of sheeting 4 to 5 inches wide and the width of the cover plus ½ inch.**

The extra ½ inch is for slack so that when the bow is cinched in, it doesn't pull awkwardly when you place it on the chair back.

Label this pattern piece "Bow Band – Cut 2" (meaning that you cut two bow band pieces to create one bow per chair cover).

7. **To make the bow knot pattern piece, cut a strip of sheeting 3 inches wide by 7 inches long and label it "Bow Knot – Cut 1" (meaning that you cut one bow knot strip to create one bow per chair cover).**

Making your chair back cover

After you make the first one, you can put together these simple chair covers in under an hour each. You need the following materials in addition to your Sewing Survival Kit:

- ✔ Fabric to make covers for each of your chairs (2½ to 3 yards of 60-inch-wide fabric to make four average-sized covers with bows)
- ✔ Thread to match the fabric
- ✔ Your custom chair back pattern (made in the previous section)

Follow these steps to create your own chair back covers:

1. **Using the pattern you created in the previous section, lay out and cut your chair back cover pieces, cutting two backs, two bow band pieces, and one bow knot piece per cover.**

2. **Set your machine like this:**
   - **Stitch:** Straight
   - **Length:** 3 mm/9 spi
   - **Width:** 0 mm
   - **Foot:** All-purpose

3. **With the right sides joined, pin and stitch the bow band pieces together and sew along the long edges as shown in Figure 18-4.**

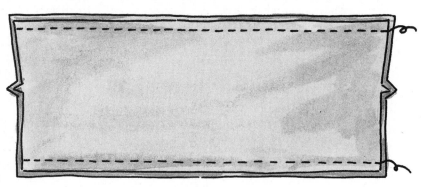

Figure 18-4:
Stitch the long edges of the bow band pieces together.

4. **Turn the bow band right side out and press it.**

5. **Set your machine like this:**
   - **Stitch:** Straight
   - **Length:** 4 mm/6 to 8 spi
   - **Width:** 0 mm
   - **Foot:** All-purpose

6. **Sew a row of gathering stitches down the center of the band, leaving thread ends loose, as shown in Figure 18-5 (see Chapter 8 for more on gathering).**

7. **Reset your stitch length to 3mm/9 spi.**

8. **Pull up the stitches for a soft gather (see Chapter 8 for more on gathering).**

9. **To make the bow knot ring, fold the small fabric strip in half the long way and sew a ½-inch seam as shown in Figure 18-5.**

10. **Press the seam open and then turn the fabric strip right side out and press it so the seam is centered down the length of the strip.**

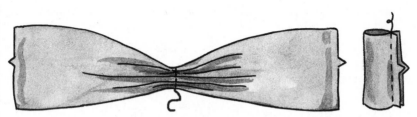

Figure 18-5:
Sew gathering stitches in the center and ½-inch seams at the ends.

11. **Place the fabric strip, right sides together around the bow band, so that it covers up the gathering stitches made in Step 6.**

    Cinch in the fabric strip, creating the bow knot ring. Adjust the size until you like the look it creates over the bow band, and then pin it so that the pin is parallel with the short sides. This is where you sew the seam on the bow knot ring.

12. **Slide the bow knot ring off the bow band and stitch it together, creating a ring.**

    Trim the seam allowance to ½ inch and press the seam open. Turn the bow knot ring right side out so that the seamline is on the inside of the ring.

13. **Slip the bow knot ring over the bow band again, centering the ring over the gathering stitches made in Step 6.**

14. **Pin the bow band on one of the chair cover pieces so that the bottom of the bow band is 1½ inches from the opening at the bottom of the cover as shown in Figure 18-6.**

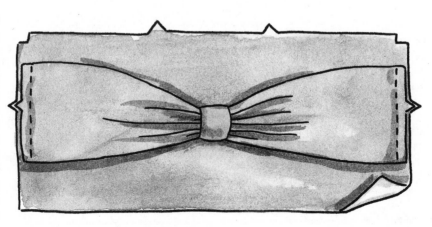

Figure 18-6:
Pin the bow band on one of the chair cover pieces so the bottom is 1½ inches from the opening at the bottom of the cover.

15. **With the right sides together, stitch the chair back cover pieces together up one side, across the top and down the other side, using a ½-inch seam allowance, as shown in Figure 18-7. Press the seams open.**

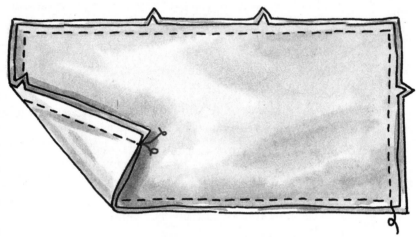

Figure 18-7:
Stitch the chair back cover together using a ½-inch seam allowance.

If your chair cover is for a square-backed chair, fold each corner so that the seam is centered in the point. From the point, measure in ½ inch, as shown in Figure 18-8. Sew across each corner. Squaring up the corners allows the cover to sit straight across the top of the chair back.

16. **Trim out the excess fabric from the corner by trimming the seam made in Step 16 to ¼ inch.**

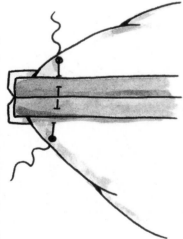

Figure 18-8:
Fold each corner so that the seam is centered in the point, and then measure in ½ inch and sew across each corner.

17. **Hem the open end of the chair cover.**

    • Fold up the hem ½ inch and press.

    • Fold the hem up another ½ inch; pin and press.

    • From the wrong side, topstitch around the hem, sewing a presser foot width from the top of the hem fold where the edge of the foot lines up with the hem fold (see Chapter 5 for more on topstitching).

18. **From the wrong side of the cover, topstitch around the hem, lining up the edge of the foot with the edge of the hem fold (see Chapter 5 for more on topstitching hems).**

19. **Turn the cover right side out and press. See Figure 18-9 for a glimpse of the finished product.**

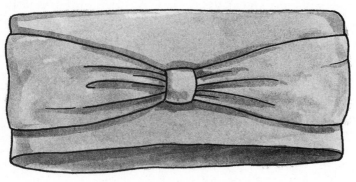

Figure 18-9:
Your chair cover turned right side out.

Dressing Up Any Old Chair with a Fit-to-be-tied Cover

Slipcover options abound in the world of chair fashion, but one of my favorite ways to dress up an old upholstered chair is with an easy-to-make throw cover. These slipcovers are made by using large pieces of fabric, called *throws,* that you seam together. You pleat, tuck, and pin the fabric in place so that it fits your chair perfectly.

I know what you're thinking — you're picturing a whole new room! You want to slipcover everything in sight! Slow down and do yourself a favor: Slipcover a chair before tackling the sofa and love seat. Before digging into these bigger projects, you need the skill and confidence you get from finishing a small project (and one that uses less fabric, should you determine slipcovering isn't your bag of chips).

Considering fabric

Because of the way throw-type slipcovers are designed, you can't make them with just any old fabric. Trust me when I tell you that fabric sporting an uneven stripe or plaid or a jungle scene with herding giraffes is *not* your best fabric option — for many reasons, most of which is the trouble you have in matching the pattern.

Keep the following tips in mind when selecting your fabric for a throw-type slipcover:

- ✔ **Stay away from obvious stripes and plaids.** These fabrics are too hard to match. All-over, medium-scale (4- to 5-inch repeat — see "Making the throw," later in this chapter, for more on pattern repeats), tightly woven prints, or solids are better choices. This way, when you shape the throw to fit the furniture, the tucking, pleating, and pinning almost disappear.

- ✔ **Choose a print that has an all-over, nondirectional design.** If you choose a print with tulips all printed in the same direction, they may line up across the sofa horizontally. A better choice is a print where the flowers float in several directions. When you turn this type of fabric, it looks as good in one direction as it does in another.

- ✔ **Use sheets or home decor fabrics 60 to 72 inches wide.** Sheets and these wider fabrics require two fabric panels and often only one seam to cover either a chair or sofa. Home decor fabrics also have color bars screened on the selvages as match points (see Chapter 13 for more on matching a design using home decor fabric).

   If you use sheets, remove the top and bottom hems for more length. Remove the hem creases by pressing with a damp press cloth that you spritz with a half-and-half mixture of water and white vinegar.

- ✔ **Buy enough fabric.** Nothing is worse than running short in the middle of a project, so double-check your measurements by using the guidelines in Table 18-1.

   If you don't see your furniture size in Table 18-1, check out the upcoming section, "Making and securing the throw," to figure out how much fabric you need.

- ✔ **Cover the furniture with quilt batting first.** Without batting, the throw tends to shift when the furniture is in use. Batting clings to the throw fabric and sort of sucks it into the upholstery.

   Batting is available by the yard or in packages at your local fabric or quilting store for standard mattress sizes. After you know the furniture dimensions, find the batting size that best fits the dimensions you need.

Don't measure your furniture until after you put the batting on. (See the upcoming section, "Batting the furniture.") Batting doesn't take up much space, but it can be enough to throw off your measurements in a big way.

Table 18-1	**Finding Proper Measurements for Your Fabrics**		
Type of Fabric	**Easy Chair (One Cushion)**	**Love Seat (Two Cushions)**	**Mid-Sized Sofa (Three Cushions, 80 Inches Wide x 30 Inches High)**
Fabrics	7 yards of 60-inch-wide fabric	9 yards of 60-inch-wide fabric	12 yards of 60-inch-wide fabric
Flat sheets	1 king-sized sheet for the throw, 1 twin-sized sheet for the cushion	2 double-sized sheets for the throw, 1 twin-sized sheet for the cushion	2 double-sized sheets for for the throw, 1 double-sized sheet for the cushion

Batting the furniture

Batting your furniture helps in lots of ways, especially when you want your throw to stick to the furniture. Without batting, your throw can shift and become uneven, and besides, extra batting makes any seat more comfortable!

You need the following materials in addition to your Sewing Survival Kit:

- ✔ Iron and ironing board
- ✔ Slipcover fabric (see the section "Making the throw" later in this chapter)
- ✔ Batting (see the previous section, "Considering fabric")
- ✔ 25-foot, flexible measuring tape
- ✔ One box of large safety pins
- ✔ One large package of twist pins (the pins with large, flat heads and a curlicue point) available at your local fabric store
- ✔ One large package of size 100 T-pins (pins that have a T-shaped head) available at your local fabric store
- ✔ One large roll of 3-inch-wide packing tape (like what movers use to tape moving boxes; if the tape is in a dispenser, all the better) available at an office supply store
- ✔ Thread to match the fabric
- ✔ Pencil and paper to record measurements

If you start slipping and can't stop . . .

Other slipcovers are shaped to the contours of the furniture with seams that may or may not be piped. This custom-type slipcover is secured to the furniture by zipping it on. Custom slipcovers are more complicated to make than the throw-type because you need a custom-made pattern that fits each section of the furniture. After you're comfortable with sewing, you may want to investigate the custom pattern instructions available in the pattern catalogs at your local fabric store.

Many of these patterns do not have tissue pattern pieces like a traditional pattern. Instead, they have comprehensive instructions that walk you step-by-step through the slipcovering process for a truly custom fit.

Follow these instructions to bat your furniture:

1. **Remove the cushions from the furniture and set them aside.**

2. **Unroll your batting about two inches and place it on the floor on one side of your chair or sofa.**

   The long edge of the batting should be even with the front edge of your furniture.

3. **Leaving two inches on the floor, start unrolling the batting so it goes up, over, and down the arm and then over the seat.**

   Fit the batting snugly into the crevices and smoothly over the surfaces of the furniture.

4. **Continue unrolling the batting so that it goes up, over, and down the other arm as before and then back to the floor.**

5. **Cut off the batting, leaving two inches to tuck, pin, and tape under the furniture.**

6. **Pin the batting to the furniture.**

   Use twist pins to secure the batting in the crevices at the back and arms.

   Use T-pins and tape to pin and tape the batting to the underside of the furniture.

   Use safety pins to pin the batting to the high-wear areas as shown in Figure 18-10. (You don't want the other types of pins poking into anyone sitting on the furniture.)

7. **Repeat this batting technique over the rest of the furniture, butting one edge of the batting to the next.**

The furniture is batted, so take a breather.

Figure 18-10:
Pin the
batting to
the furniture.

Making and securing the throw

In this session you actually make the throw. You also find out about a mysterious thing called a fabric repeat. After you measure, cut, and stitch the panels
together into a throw, you're ready to attach the throw to your furniture.

Don't cut the fabric until you read Steps 1 through 4. You've invested your time
and money in fabric and other materials, and you don't want to trudge back
to the fabric store to buy more fabric so you can fix an unfortunate mistake.

Making the throw

Before making the throw, you need to know how big to make it. Here's how to
measure the furniture and calculate the dimensions for your throw.

Inaccurate measurements doom your project to failure. Get off on the right foot
with precise length and width measurements. Pushing the tape measure firmly
into the crevices around the seat ensures that you get accurate measurements.

1. **Figure out how many fabric panels you need.**

   • Measure the furniture from front to back. Start the tape at the
     floor; go up across the seat and then up, over, and down the back
     of the piece and to the floor. Add 6 inches so you later have room
     to secure the throw to the underside of the furniture. Record this
     measurement.

   • Divide the front-to-back measurement by the width of your fabric.
     Doing so tells you how many fabric widths or *panels* you need.
     Assume that the furniture measurement is 120 inches and your
     fabric is 60 inches wide. 120 divided by 60 equals 2, so you need
     2 panels of fabric. Record the number of panels you need.

2. **Find the pattern repeat in the fabric.**

   - Take a look at your fabric and find a dominant design — maybe you see an orange mum. Now look down the lengthwise grain of the fabric (see Chapter 4 to read more about grainlines) until you see the next identical orange mum. This is where the print *repeats*.

   - Measure the repeat starting at the top of the first mum to the top of the next mum. Say that it measures 10 inches. This fabric, therefore, has a 10-inch repeat.

The smaller the repeat, the easier the fabric is to match, and the more forgiving it is on your furniture — not that you need to be forgiven for putting orange mums on your sofa, but the smaller repeat easily camouflages furniture flaws. When you start tucking and pleating the throw in place, the tucks almost disappear.

3. **Calculate the yardage you need by measuring from one end of the chair, sofa, or love seat to the other.**

   - Starting on the floor at one end, measure up and over the arm, back down and across the seat and then back up and over the arm to the floor at the other end. Add 6 inches so that you can later secure the throw to the underside of the furniture. Record this measurement.

   - Add the repeat measurement (see Step 2 for pattern repeat information) and multiply the total inches by the number of panels needed.

   - Divide by 36 to find the yardage you need for your project.

     For example, if your sofa measures 240 inches, you add 6 inches, getting 246, and then add the number of inches over which your pattern repeats (say, 12) to get 258. If you need 2 panels, multiply 258 by 2 to get 516. Divide this by 36 to get the yardage: 14.3. Round up to 14.5 yards.

4. **Plan the print and seam placement.**

   The seam should be as invisible as possible, so decide where you want the dominant part of the print to be by draping your fabric on the batted furniture. Maybe those orange mums look great centered on the back of the chair.

   If the seam runs vertically over the furniture, it looks better if you don't put it smack dab in the middle, so cut one panel in half and then seam the half-panels to either side of the full-width panel as shown in Figure 18-11 (see the next section, "Securing the throw," for more on seaming fabric panels).

5. **Place and pin the fabric panels, right sides together, matching the color bars; if you're using sheets, match the designs in the fabric.**

   The selvages on printed home decor fabric are about ½ to ¾ inch wide before the print starts. To prevent the white part of the fabric from showing at the seamline, seam the fabric panels together just inside the print.

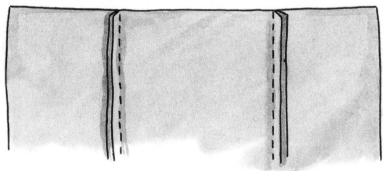

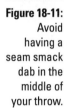

Figure 18-11:
Avoid
having a
seam smack
dab in the
middle of
your throw.

6. **Set your machine like this:**

   • **Stitch:** Straight

   • **Length:** 3 mm/9 spi

   • **Width:** 0

   • **Foot:** All-purpose

7. **Sew the fabric panels together, backstitching at the beginning and end of each seam.**

Securing the throw

Are you excited yet? You should be . . . you're just about to secure your throw to your furniture.

1. **Try the throw on the batted furniture, adjusting the seam placement to an inconspicuous area (see Step 4 in the "Making the throw" section earlier).**

   Study the seamlines on the throws pictured in Figure 18-12. The most invisible places for seamlines are across the arm (at the back where the cushion sits), from end to end across the back, or at either end of the furniture.

2. **Push the throw into the crevices at the back of the seat and at the back and base of the arms, and then pin the throw to the furniture using twist pins.**

   A twist pin has a curlicue point, so when pinning the throw into the furniture, twist the pin as if you were tightening down a screw.

3. **Lay the furniture on its back.**

4. **Pleat the fabric fullness over the arms to shape the throw. Pull the pleats taut over one arm and then pin and tape the fabric under the bottom of the furniture at the base of the arm at one end.**

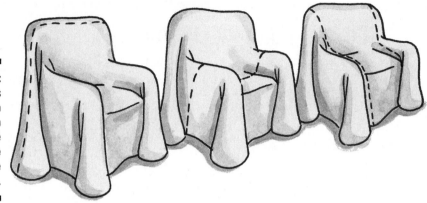

Repeat with the other arm and across the front of the furniture, securing the throw under the bottom of the furniture at the other end (see Figure 18-13).

When covering a sofa, keep the furniture flipped to the front and then fit and secure the throw to the ends, keeping it in the same position.

5. **Flip the furniture over to its front.**

6. **Pull the back of the throw tautly across and over the back of the furniture, pinning and taping it under the bottom.**

After the throw has been secured, stand your furniture piece right side up and place it in the room. What do you think? All you have left is covering the cushions, and then you're done. The following section shows you the easiest way to do this — it's as easy as wrapping a gift.

Figure 18-13:
Pleat, pull,
pin, and
tape the
throw to
the bottom
of your
furniture.

Covering furniture without falling apart

Slipcovering is a big job with lots of fabric to move around on large objects. To make it more manageable, I like to break it down into three steps, or three sessions. Do each step, and then take a breather. The fourth step is optional.

1. **"Batt" the furniture.**

2. **Make and attach the throw.**

3. **Gift-wrap the cushions.**

4. **Put on the skirt (optional).**

Of course, you may also want to enlist the help of a decorating buddy — someone who can give you a hand with all that fabric and furniture rearranging.

Gift wrapping the cushions

Rather than sew a cushion cover, you can wrap the fabric around the cushion and secure it with safety pins. If you want to make a traditional slipcover for the sofa cushions, see Chapter 15 and follow the instructions for the box-edged pillow.

You need the following materials in addition to your Sewing Survival Kit:

✔ Iron and ironing board

✔ 1½ to 2 yards of fabric per cushion

✔ Two to three large safety pins per cushion

Follow these steps to gift-wrap your cushions:

1. **Before cutting the fabric for the cushions, try it on by centering or matching the dominant design with the throw.**

   For smaller pattern repeats, this design-matching consideration isn't as important.

2. **Cut out a rectangle of the cushion fabric that is twice the width of the cushion plus 6 inches and twice the length of the cushion plus 6 inches.**

   You want all the cushions to match, so after you cut one cushion cover, use this as a pattern for the others.

3. **With the right side of the fabric up, lay the cut cushion cover on top of the uncut fabric, matching the design from the cut piece to the design on the fabric underneath.**

4. **Cut a piece of fabric for each cushion cover, being sure to match up the design on each piece.**

5. **Wrap the cushions like gifts, folding hospital corners and securing each cushion cover with one or more large safety pins as shown in Figure 18-14.**

   • Place the cushion top side down, centering the cushion over the design in the fabric (if you're using a solid or small-scale print, this step is not that critical).

   • Wrap one side of the fabric over the opposite side, and secure the join with one or two safety pins.

   • Using your thumbs and forefingers, fold the cushion fabric at the corners the way you would wrap a gift (see Figure 18-14). Wrap the other two opposite sides of the cushion, pulling one side over the other; secure the ends with several safety pins.

Stand back and admire your work. Your furniture has wrapped cushions and a throw. Does it look finished? Are you impressed?
If so, you're done. If not, make a skirt for it.

Figure 18-14:
Gift wrap
your
cushion.

Making a skirt

You can attach a skirt around the bottom of your furniture to disguise unsightly furniture legs, create a concealed storage area, or add a more finished look to your furniture.

Follow these steps to create your skirt:

1. **Start at one leg and measure all the way around your furniture, keeping the measuring tape parallel to the floor.**

2. **Add 4 inches to the measurement you took in Step 1; record this measurement.**

3. **For a 6-inch skirt, cut a fabric strip 16 inches wide x the length recorded in Step 2. For a longer or shorter skirt, calculate the width of the skirt strip.**

   Measure the length of the skirt you need from where it attaches to the furniture down to the floor. Double that length and add 4 inches. This is the width of the fabric strip you need to make your skirt. For example, if your skirt needs to be a finished length of 10 inches, your skirt strip needs to be 24 inches wide.

4. **Finish one short end of the strip (see Chapter 6 for more on finishing raw edges).**

5. **Fold the strip in half lengthwise and press it (see Figure 18-15).**

6. **Fold and press a 1-inch hem on the unfinished short end.**

7. **Set your machine like this:**
   - **Stitch:** Straight
   - **Length:** 3 to 4 mm/6 to 9 spi
   - **Width:** 0
   - **Foot:** All-purpose

8. **Topstitch the hem, sewing ¾ inch from the hem fold (see Chapter 5 for more on topstitching).**

9. **Set your machine like this:**
   - **Stitch:** 3-step zigzag
   - **Length:** 1 to 1.5mm/13 to 14 spi
   - **Width:** 0
   - **Foot:** All-purpose

   If you're using a serger, set it like this:
   - **Stitch:** Balanced 3-thread overlock
   - **Length:** 2.5 to 3 mm
   - **Width:** Wide
   - **Foot:** Standard

10. **Overcast the two long edges together as shown in Figure 18-15. (Check out Chapter 6 for more on overcasting.)**

11. **Tie off the threads at both ends of the skirt strip (see Chapter 5 for more on tying off threads) or apply seam sealant to them.**

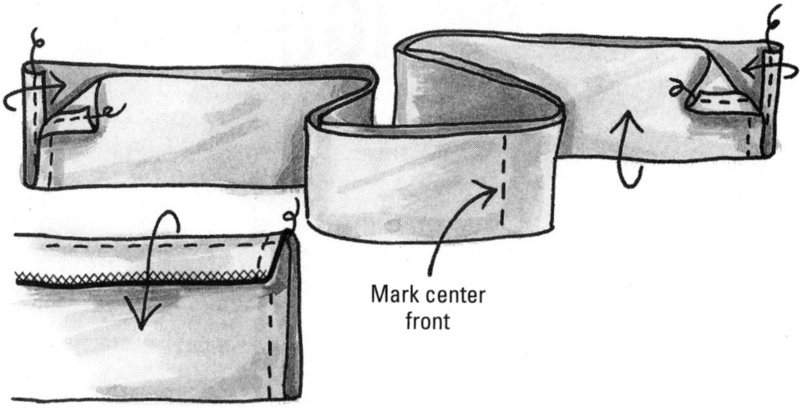

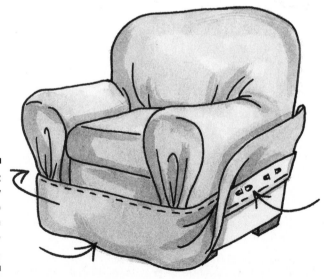

Figure 18-15:
Topstitch the hem and overcast the two long edges together.

Mark center front

12. **Fold down and press a 2-inch lip edge from the finished edge as shown in Figure 18-15.**

13. **Edgestitch along the folded lip edge (see Figure 18-15 and Chapter 6 for more on edgestitching).**

14. **Using large safety pins, pin the skirt to the bottom of the furniture, as close to the edgestitched lip as possible and so the hemmed edge laps over the overcast edge and the skirt laps at one of the back corners (see Figure 18-16).**

Celebrate and initiate your newest decorating accomplishment by sitting down in your chair with a good book.

Figure 18-16:
Use safety pins to attach the skirt to your chair.

Part V
Alterations and Quick Fixes

The 5th Wave   By Rich Tennant

"The black spots? That's where he has holes in his pants. And he has the nerve to call his felt tip marker a 'sewing' tool."

In this part . . .

You know the old expression. Stuff happens. Well, it happens to your clothes, too. Holes show up in your favorite shirt, and one day you may try on your lucky pair of pants and discover that the fit just isn't the same.

When bad stuff happens to your favorite garments, don't throw them away. Read the chapters in this part and give them a second lease on life.

And hey — some of the projects I show you in this part may actually make your garments look better than they did before the bad stuff happened!

Chapter 19

Too Short, Long, Tight, or Loose? 12 Ways to Fix It Quick

In This Chapter

▶ Lengthening and shortening pants and skirts

▶ Adjusting the rise in pants

▶ Giving yourself some breathing room

▶ Pulling in the reins on oversized clothes

▶ Creating a fabulous belt that fits almost everyone

A re you suffering from the *terrible too's* — you know, clothes that are too long, too short, too tight, or too loose? I have the toughest time getting rid of clothes that are still wearable, especially when I know if I just lose five pounds, they fit. So if you're like me and don't want to throw away perfectly good clothes despite their imperfect fit, you can use the creative shortcuts in this chapter to whip them back into shape — your shape, that is.

When It's Too Short

You can reduce shrinkage of most fabrics by not cooking washable fabrics in the dryer on the hottest, cotton setting. Fabrics last longer and don't shrink as much when you dry them on your dryer's perma-press setting.

But what if that information is water under the bridge and your garment is too short to be respectable? Read on to find out what to do.

Cutting off pant legs and rehemming them

You can turn some short pants into shorts by simply cutting off the legs and rehemming them (see Chapter 7 for more information on hemming). Look at the width of the pant legs and imagine them cut off at the length where you normally wear your shorts. Are the pant legs in question full enough for you to cut off? Are they narrow like you like them? The answer lies in your personal preference. As for the fabrics, stick with woven fabrics, such as denim, corduroy, gabardine, or poplin.

Some pant legs just look funny when you make them into shorts, so why not cut them off to a cropped or capri length instead, and then rehem them? See the hemming how-to's in Chapter 7.

Letting down and facing the hem

If your pants or skirt are too short, the hem allowance may be generous enough that you can let it down and increase the length. Look at the hem allowance on the garment:

✔ Is the hem double turned and then stitched?

✔ Is the hem allowance a generous 2 inches or more?

If so, you may be able to let down the hem. You can add some extra length by facing the hem.

For this project, you need *hem facing tape,* which you can find in a rainbow of colors at your local fabric store. Look for a color that comes as close as possible to matching your fabric. Even though the tape doesn't show, you still want it to be as close a color match as possible.

Follow these steps to lengthen your hem by facing it:

1. **Using your seam ripper, rip out your hem (see more about ripping in Chapter 6).**

2. **Using a steam iron, press over the hem to press out the old hem crease.**

   Sometimes the hem crease doesn't disappear entirely. You can usually press out a tough crease by sprinkling a half-and-half mixture of white vinegar and water on a press cloth (see Chapter 1), laying the dampened press cloth over the hem crease and then pressing until the press cloth is dry.

3. **Unfold one edge of the pre-folded hem facing tape and pin the tape edge even with the hem edge, placing the right sides together as shown in Figure 19-1.**

   The hem facing tape should end up lying on top of the garment fabric.

   Leave the hem tape in one long piece. You cut it off after you seam the ends.

Figure 19-1:
Unfold the hem facing tape, sew it to the hem edge and then sew the ends of the hem facing tape together.

4. **Set your machine like this:**

   - **Stitch:** Straight

   - **Length:** Appropriate for the fabric (try some test stitches to find the one that most closely matches the stitch length used in the other seamlines)

   - **Width:** 0 mm

   - **Foot:** All-purpose

5. **Sewing with the tape side up, stitch the tape around the hem on the fold of the hem tape (see Figure 19-1).**

6. **Stop sewing on the tape about 1 inch from where you started.**

   Don't cut the tape yet. This way, you don't end up cutting the tape off too short. Remove your work and head to the ironing board.

7. **Fold up the faced hem (as you would turn up a normal hem) and, using a steam iron, gently press over the hem facing.**

   Press from the wrong side of the garment, using a little steam. This step helps shape the hem facing so that it becomes part of the garment.

8. **Cut off the extra length of hem facing tape, leaving enough length on the short ends for a seam allowance.**

9. **Sew together the short ends of the hem facing tape, press the seam open, and then finish stitching the hem facing to the hem edge (see Figure 19-1).**

10. **Rehem the garment by using one of the hemming methods I describe in Chapter 7.**

When It's Too Long

Of course, you can simply rehem pants and skirts that you find too long to the right length (see Chapter 7). But when it comes to sleeves and thicker fabrics like denim, the following solutions are my favorite ways of solving the too-long problem.

Moving the button on the sleeve's cuff

A fast way to take care of a slightly too-long sleeve is to move the button over so that the cuff fits snugly around the wrist, keeping it from sliding down over your hand. Review the information in Chapter 5 on the ways to sew a button.

Taking up a tuck in the sleeve

For sleeves that you feel are 1 to 2 inches too long, take up the slack by stitching tucks. Just follow these steps:

1. **Decide how much excess fabric you want to put up into the tucks.**

A tuck takes up twice as much fabric as its actual width. For example, a ¼-inch tuck takes up ½ inch of fabric. For heavier fabrics, tucks take up slightly more than double because the turn of the cloth folds over a wider distance.

2. **Set your machine like this:**

   • **Stitch:** Straight

   • **Length:** 3 mm/9 spi

   • **Width:** 0 mm

   • **Foot:** All-purpose

3. **Sew the tuck in place, guiding the folded edge along the line on the needle plate.**

   Guiding the tucks this way helps keep your sewing straight so that the stitches are an even distance from the fold.

4. **Repeat the process on both sleeves for as many tucks as you need.**

   The finished sleeve looks something like Figure 19-2.

Figure 19-2:
Sew tucks to shorten sleeves that are too long.

Removing the cuff to shorten the sleeve

My husband's arms are shorter than manufacturers think they should be, apparently, so I constantly shorten shirtsleeves for him. I offered to take up some tucks in his sleeves, but he just wasn't interested — go figure.

Thankfully, you can easily shorten sleeves at the cuff when you follow these steps:

1. **Using a seam ripper, rip off the cuff, carefully cutting the stitches that hold it onto the sleeve.**

   Leave the cuff with the seam allowance pressed toward the inside.

   As a frame of reference, remove one cuff at a time. This way, if you need to check how the shirt manufacturer stitched on the cuff in the first place, you can check the one that you haven't removed.

2. **Pin the cuff back onto the sleeve so that the finished edge of the cuff is in the desired position.**

   Try on the shirt and bend your arm to be sure that the cuff is positioned in exactly the right spot.

3. **Using a fabric marker, mark along the top of the cuff, establishing the new cuff position.**

4. **Unpin the cuff and cut away the excess sleeve fabric, leaving a ½-inch seam allowance at the bottom of the sleeve, below the cuff placement marks that you made in Step 3 (see Figure 19-3).**

Figure 19-3: Mark the new cuff position and trim off the excess sleeve fabric.

5. **Repleat the bottom of the sleeve by using the original pleats as a guide.**

   You have to make deeper pleats so that the fullness of the shorter sleeve fits the cuff. After shortening one cuff, repeat Steps 1 through 5 for the other cuff. Double-check that you pleated the other sleeve like the first. Read more about pleats in Chapter 8.

6. **Pin on the cuff (see Figure 19-4) so that the seamline is even with the marks you made in Step 3.**

Figure 19-4: Pin on the cuff.

7. **Set your machine like this:**

   • **Stitch:** Straight

   • **Length:** 2.5 to 3 mm/10 to 12 spi

- **Width:** 0 mm

- **Foot:** All-purpose

8. **Edgestitch the cuff to the sleeve, guiding the stitches so that they sew over the original stitching line (see Chapter 6 for more on edgestitching). Repeat for the other sleeve.**

Shortening jeans

Shortening and rehemming jeans presents some real challenges unless you have the right tools and technique. Some double jean seams can bind home-use sewing machines. And if the presser foot coasts down off the thicknesses, you've got a big mess — unless you use a wedge.

You put a wedge under the presser foot to help you sew over an uneven fabric thickness. A sewing wedge works kind of like a shim under a dresser leg because it stabilizes the presser foot over that pesky seam. You can find several commercial wedges used for sewing.

Follow these steps to shorten too-long jeans:

1. **Before taking up the hem on your jeans, wash and dry them on the high cotton setting.**

   After rehemming, dry your jeans on the perma-press setting. This way, they don't shrink any further.

2. **Measure and mark the hemline with your dressmaker's chalk.**

3. **Cut off the excess fabric, leaving at least ½ to ⅝-inch hem allowance.**

4. **Finish the raw edge, using one of the overcasting stitches on your sewing machine or a three-thread overlock on your serger (see Chapter 6 for the best way to finish raw edges).**

5. **Fold up and press the hem allowance on the mark you made in Step 2.**

   Even though your jeans may have been double-hemmed, this excess thickness is often too much for many sewing machines. You can sew your hem more easily, and it looks better, when you turn it up only once.

6. **Set your machine like this:**

   - **Stitch:** Straight

   - **Length:** 3 to 4mm (6 to 9 spi)

   - **Width:** 0mm

   - **Foot:** All-purpose, Teflon(tm), or roller

- **Needle:** Size #90/14 Jeans

- **Accessories:** Button reed (sometimes called a wedge) or a Jean-a-ma-Jig (brand name)

7. **Use the wedge under the heel of the presser foot.**

   - Start sewing until the toe tips up on the fabric thicknesses created by the seam allowances.

   - Stop with the needle in the fabric and lift the foot.

   - Place the wedge under the heel and lower the foot. The wedge lifts up the back of the foot, so that the foot and fabric thicknesses are even and the foot is parallel to the feed dogs (see Chapter 1 for more on feed dogs).

8. **Stitch across the thickness until the toes start tipping down.**

   Stop with the needle in the fabric and lift the foot again.

9. **Use the wedge under the toe of the foot.**

   Slip the wedge under the toe and lower the foot, as shown in Figure 19-5.

Figure 19-5:
Use a wedge to maneuver over thick seams without bogging down your machine.

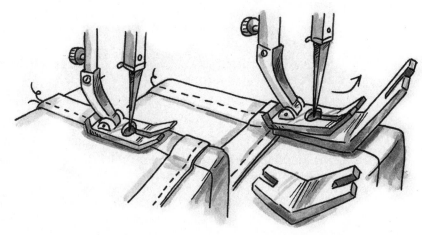

10. **Sew until the needle and the back of the foot are off the thickness.**

    As you come off the thickness, the wedge levels the foot for even feeding and even better stitching.

11. **Lift the foot and remove the wedge, and then lower the foot and sew until you get to the next thick seam.**

    Repeat Steps 7 through 10 until you finish hemming.

When Pants Don't Fit Well in the Rise

Pants can be too long or too short in the *rise* (the part of the pants between the legs). Before giving them away, try one of these tried-and-true comfort alterations.

Lowering the crotch curve

Do you feel like your pants ride up on you every time you move? Follow these steps to give yourself a little more room:

1. **Turn the pants inside out so that one leg is inside the other.**

   - With one hand, hold the pants upside down by the hems.

   - Using the other hand, reach into the waist opening, guiding your hand all the way down one pant leg.

   - Let that same hand come out of the leg hole and grab both pant hems at the inseams.

   - Pull your arm out through one leg hole, holding onto the inseams, until the pants are turned inside out.

2. **Slip the pants over the narrow end of the ironing board so that the *crotch point* (where all the seams come together) is centered on the board.**

3. **Using a fabric marker, make a mark ¼ inch lower, toward the leg, than the original seamline at the seam intersection.**

4. **Measure 3 to 4 inches up toward the waistband from either side of the new crotch point and draw a new crotch curve by using your fabric marker or dressmaker's chalk, as shown in Figure 19-6.**

5. **With a basting-length stitch, restitch the crotch curve on the new line you made in Step 4 (see Chapter 5 for the particulars on machine basting).**

6. **Trim the seam allowance to ⅝ inch and try on your altered pants.**

   If the pants fit comfortably, go on to the next step. If you need to lower the crotch another ¼ inch, repeat Steps 1 through 6 until you get a comfortable fit.

7. **Restitch the new crotch curve by using a 2.5 to 3 mm/10 to 12 spi straight stitch.**

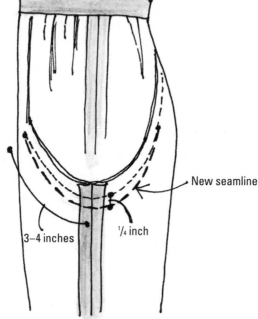

Taking in the inseam

Do you feel like the crotch of your pants hangs just above your knees? Fix the too-long rise by shortening the crotch depth at the *inseam* (the inner leg seam). The following technique shortens the crotch depth while leaving the circumference of the leg intact, meaning the pants still fit around your thighs. Just follow these steps:

1. **Turn your pants inside out, holding the crotch seam so that you can pin and take in the inseams.**

2. **Starting 7 inches down from the crotch seam on one side of the in-seam, sew a gradual row of basting stitches tapering out and up ⅛ inch from the original seamline, as shown in Figure 19-7. (See Chapter 5 for more on machine basting.)**

3. **Repeat for the other side of the in-seam, sewing from the crotch inter-section, tapering the seamline to 7 inches below the intersection.**

4. **Put on your altered pants and sit in them.**

   Are they more comfortable? If so, go on to the next step. If not, repeat Steps 1 through 3, taking out another ⅛ inch with each row of basting until the pants fit you comfortably.

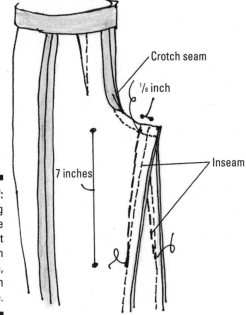

Crotch seam

⅛ inch

Inseam

7 inches

Figure 19-7:
Begin taking
in the
inseam at
the crotch
intersection,
¼-inch
at a time.

5. **Restitch over the basting stitches by using a 2.5 to 3 mm/10 to 12 spi stitch length, and then trim the excess seam allowance to within ¼ inch of the new seamline.**

6. **Remove the basting stitches.**

When It's Too Tight

The tidbits in this section can help you get just a little bit more wear out of your clothes without forcing you to lose weight or start that exercise program.

Moving the buttons over on a jacket

An easy way to get more room in a jacket is to simply move the buttons over. Moving a button over even ½ inch makes a big difference in the way a garment looks and feels.

Turn a double-breasted jacket into a single-breasted jacket by eliminating one row of buttons and moving the other row so that the buttons and buttonholes are centered. You get more room, and the single-breasted styling is usually more slimming. (See Chapter 5 to find out about sewing buttons by hand and machine.)

Adding room to the waistband

You typically cut waistbands on the lengthwise grain (see Chapter 4 for more information on grainlines). When washed and dried on the high cotton setting, fabric often shrinks on the lengthwise grain, and it keeps shrinking even after you've washed the garment several times. No wonder those waistbands feel a little tight lately! Here's how to give yourself a little more room:

1. **Find a place in the garment where you can steal a little bit of fabric to make an extension.**

   Extra hem allowance, an extra belt loop, or the lower edge of an in-seam pocket all work well.

2. **Cut the extension as long as possible and the same width as the waistband and interface it with fusible interfacing (see Chapter 2).**

3. **Remove the waistband and cut it at the center back.**

   Rip out the stitching that holds the waistband to the waistline, removing the stitching 3 to 4 inches on either side of the center back. Cut through the waistband the short way, as I show you in Figure 19-8.

4. **Cut your fabric extension.**

   Try on the garment and figure out how much of an extension you need. Cut the extension long enough to fit the waistband *plus* the seam allowance.

   Add generous seam allowances so that you can press open the seams on both ends of the extension. This way, the extended waistband is smooth and comfortable.

5. **Set your machine like this:**

   - **Stitch:** Straight

   - **Length:** Appropriate for the fabric (Try some test stitches to find the one that most closely matches the stitch length used in the other seamlines.)

   - **Width:** 0 mm

   - **Foot:** All-purpose

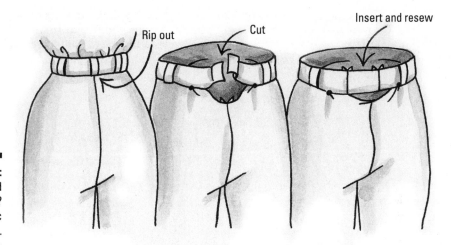

Rip out

Cut

Insert and resew

Figure 19-8:
Waistband
too tight?
Add a fabric
extension.

6. **Sew the extension to the center back of the waistband (see Figure 19-8).**

   Place the right side of the short, open end of the waistband to the right side of the interfaced extension and sew a seam. Repeat for the other end of the extension.

7. **Sew the waistband back on and attach the belt loop as it was before.**

When It's Too Loose

Here are a couple of tricks that I use when things are too loose. When hips are proportionally bigger than the waistline, this quick fix takes in the waistline. If your waistline yo-yos from season to season, using an adjustable belt over a too-big waistline just may be the ticket.

Taking in the waistline

This technique works well when taking in casual men's or ladies' slacks that have a front zipper and that don't have the traditional center back seam in the waistband. Just follow these steps:

1. **Pinch in and pin the necessary amount out of the center back and through the waistband.**

2. **Sew a wider seam allowance at the center back through the waistband so that you take in the waistline by the amount you determined in Step 1.**

3. **Starting at the crotch and sewing up through the waistband, edgestitch (see Chapter 6 for more about edgestitching) next to the seamline, which causes the seam allowance to lay down smoothly and to one side. (See Figure 19-9.)**

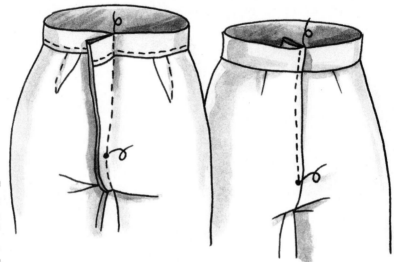

Figure 19-9:
Waistline
too loose?
Take it in.

Tightening up a look with an easy-to-make belt

Adding a belt to your outfit can help take up extra room in a shirt, blouse, or dress, creating a truly quick and easy fix to a fitting issue! Want a belt that shrinks or grows with you? Quickly craft this very comfortable belt of woven cotton belting.

In addition to your Sewing Survival Kit (which you can read about in Chapter 1), you need the following materials:

- ✔ 41 inches of 2-inch Guatemalan belting
- ✔ Two 8-inch loop-side Velcro strips
- ✔ Two 2-inch hook-side Velcro strips
- ✔ Thread to match the belting
- ✔ Fabric glue, such as Cool Gloo or FABRI-TAC
- ✔ Seam sealant, such as FrayCheck (see info about seam sealant in Chapter 1)

To create the belt, follow these steps:

1. **Dribble a bead of seam sealant on each end of the belting to prevent the ends from fraying.**

   Set the belting aside to dry for about 5 minutes.

2. **Fold, press, and pin small pleats at each end of the outside of the belting, as shown in Figure 19-10.**

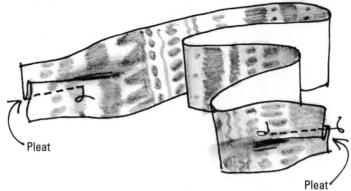

Figure 19-10: Fold small pleats at each end of the belting.

Pleat

Pleat

3. **Set your machine like this:**

   - **Stitch:** Straight
   - **Length:** 3.5 mm/7 spi
   - **Width:** 0 mm
   - **Foot:** All-purpose

4. **Pin the two short strips of hook-side Velcro over the pleats on the outside of the belting and sew the Velcro in place around all four sides (see Figure 19-11).**

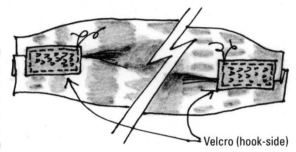

Figure 19-11: Sew Velcro over the pleats on each end.

Velcro (hook-side)

5. **Centering the two long, loop-side strips of Velcro, place and glue them 4 inches in from each end and on the inside (or the other side) of the belting strip, as shown in Figure 19-12.**

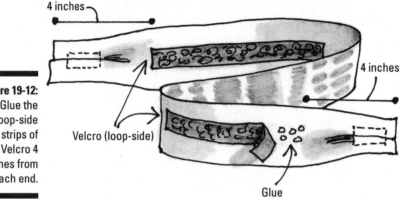

4 inches

4 inches

Figure 19-12:
Glue the
loop-side
strips of
Velcro 4
inches from
each end.

Velcro (loop-side)

Glue

You glue the long strips so that stitches don't show through to the outside of the belt.

6. **Let the glue dry as directed by the manufacturer (usually at least 24 hours for a permanent bond) before using the belt.**

7. **Place the belt around your waist, tucking the loose end under and attaching it to the Velcro, as shown in Figure 19-13.**

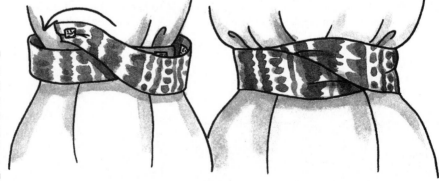

Figure 19-13:
This belt
adjusts with
you, even
when you
eat too
much.

Chapter 20

Making Repairs on the Run

*H*ave you looked in your closet to discover you have nothing to wear? Maybe you're troubled because your favorite shirt has a split seam or your jeans need a new zipper. In this chapter, I share some of my favorite short-cuts for painlessly cutting your repair pile down to size. Find out how to fix a split seam, patch a hole, repair a tear, and replace a zipper. If you're looking for information on the most basic (and common) repair of all — sewing on a new button — turn to Chapter 5.

To be prepared for any sewing emergency, always keep your Sewing Survival Kit fully stocked (see Chapter 1 for a list of all the tools your kit should include). You use essentially the same tools for repairs and fixes as you use for regular sewing. You may also want to keep a Quick-Fixes Sew-vival Kit (see the upcoming sidebar, "The amazing Quick-Fixes Sew-vival Kit") on hand.

Repairing a Seam

If you have a simple ripped seam, where the stitches in a seam are ripped or broken, your repair job is an easy one. If the fabric has deteriorated, pulled away from the stitches, or is totally obliterated at or around the seam allow-ance, you use a different technique to fix things up. Check out the next section, "Patching Holes and Rips," for more information.

The amazing Quick-Fixes Sew-vival Kit

Even though I have an entire room devoted to sewing stuff, I keep a wonderful little clothing care and repair kit that I call my Quick-Fixes Sew-vival Kit in my nightstand where I know I can always find it in a hurry. The Quick-Fixes Sew-vival Kit contains the following helpful tools and accessories, among others:

✔ **Ribbon thread braid:** A colorful braid made of 363 separate strands of thread in 28 different colors. Simply pull out the thread in the color that you need from the braid — no tangling, and good-quality thread to boot.

✔ **Self-threading hand needles:** These needles have a notch at the top, which means no more threading those pesky little needle eyes. (See Chapter 5 for more information on self-threading needles.)

✔ **Emergency shirt buttons:** These no-sew replacement shirt buttons poke through the fabric in an instant.

✔ **Safety pins and straight pins:** You can't have enough of these pins for little emergencies.

✔ **Collar extender:** This tool for the mature neck extends the collar band another ¾ inch.

✔ **Res-Q-Tape:** This sticky double-faced tape helps hold things in place. (See Chapter 7 for more on using Res-Q-Tape.)

✔ **Folding scissors:** Use them for cutting threads and Res-Q-Tape.

✔ **Snag repair tool:** Helps you pull snags through to the wrong side of the fabric easily and invisibly.

Just follow these steps to repair a simple ripped seam:

1. **Turn the item inside out so that you can easily access the seam allowances.**

2. **Using your seam ripper and embroidery scissors, remove the broken and ripped stitches (for more on un-sewing, see Chapter 6).**

3. **Pin the seam allowances back together into their original position.**

4. **Set your machine like this:**

   - **Stitch:** Straight
   - **Length:** 2.5 to 3 mm/10 to 12 spi
   - **Width:** 0 mm
   - **Foot:** All-purpose

5. **Start sewing over the intact seam, stitching ½ inch from the split in the seam and keep stitching ½ inch over the intact seam on the other side of the split.**

   Backstitch at the beginning and end of the repairing stitches.

Patching Holes and Rips

My brother is a commercial salmon fisherman in Alaska. Before he was married, he handed me a pile of mending whenever I visited. Talk about holes! He had so many shirts with holes in the elbows that he finally gave up and started cutting the sleeves off his long-sleeved shirts before they could get holey.

Even if you don't give your clothes quite the workout that a fisherman does, you may find holes in your clothes and other sewing projects from time to time.

Patching holes with patches

I find the following technique to be the very best way to patch holes. You can use this method to patch over holes in elbows, knees, or anywhere that holes find their way into a piece of fabric.

You can make patches large or small and arrange them artfully to cover other messes besides holes. Small pocket patches arranged in a collage cover an indelible ink stain (see Chapter 11 for more on sewing pockets).

Iron-on patches may be too good to be true: Experience has taught me that, after a little washing and wearing, the adhesive quits, and you have a patch that comes off. If you're using iron-on patches, also stitch them on.

Just follow these steps to sew on a patch:

1. **Find a fabric similar to the garment that you're patching.**

   If possible, steal fabric by stitching shut a pocket that doesn't get a lot of use, and cutting away the fabric from underneath.

   Save worn-out jeans so that you have a plentiful supply of used denim for patching.

2. **Cut out a patch ½ to ¾ inch larger than the hole, all the way around. You can cut the patch to any shape that you like.**

   Before cutting the patch to size, inspect the fabric around the hole. You may decide that you need a bigger patch to cover any frays in the area.

3. **Pin the patch in place, centering it over the hole so that the right side of the patch fabric is up, as shown in Figure 20-1.**

   Pin around the edges of the patch, through the patch, and the garment underneath.

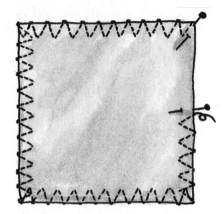

Figure 20-1:
Pin the
patch in
place and
sew it on
with a three-
step zigzag
stitch.

4. **Set your sewing machine like this:**

   • **Stitch:** Three-step zigzag

   • **Length:** 0.5 to 0.8 mm/fine setting or 60 spi

   • **Width:** 5 mm (or the widest width you have)

   • **Foot:** Embroidery

   • **Needle:** #90/14 HJ denim or jeans (for heavy fabrics); #80/12H
     Universal for everything else

5. **Place the garment and patch under the presser foot, right side up.**

   The patch should be under the foot so that the edge is slightly to the
   right of the needle.

6. **Start sewing so that, when the needle travels across the patch fabric
   to the right, the last stitch formed is on the outside edge of the patch.**

   This stitch is very dense and helps to meld the two pieces of fabric
   together (kind of like the Vulcan Mind Meld), so the patch is as strong
   as the fabric it patches.

   Remember to pull out the pins before sewing over them.

7. **If the patch is a circle, sew all the way around it. If the patch is a rectangle or square, sew to the corner and pivot.**

   • Sew to the corner, stopping with the needle in the far right side of
     the stitch. Doing so positions the patch so that you double-stitch
     and reinforce it in the corner.

- Lift the foot, pivot 90 degrees, lower the foot, and sew the second side of the patch, again stopping with the needle in the far right side of the stitch and pivoting.

- Continue like this until you've sewn the patch on.

8. **Pull the threads to the back of the fabric and tie them off (see Chapter 6 for more information on tying off threads).**

Patching with appliqués

You can get creative by making or purchasing a ready-made *appliqué* (a shaped piece of fabric completely covered by embroidery stitches) and using it as a patch in a low-stress area. Before patching with an appliqué, though, consider where you want to position it on the garment. Appliqués usually aren't large enough for patching knees, elbows, and other high-wear areas, and they can be lumpy and not very comfortable. Your best bet is to use them to disguise smaller holes.

Appliqués make short work of repairing holes. Just follow these steps to patch with an appliqué:

1. **Pin the appliqué over the hole.**

   If the appliqué is too thick to pin through, glue it into place, using your fabric glue stick.

2. **Set your sewing machine like this:**
   - **Stitch:** Straight
   - **Length:** 3 mm (10 spi)
   - **Width:** 0
   - **Foot:** Embroidery

3. **Using thread that matches the appliqué, straight stitch around it, sewing just inside the satin-stitched edge. (See Chapter 5 for more information on these two stitches.)**

4. **Pull the threads to the wrong side and tie them off.**

Sometimes you can disguise your appliqués and make them look like decorations. I've patched a hole with an appliqué and then placed another appliqué or two on the garment in other places so that the appliqués looked like they were on the garment all along.

Mending Tears on Woven Fabric

The goal in mending a tear on woven fabric is to make the repair as flat and invisible as possible. You accomplish this smooth repair using the three-step zigzag stitch and some lightweight fusible interfacing. (See Chapter 2 for more information on interfacing.)

If you're lucky enough to find a lightweight darning or embroidery thread through your local sewing machine dealer in the color that matches your garment, buy it. This finer weight of thread works beautifully for mending because it buries itself into the fabric for an almost invisible repair.

To mend tears on woven fabric, just follow these steps:

1. **Cut a ½-inch-wide strip of lightweight fusible interfacing the length of the tear plus 1 inch.**

   For example, if the tear is 5 inches long, the strip of interfacing should be ½ inch wide x 6 inches long.

2. **Trim off the loose threads from the tear.**

3. **Using your iron, fuse the interfacing to the back of the tear.**

   • Lay the repair wrong side out on the ironing board.

   • Push the raw edges of the tear together; place the interfacing over the tear.

   • Fuse the interfacing to the fabric according to the manufacturer's instructions.

4. **Set your machine like this:**

   • **Stitch:** Three-step zigzag

   • **Length:** 0.5 to 0.8 mm/fine setting or 60 spi

   • **Width:** 5 to 7 mm

   • **Foot:** Embroidery

5. **With the fabric right side up, position your needle ½ inch before one end of the tear and lower the foot, centering it over the tear.**

6. **Sew so that the stitches go back and forth over the tear as shown in Figure 20-2.**

   If the tear is wider than the width of the mending stitch, sew two rows of stitching next to each other so that the second row meshes into the first.

7. **Pull the threads to the back and tie them off.**

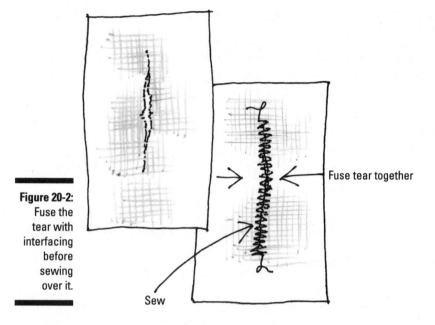

Fuse tear together

Figure 20-2:
Fuse the tear with interfacing before sewing over it.

Sew

Replacing Zippers (It's Easier Than You Think)

The fabric is already shaped, pressed, and stitched with the original zipper, so the work is all figured out for you. You just have to rip out the old zipper and then slip in and stitch the new one. Easy as pie.

Replacing a fly-front zipper

I bet you have a pair of pants, jeans, shorts, or a skirt in the repair pile badly in need of a zipper replacement. Don't put off this repair another minute!

You don't have to find a zipper that measures exactly the same length as the one you want to replace. Use a zipper that measures longer than the opening. (It doesn't matter how much longer because you eventually cut it to fit.) Using a longer zipper allows you to maneuver the presser foot without running into the pull.

Follow these instructions to replace a zipper:

1. **Remove the old zipper by ripping out the stitching that attaches the zipper to the garment (check out Chapter 6 for more on ripping).**

   Unzip and remove the old zipper by carefully ripping out the stitches with a sharp pair of embroidery scissors or a seam ripper.

   Take notes or make sketches of how the manufacturer originally installed the zipper. Those notes come in handy when you put everything back together.

2. **Rip back the waistband just far enough to remove the old zipper.**

3. **Mark the original topstitching line with transparent tape (see Figure 20-3).**

   Even though you have removed the stitches, you can still see where the topstitching used to be.

4. **Set your machine like this:**

   - **Stitch:** Straight
   - **Length:** 2.5 to 3 mm/10 to 12 spi
   - **Width:** 0 mm
   - **Foot:** Zipper

5. **Secure the zipper to the fly-front facing extension.**

   Open the fly-front facing extension (the part of the garment used to make the flap that covers up the zipper). With the right side of the zipper to the right side of the extension, pin or hand-baste the zipper so that the left edge of the zipper tape is even with the left edge of the facing extension, as shown in Figure 20-3.

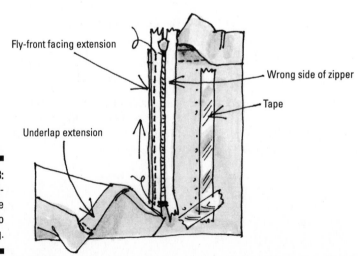

Fly-front facing extension

Wrong side of zipper

Tape

Underlap extension

Figure 20-3:
Pin or hand-baste the zipper into the opening.

6. **Sewing from the bottom of the zipper tape, stitch all the way along the left edge of the zipper tape, sewing about ⅛ inch from the edge.**

7. **Pin the other side of the zipper.**

   Unzip the zipper. Pin the side that you haven't sewn yet so that the zipper tape is sandwiched between the underlap and the underlap extension (the fabric piece behind the zipper that keeps you from catching your underwear in the zipper), and the fold is next to the zipper teeth, as shown in Figure 20-4.

Underlap extension

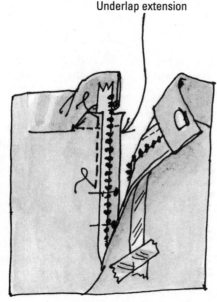

Figure 20-4:
Unzip the zipper and stitch it between the under-lap and underlap extension.

8. **Zip the zipper and check that the zipper and the fly front are smooth.**

   If they aren't smooth, reposition the pins.

9. **When everything is smooth, unzip the zipper again and stitch the other side of the zipper, sewing close to the teeth.**

10. **Unzip the zipper, cut off the excess zipper tape, tuck the underlap end of the zipper under the waistband, and pin the waistband back to the top of the pants with right sides together.**

11. **Set your machine like this:**

    - **Stitch:** Straight
    - **Length:** 2.5 to 3 mm/10 to 12 spi
    - **Width:** 0 mm
    - **Foot:** All-purpose

12. **Replace the all purpose presser foot with the zipper foot.**

    Leave your other machine settings as you set them in Step 11.

13. **Topstitch the fly front as shown in Figure 20-5.**

    Slide the toe of the foot to one side so that it avoids the zipper teeth. Lower the foot, placing it on the fly front and guiding the needle next to the transparent tape on the inside edge. The tape is a template to keep you sewing straight.

14. **Put your all-purpose foot back on the machine.**

15. **Pin the top of the zipper opening to one side of the waistband so that the right sides are together.**

16. **Sew the other side of the zipper, guiding the needle over the stitching line that was there before you replaced the zipper.**

17. **Restitch the back of the waistband to the opening on both sides of the zipper opening by stitching-in-the-ditch in the crack of the waistband seamline as shown in Figure 20-5 (see Chapter 5 for the how-to's of stitching-in-the-ditch).**

Stitch-in-the-ditch

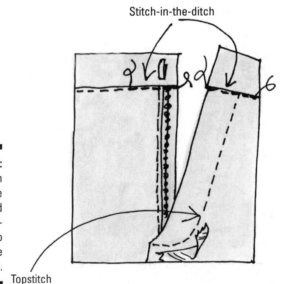

Figure 20-5: Topstitch over the zipper and stitch-in-the-ditch to reattach the waistband.

Topstitch

Replacing a separating zipper

You can find separating zippers on cardigan-style shirts, jackets, and sweaters. When you unzip them, the jackets open completely down the center front because the zipper teeth or coils separate from each other. In this section, I show you how to get rid of those old zippers that aren't doing the job anymore.

When repairing zippers in a leather, suede, or pigskin jacket, use a leather machine needle (available through your local sewing machine dealer) and set your stitch length so that the stitches land in the exact same holes as the original topstitching — otherwise, the stitches perforate and tear the leather.

Use this easy procedure to replace an ailing zipper with one that can hold things together:

1. **Buy a replacement zipper the same length as the zipper opening.**

2. **Rip out the stitches of the old zipper carefully, using sharp embroidery scissors or a seam ripper.**

3. **Separate the replacement zipper.**

4. **Open the lining, making it flat.**

5. **Pin the first side of the zipper to the lining with the right sides together so that the zipper pull faces to the outside, as shown in Figure 20-6.**

6. **Set your machine like this:**

   - **Stitch:** Straight
   - **Length:** 3 to 3.5 mm/10 to 12 spi
   - **Width:** 0 mm
   - **Foot:** Zipper

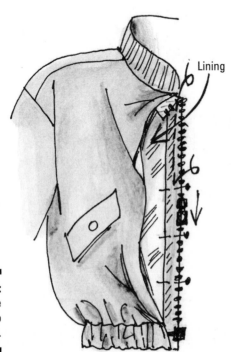

Lining

Figure 20-6:
Pin the
zipper to
the lining.

7. **Stitch the first side of the zipper, sewing through one layer of the lining.**

   Guide the foot so that you sew down the center of the zipper tape.

8. **Pin the garment front opening over the first side of the zipper and through all the fabric layers.**

9. **Topstitch over the original topstitching line, as shown in Figure 20-7.**

Figure 20-7:
Topstitch
the zipper.

Stitch on original stitching line

10. **Pin and sew the second side of the replacement zipper to the front jacket opening as explained in Steps 4 through 9.**

You feel like you have a bunch of new clothes after you use these techniques to get to the bottom of your repair basket. The trick is to keep ahead of those repairs, now that you know what to do.

Part VI
The Part of Tens

The 5th Wave   By Rich Tennant

"If it's any consolation, you hemmed the length on this leg perfectly."

In this part . . .

This part of the book is the shortest, but it runs long on information. These chapters include sewing tips and hints that I wish I had known when I was learning to sew. Each one of the tips saves you unwanted mistakes, wasted time, and untold irritation. If you find that just one of these hints keeps you on the straight and narrow and helps your sewing experience, my work here is done!

Chapter 21

Ten Tips for Mixing Prints

Do you remember Mom telling you not to mix a print with a plaid, not to put polka dots with stripes? If you follow this rule, *STOP*. Pick up any decorating magazine and see how many beautifully decorated rooms break this rule. Here are some guidelines that you *should* follow, though.

Stick with One Base

Several years ago, I found a new sofa on sale that I thought would go with the carpet. Both had shades of mauve and blue. (It was the 80s — what can I say?) When I put the sofa fabric together with the carpet, something looked off. At the time, I didn't know what it was. Later I realized that I was putting a warm color base with a cool color base. Even though the colors running through the sofa and the rug were similar, they clashed.

Prevent this dilemma and keep the same color bases together in your home. Check out the section "Understanding color" in Chapter 13 to get the lowdown on color bases.

Run a Background Check

The background color of each print fabric should match the others in the room. If the background of one print fabric is white, the background of the other coordinate fabrics should also be white. If the background of one print is off-white or cream, the background of the coordinate fabrics should also be off-white or cream.

Go Solid and Save Money

Stick with a solid-colored fabric for your big-ticket upholstered pieces. The fabric may have several colors woven into it in a pleasing texture, but when you stand back and squint at it, your sofa or love seat should look like a solid color. If your piece of furniture is upholstered with a large-scale print, you are apt to tire of the print before the sofa or chair is ready for the secondhand store. So go solid, accenting with throw pillows and table linens you'll find easier and less expensive to replace using the prints you love.

Mix 'n' Match Manufacturers

Even though two different fabric manufacturers may make your fabrics, you can still use the pieces in the same room, as long as they have the same colors and backgrounds in them. I once teamed a beautiful large-scale floral print that had a white dogwood blooming on a black background with a ½-inch black-and-white gingham check. Different manufacturers made both fabrics, but they looked great together because the colors were the same and the scales of the prints were different (see below for more on mixing different scaled prints).

Stare Down Your Prints

When mixing patterns, stand back and squint. Depending on where you stand, small-scale prints look almost like solid-color fabrics, which can affect the overall color scheme in the room.

For example, a small red-and-white checked fabric can look like a lighter shade of the red in the pattern — or it may even look pink — when you stand back eight feet. And, although the red of the small check exactly matches the larger red tulip in another fabric, the colors may not look like they match when you check them out from across the room.

Weigh the Scales Before Mixing Your Prints

When mixing different patterns such as florals, plaids, or polka dots, don't use designs that have the same scale. For example, look at two fabrics with the same color scheme, both printed with 3-inch flowers. From across the room, you can't really tell them apart because the fabrics have the same scale — the same-sized flowers. For a more interesting contrast, combine scales and patterns. Use a small-scale print with a mid-scale print of a different pattern, for example. Try a ½-inch flower print with a 1½-inch windowpane plaid that has the same colors as the floral. Wow!

Follow these guidelines to mix your prints in high style:

- ✔ Use only one print with a large repeat per room (the repeat is the distance between the same design along the length of a piece of fabric). A 15- to 24-inch repeat is considered large. Using more than one large-scale print confuses the eye.

- ✔ Use the same large-scale print in several areas in the same room.

- ✔ Complete the room using smaller scale accent fabrics such as florals, stripes, plaids, or polka dots on throw pillows or an ottoman.

Try Before You Buy

Ask the fabric salesperson for a swatch of home decor fabric to take home to see what it looks like against your tile, carpet, and wall color. Better yet — buy a square of fabric (if the fabric is 54 inches wide, buy 1½ yards of it to make a square). Simply drape the large fabric square over your sofa or chair and live with it for a couple of days. Besides getting a chance to try out a fabric in the room before making a serious commitment and buying several yards, you can hem your sample and use it as a square table topper.

Rely on a Collection

Puzzled by prints? Some fabric manufacturers make it easy on you by designing collections of companion fabrics that work together in the same room or in the same home. Using these fabrics, you can successfully create a pulled-together look in a room while having the color flow effortlessly from one room to the next.

Check out the color section of this book to see how I used a collection in my guest bedroom. I used the large-scale print on the duvet and the pillow shams; the smaller-scale floral and the coordinate stripe in the window treatment and dust ruffle; and the coordinate stripe to make the knotted neck pillow on the bed. Notice that the stronger colored stripe carries your eye from the window, to the bed, and then to the floor for a really pulled-together look.

Buy More, Use Less

You've heard less is more, right? That rule applies when planning the number of fabrics for your home, too. After you choose the color scheme and fall in love with just the right primary fabric, find two — not four or five — others that work with it. Make use of all three fabrics throughout the room or in adjoining rooms, and buy enough of each for the projects you plan to make this month and those you may want to make next year. Manufacturers frequently drop fabrics from their lines, and dye lots vary, so I find it best to get all your fabric at once.

When you buy more of your core fabrics to begin with, you have enough the next time inspiration strikes. Make a new throw pillow to replace the one that the dog ate, another table runner to take over for the one that has faded with many washings, a new throw so you can throw away the one with the coffee stain — you get the picture.

Consult a Pro

If you are still unsure about whether one color goes with another, or whether the colors you choose create the mood you are looking for in a room, check out www.deweycolorsystem.com. The innovative Dewey Color System helps you to find out what colors you are naturally attracted to and why, and then helps you choose a color scheme using the foolproof Dewey Color Coordinator.

Chapter 22

Ten Mistakes Beginners Often Make

. . . .

In This Chapter

▶ Matching your projects to your skill level

▶ Rejecting troublesome fabrics and unflattering styles

▶ Avoiding common sewing pitfalls

▶ Easing up on yourself

. . . .

*T*his chapter alerts you to ten of the most common sewing mistakes and pitfalls — stumbling blocks that I and my students have tripped over. If you know what to watch out for, you're more likely to have a wonderful sewing experience.

Attempting a Project beyond Your Skill Level

I like challenges as much as the next person, but when it comes to sewing, I draw a fine line between challenging and frustrating. The bottom line for your first project: Don't even think about making a suit jacket with notched lapels out of an uneven wool plaid. Starting at that level is a recipe for disaster. You'll probably waste your time and money — and you may never wear the thing after you finish it. You may never even sew again. Instead, look for projects with few seams, such as the easy envelope pillow in Chapter 15 or the place mat vest project in Chapter 3. Both projects have just a few seams and don't need a lot of fitting; you can sit down, have fun, and make each one in a couple hours or less.

Also know that the first time you make something, you're on a learning curve, and the result probably won't be perfect. In fact, you may never wear the garment, which is okay. Your skills improve with every project. After you master the basics, you can move on to more challenging projects that have a little bit more style.

Choosing Difficult Fabrics to Work With

Don't choose fabrics that may be too heavy, too fine, too complicated (such as plaids, stripes, and 1-inch gingham checks), or too expensive (with the proviso that using the best fabrics you can afford adds to the tactile experience of sewing). Read the information on fabrics and fibers in Chapter 2, and choose those fabrics that work with your lifestyle, personal style, and comfort requirements.

Also stay away from lightweight slippery fabrics such as polyester faille, silk crepe or charmeuse, sand-washed rayon, acetate linings, and the entire category of microfibers. These fabrics scoot around during cutting, attract static electricity, slip when you pin them together, and need special handling during sewing and pressing.

Because of their *nap,* or fuzzy texture, fabrics such as corduroy and velvet are also challenging because you can lay out and cut the pattern pieces only in one direction. I suggest that when you're ready to make a project out of a napped fabric, choose a fabric such as Polarfleece and make the throw in Chapter 17. When you have a little more experience, go on to the corduroys and velvets. But when you're starting out, stick with easier fabrics like cotton poplin, chambray, and cotton twill.

Choosing an Unflattering Style

Choose clothing styles that look good on you when you shop for ready-to-wear. Chances are that if elastic-waist, pull-on pants from your local department store don't look good on you, elastic-waist, pull-on pants that you make for yourself won't look good on you, either. Check out Chapter 4 to determine your figure type.

Using the Wrong Fabric for the Pattern

If the pattern says "For Knits Only" and you decide to use a woven poplin because you find it to be a perfect color, the project won't fit. Knits stretch and contribute to the overall fit of the garment. So read the back of the pattern envelope and choose from the list of recommended fabrics.

Laying Out the Fabric Incorrectly

Have you ever had your pants' legs twist uncomfortably around your legs while you walk? And perhaps this same pair of pants makes you look bow-legged even when you carefully press the creases. Chances are good that the fabric was cut off-grain.

Before cutting, lay out the pattern as your pattern guide sheet instructions recommend and read Chapter 4. Remember the old adage: "Measure twice and cut once." You avoid costly mistakes.

Neglecting to Use Interfacing

I remember my mom complaining about using interfacing in projects. "After all, it really doesn't show," she'd say, "and I don't want to spend the money on it." We agreed to disagree.

Interfacing is a layer of fabric that gives body and oomph to collars, cuffs, and front plackets. It doesn't show on the outside of the garment, but it makes a world of difference in the project's final look. If I'm spending my time and effort making something, I want it to look as professional as possible. Interfacing helps me do that. See Chapter 2 for information about interfacing and plan on using it in your next project. You'll love the results.

Failing to Press as You Sew

I remember one of my favorite college professors at the State University of New York's Fashion Institute of Technology (FIT for short) telling me to "have a love affair" with my iron. I never really thought too much about the value of pressing garments-in-progress until he said it, but he was right. When you press a project after each seam, you shape a flat, shapeless piece of fabric into something that fits the forms and curves of whatever is under it — almost like pressing the fabric into submission. See the section in Chapter 5 on pressing and have a love affair with your iron when you sew.

Using an Old, Beat-Up Sewing Machine

I work with a friend who used to sew and has an oldie but moldy sewing machine. It has been hidden away in the garage, never seeing the light of day for the last 10 to 15 years. Every so often I hear her say, "I think I'll dig out the machine and start sewing again." She never does, and I can only imagine how well it works after all this time in retirement.

When I sew, part of the joy for me is sitting down in front of the machine, knowing that it works perfectly every time. So, instead of borrowing Grandma's old clunker, get a sewing machine that sews in good working order by

✔ Renting or borrowing a machine from your local dealer

✔ Taking a sewing class

✔ Buying a new or reconditioned machine

No, you don't have to buy one of those $4,000 do-everything models. You just need one that provides good, reliable service. Trade up to a better model as your skills improve and as your budget permits.

When you use a machine that sews in good working order, you also need to maintain it to keep it that way. See the section in Chapter 1 about sewing machine care, and then treat yours with the TLC it deserves.

Neglecting to Use a New Needle on Every Project

I once met a woman who complained about her needle unthreading each time she sewed. I asked her to bring the machine to me so that I could diagnose the problem. When she did, I discovered that she'd worn the needle down to the eye! No wonder she was having trouble. We put in a new needle, and the machine worked perfectly.

I worked with another woman who was having a terrible time with skipped stitches (where the line of stitching had two or three short stitches followed by one long stitch, which isn't supposed to happen). I suggested that she change the needle. She pulled a different one out of her pincushion and put it in the machine. Again, she experienced the same problem. This happened two more times that afternoon. She was ready to take the machine to the local service center until I insisted that she use a brand-new needle from the package — no more skipped stitches.

Even though the needle looks perfect to the naked eye, the point bends, gets all boogered up, and just plain wears out with use, like a razor blade. So change your needle and throw away the old one after each project.

Refusing to Cut Yourself Some Slack

Remember when you first started riding a bike? You weren't perfect, were you? I spent my first bike-riding summer with scabs on both knees until I figured out what I was doing.

Sewing is like anything new. You can't be perfect from the get-go, so cut yourself some slack. If you can live with a sewing mistake, *don't* rip it out.

Chapter 23

Ten Sewing Fundamentals to Remember

*I*n this chapter, I give you some tips that I wish someone had shared with me when I first started sewing. Post these hints on a bulletin board in front of you when you sew, or write them on stick-on notes and put them on your sewing machine.

Buy the Best Fabric You Can Afford

Sewing is a tactile craft. For me, one of the pleasures of sewing is working with the best fabric I can afford. Better fabrics are easier to work with; are woven, knitted, or printed on grain; hold up to frequent washing and wearing; and usually produce a better end product. (See Chapter 4 for more information about grain.)

What makes a good quality fabric? Several factors do. Find out if a fabric makes the cut by

✔ **Checking the fiber content.** Reread the information in Chapter 2 about fabrics and fiber content and then preshrink the fabric. If the fabric looks like a droopy dishrag after you preshrink it, chances are the fabric will look like a dishrag when it becomes a finished project. So return the fabric to the store before putting your time into it.

✔ **Considering what you pay per yard.** Although I can think of exceptions, I've discovered that you usually get what you pay for.

✔ **Examining the fabric's *hand*.** The way the fabric feels and drapes in your hand or against your body is its *hand*. Gather up a width of fabric in one hand and then drape a length of it over your arm, around your neck, or over one shoulder. Does it drape in smooth folds or bend in stiff creases? Does it bend at all? If it drapes in smooth folds, it has a soft hand. If it bends and creases, or doesn't bend at all, it has a hard or stiff hand.

When making a garment, I usually buy the yardage recommended on the back of the pattern envelope because the pattern companies are generous with their recommendations. When it comes to home decor projects, though, I usually buy fabric for one more pattern repeat than I think I need. (See Chapter 4 for determining the pattern repeat in a fabric.)

Know Your Fabric Terminology

Fabrics have *selvages,* a *crosswise grain,* a *lengthwise grain,* and a *bias.* You need to know these terms in order to understand the pattern layout and cutting instructions, the basic project construction, how to buy the proper amount of fabric, and how to plan your project. I give you a handy run-down in the following list:

✔ **Selvages:** The finished edges of the fabric (Selvages run the length of the fabric.)

✔ **Crosswise grain:** The width of the fabric, perpendicular to the selvages

✔ **Lengthwise grain:** The length of the fabric from one cut end to the other cut end, parallel to the selvages

✔ **Bias:** The 45-degree angle between the crosswise grain and the lengthwise grain

See Chapter 4 for more details on these terms.

Know the Difference between Right and Wrong

After one of my two-hour seminars for beginning sewers, a guy stood up in the back of the room and said (with the most perplexed expression on his face), "What's all this about the right and the wrong sides? I think it would be better if you said the top and the bottom or the front and the back. I don't get it."

This experience reminded me never to skip over the basics with someone new to the craft. The following list gives you the lowdown on the right and wrong sides:

- **The right side of the fabric:** The pretty side that faces the outside of the project and usually has the brightest colors and more defined textures
- **The wrong side of the fabric:** The side that faces the inside of the project where the seams are

For more information on fibers and fabrics, see Chapter 2.

Place Right Sides Together

When sewing, place the right sides of the fabric together to make a seam. This concept is as basic to sewing as the needle and thread. In other words, place the right side of one piece of fabric against the right side of another piece of fabric (usually matching the notches along the seamline). See Chapter 6 for more information on making perfect seams.

Put Your Foot Down before Sewing

Put the presser foot down, that is. The presser foot firmly holds the fabric under the needle. Without the presser foot, the fabric just flops around, and you can't sew straight. When you lower the foot onto the fabric, the upper thread tension also engages so that the stitches form properly. Use these handy tips to know when to put your foot down:

- Lower the foot when you start to sew
- Raise the foot to remove your work after you finish sewing

Remember that your sewing machine comes with several different presser feet designed for different uses. Review your machine's operating manual and Chapter 1 to find out the benefits of sewing with your feet.

Stop and Start Sewing the Right Way

I can't think of anything more frustrating than getting ready to sew a nice long seam, stomping on the foot pedal, and having the needle come unthreaded.

The following tips help you stop and start sewing the right way to avoid this problem:

- ✔ **Stop sewing at the end of the stitch cycle.** If you don't, the take-up lever pulls out a length of thread for the next stitch and unthreads the needle. By stopping when the needle is out of the fabric and the take-up lever is at the highest position, you eliminate the problem. Newer sewing machine models have this feature built in. See Chapter 5 for more information on taking the first stitch.

- ✔ When stitching a corner, stop with the needle in the dead-lowest position before pivoting at the corner to avoid a skipped stitch.

Righty, Tighty; Lefty, Loosey

This little rhyme refers to the tension knobs on your sewing machine and serger.

Turning the tension dials to the right makes them tight. Turning them to the left makes them loose — this trick works with pickle and peanut butter jars, too. (You can find more about balancing thread tensions in Chapter 1.)

Test-Stitch First

When sewing, you want the seams and buttonholes to turn out as flat and as good-looking as possible so that, when you press, you aren't fighting with them.

The best way to make sure that the seamlines behave is to test the stitch you intend to use for the seam on a scrap piece of fabric before you sew the real deal. This rule works with not only the straight stitch but also all the other stitches available on your sewing machine and serger.

Use the following guidelines to help you adjust the stitch length as necessary:

- ✔ **If your fabric puckers, shorten the stitch length.** Shortening the stitch length puts more thread into the stitch so that the fabric relaxes and goes back to the original shape.

- ✔ **If your fabric waves out of shape, lengthen the stitch.** Lengthening the stitch removes thread from the stitch so that the fabric returns to the original position.

See Chapter 5 for more of the particulars on taking the first stitch.

Sew from the Bottom Up and from the Center Out

Remember these hard and fast rules when working with vertical seams and horizontal seams (they also apply to any project):

✔ When you sew a vertical seam (like a side seam on a skirt or a pair of pants), sew from the hem edge up to the waistline.

✔ When you sew a horizontal seam (like a shoulder seam), sew from the outside edges toward the center.

✔ When you sew a collar or facing, sew from the center out to the point or raw edge on one side, and then from the center out to the point or raw edge on the other side.

Press Seams Flat and Together — and Open or to One Side

Proper pressing and ironing techniques transform homemade projects into custom-made masterpieces. To understand the difference, please review the information in Chapter 5 under "Pressing Matters." Your project's instructions may tell you to press in any of the following ways:

✔ **Press the seam flat and together:** Press the iron over the seamline from the wrong side of the fabric. Doing so sets or *blends* the stitches in the fabric. Position the iron so that you press the seam allowance together from the seamline out toward the edge.

✔ **Press the seam open:** Press a ⅝-inch seam from the wrong side of the fabric so that one seam allowance falls to the right and the other seam allowance falls to the left. The seamline itself ends up centered between the seam allowances. Using a seam roll makes pressing seams open easier (see Chapter 1 for more on pressing tools).

✔ **Press the seam to one side:** Press a ¼-inch seam from the wrong side of the fabric to one side or the other so that the crack of the seam faces the back of the project.

For more information about the art of pressing, see Chapter 5.

Clip with Your Scissors' Tips

Don't cut a hole in your project where you don't want one! Any time you cut from an edge into a seam allowance (for example, when you clip or notch a curve — see Chapter 6 for info on clipping and notching) and toward a seam-line, use the very tips of your scissors or shears. This way, you don't accidentally cut into the seamline.

Appendix

Sewing Resources

Sewing Organizations

American Sewing Guild
9660 Hillcroft, Suite 510
Houston, TX 77096
Phone: 713-729-3000
Fax: 713-721-9230
Web site: www.asg.org

Home Sewing Association
P.O. Box 1312
Monroeville, PA 15146
Phone: 412-372-5950
Fax: 412-372-5953
Web site: www.sewing.org

Sewing Publication

Sew News
741 Corporate Circle, Suite A
Golden, CO 80401
Phone: 800-289-6397
Fax: 303-277-0370
Web site: www.sewnews.com

Sewing Machine Companies

Baby Lock USA
1760 Gilsinn Lane
St Louis, MO 63026
Phone: 636-349-3000
Fax: 636-349-2333
Web site: www.babylock.com

Bernina of America, Inc
3702 Prairie Lake Court
Aurora, IL 60504-6182
Phone: 630-978-2500
Fax: 630-978-9529
Web site: www.berninausa.com

Brother International
100 Somerset Corporate Boulevard
Bridgewater, NJ 08807-0911
Phone: 908-704-1700
Fax: 908-704-8235
Web site: www.brother.com/usa/hsm/hsm_cntr.html

Elna, USA
1760 Gilsinn Lane
Fenton, MO 63026
Phone: 636-349-3000
Fax: 636-349-2333
Web site: www.elnausa.com

Pfaff American Sales Corp.
P.O. Box 458012
Westlake, OH 44145
Phone: 440-808-6550
Fax: 440-250-3550
Web site: www.pfaffusa.com

Singer Sewing Company
1224 Heil Quaker Boulevard
P.O. Box 7017
LaVergne, TN 37086
Phone: 800-474-6437
Fax: 615-213-0994
Web site: www.singer.com

Viking Sewing Machines, Inc.
31000 Viking Parkway
Westlake, OH 44145
Phone: 800-358-0001
Fax: 440-847-0001
Web site: www.husqvarnaviking.com

Pattern Companies

Kwik Sew Pattern Company, Inc.
3000 Washington Avenue North
Minneapolis, MN 55411-1699
Phone: 800-594-5739
Fax: 612-521-1662
Web site: www.kwiksew.com

McCall Pattern Company
11 Penn Plaza
New York, NY 10001
Phone: 212-465-6800
Fax: 212-465-6814
Web site: www.mccall.com

Simplicity Pattern Company, Inc.
2 Park Avenue, 12th Floor
New York, NY 10016
Phone: 212-372-0500
Fax: 212-686-3214
E-mail: info@simplicity.com
Web site: www.simplicity.com

Vogue/Butterick
161 Sixth Avenue
New York, NY 10013
Phone: 212-620-2500
Fax: 212-620-2746
Web site: www.mccall.com

Home Accessory Company

Southern Living At HOME®
(Makers of home accessories featured in the color pages of this book.)

P. O. Box 830951
Birmingham, AL 35283
Phone: 360-833-1213
Web site: www.southernlivingathome.com/sunsetstyle

Notion Companies

Creative Feet
(Makers of piping foot and other creative presser feet)
P.O. Box 26282
Prescott Valley, AZ 86312-6282
Phone: 800-776-6938
Fax: 928-772-7164
Web site: www.creativefeet.com

Prym/Dritz Corporation
(Makers of sewing notions and home decor trims)
P.O. Box 5028
Spartanburg, SC 29304
Phone: 800-845-4948
Fax: 800-574-3847
Web site: www.dritz.com

The Snap Source
(Makers of sport snaps and snap tools)
P.O. Box 99733
Troy, MI 48099-9733
Phone: 800-725-4600
Fax: 248-280-1140
Web site: www.snapsource.com

William. E. Wright, LP
(Makers of trims and tapes for fashion and home decor)
85 South Street
West Warren, MA 01092
Phone: 413-436-7732
Web site: www.wrights.com

Sewing Notion Mail-Order Companies

Clotilde, Inc.
P.O. Box 7500
Big Sandy, TX 75755-7500
Phone: 800-545-4002
Web site: www.clotilde.com

Nancy's Notions
333 Beichl Avenue
Beaver Dam, WI 53916
Phone: 800-833-0690
Fax: 800-255-8119
E-mail: nzieman@aol.com
Web site: www.nancysnotions.com

Thread Companies

Coats & Clark
Consumer Service
P.O. Box 12229
Greenville, SC 29612
Phone: 800-648-1479
Web site: www.coatsandclark.com

Sulky of America, Inc.
3113 Broadpoint Drive
Punta Gorda, FL 33983
Phone: 800-874-4115
Fax: 941-743-4634
Web site: www.sulky.com

Kits

Naked Room Solutions, Inc.
(Makers of the Quick-Change Window Cornice and Infinity Rings)
4420 NW Dahlia Drive
Camas, WA 98607
Phone: 360-833-9553
Fax: 360-833-9553

Index

• *C* •

• T •

FOR DUMMIES®

The easy way to get more done and have more fun

PERSONAL FINANCE & BUSINESS

Investing FOR DUMMIES

0-7645-2431-3

Home Buying FOR DUMMIES

0-7645-5331-3

Grant Writing FOR DUMMIES

0-7645-5307-0

Also available:

Accounting For Dummies
(0-7645-5314-3)

Business Plans Kit For Dummies
(0-7645-5365-8)

Managing For Dummies
(1-5688-4858-7)

Mutual Funds For Dummies
(0-7645-5329-1)

QuickBooks All-in-One Desk Reference For Dummies
(0-7645-1963-8)

Resumes For Dummies
(0-7645-5471-9)

Small Business Kit For Dummies
(0-7645-5093-4)

Starting an eBay Business For Dummies
(0-7645-1547-0)

Taxes For Dummies 2003
(0-7645-5475-1)

HOME, GARDEN, FOOD & WINE

Feng Shui FOR DUMMIES

0-7645-5295-3

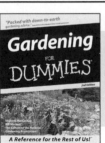

Gardening FOR DUMMIES

0-7645-5130-2

Cooking FOR DUMMIES

0-7645-5250-3

Also available:

Bartending For Dummies
(0-7645-5051-9)

Christmas Cooking For Dummies
(0-7645-5407-7)

Cookies For Dummies
(0-7645-5390-9)

Diabetes Cookbook For Dummies
(0-7645-5230-9)

Grilling For Dummies
(0-7645-5076-4)

Home Maintenance For Dummies
(0-7645-5215-5)

Slow Cookers For Dummies
(0-7645-5240-6)

Wine For Dummies
(0-7645-5114-0)

FITNESS, SPORTS, HOBBIES & PETS

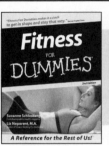

Fitness FOR DUMMIES

0-7645-5167-1

Golf FOR DUMMIES

0-7645-5146-9

Guitar FOR DUMMIES

0-7645-5106-X

Also available:

Cats For Dummies
(0-7645-5275-9)

Chess For Dummies
(0-7645-5003-9)

Dog Training For Dummies
(0-7645-5286-4)

Labrador Retrievers For Dummies
(0-7645-5281-3)

Martial Arts For Dummies
(0-7645-5358-5)

Piano For Dummies
(0-7645-5105-1)

Pilates For Dummies
(0-7645-5397-6)

Power Yoga For Dummies
(0-7645-5342-9)

Puppies For Dummies
(0-7645-5255-4)

Quilting For Dummies
(0-7645-5118-3)

Rock Guitar For Dummies
(0-7645-5356-9)

Weight Training For Dummies
(0-7645-5168-X)

Available wherever books are sold.
Go to www.dummies.com or call 1-877-762-2974 to order direct

WILEY

FOR DUMMIES®

A world of resources to help you grow

TRAVEL

0-7645-5453-0

0-7645-5438-7

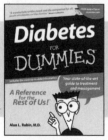

0-7645-5444-1

Also available:

America's National Parks For Dummies
(0-7645-6204-5)
Caribbean For Dummies
(0-7645-5445-X)
Cruise Vacations For Dummies 2003
(0-7645-5459-X)
Europe For Dummies
(0-7645-5456-5)
Ireland For Dummies
(0-7645-6199-5)

France For Dummies
(0-7645-6292-4)
Las Vegas For Dummies
(0-7645-5448-4)
London For Dummies
(0-7645-5416-6)
Mexico's Beach Resorts For Dummies
(0-7645-6262-2)
Paris For Dummies
(0-7645-5494-8)
RV Vacations For Dummies
(0-7645-5443-3)

EDUCATION & TEST PREPARATION

0-7645-5194-9

0-7645-5325-9

0-7645-5249-X

Also available:

The ACT For Dummies
(0-7645-5210-4)
Chemistry For Dummies
(0-7645-5430-1)
English Grammar For Dummies
(0-7645-5322-4)
French For Dummies
(0-7645-5193-0)
GMAT For Dummies
(0-7645-5251-1)
Inglés Para Dummies
(0-7645-5427-1)

Italian For Dummies
(0-7645-5196-5)
Research Papers For Dummies
(0-7645-5426-3)
SAT I For Dummies
(0-7645-5472-7)
U.S. History For Dummies
(0-7645-5249-X)
World History For Dummies
(0-7645-5242-2)

HEALTH, SELF-HELP & SPIRITUALITY

0-7645-5154-X

0-7645-5302-X

0-7645-5418-2

Also available:

The Bible For Dummies
(0-7645-5296-1)
Controlling Cholesterol For Dummies
(0-7645-5440-9)
Dating For Dummies
(0-7645-5072-1)
Dieting For Dummies
(0-7645-5126-4)
High Blood Pressure For Dummies
(0-7645-5424-7)
Judaism For Dummies
(0-7645-5299-6)

Menopause For Dummies
(0-7645-5458-1)
Nutrition For Dummies
(0-7645-5180-9)
Potty Training For Dummies
(0-7645-5417-4)
Pregnancy For Dummies
(0-7645-5074-8)
Rekindling Romance For Dummies
(0-7645-5303-8)
Religion For Dummies
(0-7645-5264-3)